Perplexities of Consciousness

Life and Mind: Philosophical Issues in Biology and Psychology
Kim Sterelny and Robert A. Wilson, Series Editors

Perplexities of Consciousness

Eric Schwitzgebel

A Bradford Book
The MIT Press
Cambridge, Massachusetts
London, England

© 2011 Massachusetts Institute of Technology

For information about quantity discounts, email special_sales@mitpress.mit.edu.

Set in Stone Sans and Stone Serif by Toppan Best-set Premedia Limited. Printed and bound in the United States of America.

Library of Congress Cataloging-in-Publication Data

Schwitzgebel, Eric.
Perplexities of consciousness / Eric Schwitzgebel.
    p. cm.
"A Bradford book."
Includes bibliographical references and index.
ISBN 978-0-262-01490-8 (hardcover : alk. paper) 1. Consciousness. 2. Philosophy of mind. I. Title.
B808.9.S39   2011
126—dc22

                                                            2010015780

10 9 8 7 6 5 4 3 2 1

to Pauline

Contents

Preface

I have two aims in this book. First, I aim to persuade you that people in general know very little about what might seem to be obvious features of their stream of conscious experience—where by "conscious experience" I mean sensory experience, visual imagery, inner speech, emotional experience, and the whole variety of subjective phenomena that constitute what we sometimes think of as our inner lives. Second, I aim to persuade you that you yourself know very little about such matters. Obviously, these two aims intertwine and support each other. My scholarly emphasis is on the general claim, but I've found in the course of writing these chapters that I care at least as much about the reader's conception of his or her own self-knowledge. I want to undermine your self-confidence. I want to make it seem not obvious to you where the truth lies on various issues you might have thought straightforward.

Currently ongoing conscious experience—what contemporary philosophers of mind call *phenomenology*—might seem a singularly unpromising topic for doubt. Even Descartes in his first two *Meditations* and Hume in the first book of his *Treatise*, despite their great talent for skepticism, couldn't bring themselves to doubt such matters. Both thought, or appear to have thought, that no matter how great our errors may be about the outside world, we can't err in the same way about the current contents of our own consciousness. I might not know whether there is a red tomato in front of me (maybe I'm being systematically deceived in my sensory inputs by some powerful being), but I know for sure what the character of my *visual experience* of that tomato is—that I *seem* to be seeing a red thing, in this hue or hues, in this shape, over this apparent distance. Likewise, if a prankster has made a clever swap, I may be wrong about having dropped a barbell on my toe, but surely I cannot be wrong about the severe pain I now feel. The Western philosophical tradition is nearly univocal on the special privilege, or at least excellent accuracy, of our knowledge of our currently ongoing stream of experience. Though Sigmund Freud, Richard Nisbett, and many others have embarrassed us with our errors about *some* features of our minds, such as our motives and traits, most philosophers have thought that nonetheless current conscious experience is a special aspect of the mind about which our knowledge is remarkably secure.

The chapters of this book are not cumulative; with the exception of chapter 7 (and the partial exception of chapter 5), each serves as a kind of case study of our ignorance in some particular domain. As case studies, they can be read in any order. I recommend starting with the topic you find most interesting. Chapter 7 is the most general statement and defense of my pessimism; it draws force from three brief case studies embedded within it and, more powerfully I hope, from the more detailed case studies that constitute the bulk of the book. The chapters sometimes become descents into confusion, with no clear final thesis but rather a tossing up of the hands; you will either share my uncertainty or think I'm dense.

I will not have much to say about the *metaphysics* of consciousness—the question of whether we are purely material beings, and if so what aspect of materiality is responsible for the stream of conscious experience. I am, however, skeptical about metaphysical accounts of consciousness too. In part this is because I think it became evident in the late twentieth century (if it wasn't evident earlier) that all metaphysical accounts of consciousness will have some highly counterintuitive consequences if confronted frankly. (If functionalism is true, some weird assemblages with the right functional properties will be conscious; if consciousness depends on the stuff we're made of, then aliens behaviorally indistinguishable from us might nonetheless be totally unconscious; and so on.) *Something* apparently preposterous, it seems, must be true of consciousness. Thus, our ordinary untutored intuitions cannot be a reliable guide to what kinds of systems are conscious, nor is there any evolutionary or developmental reason to think that they would be a reliable guide. Furthermore, we appear to have no solid basis for choosing among the various metaphysical alternatives: Armchair philosophical reflection leaves us only idiosyncratic hunches about equally unsupported half-intuitive theories, while empirical observation of physical structure and behavior is uninterpretable—cannot be accepted as showing the presence or absence of conscious experience—without a prior theory of consciousness, creating a tight vicious circle. (For more on this last point, see chapter 6.)

Nothing important in this book, I hope, turns on a complex, abstract philosophical argument. History has not been kind to such arguments; evidently the cognitive powers of even the best philosophers are generally too frail for such arguments to help them gain much purchase on the truth. The problem does not generalize across fields: Complex mathematical and scientific arguments do often survive scrutiny. The difficulty, I suspect, is principally in the background assumptions, which are more easily agreed upon by mathematicians and scientists than by philosophers, and which are too shaky in the case of philosophy to support grand edifices.

Jakob Hohwy has pointed out to me three recurring structures in my skeptical reflections. The argument types are simple enough, I hope, and employed often enough with different examples, to support my overall perspective even if several particular examples fail. First is the *argument from variation*: People often differ greatly in their judgments about their stream of experience (across cultures, between individuals within the same culture, or within the same individual over time). Sometimes, in such cases, it seems unlikely that their actual underlying experiences vary correspondingly. Consequently, some of their judgments—we don't necessarily know which ones—are probably wrong. Second is the *argument from error*: Ordinary people often think that their experience has some feature that more careful introspection, perhaps combined with other evidence, suggests it does not have. Ordinary reflection, in such cases, is therefore prone to error. Third is the *argument from uncertainty*: When instructed to reflect carefully and asked probing questions, people often find they feel uncertain about even the most basic aspects of their stream of experience. Such doubt suggests a substantial possibility of error in judgments of that general type, not only when people are reflecting carefully and are asked probing questions but also when they are reflecting more casually. I ask you not to evaluate these arguments now. I wouldn't expect you to find them compelling, independent of detailed examples. I am merely noting their general form, which may be of help in understanding the argumentative structure of the book.

Timothy Gann, Linus Huang, Alan Moore, Russell Pierce, Cati Porter, and Daniel Price all provided comments on the entire book as it was first being shaped into a whole. The following people helped me in thinking about one or more individual issues or chapters: Donald Ainslie, David Barlia, José Bermúdez, Richard Bett, Ned Block, Jorg Büchholz, Curt Burgess, Peter Carruthers, Mason Cash, Dave Chalmers, Jonathan Cohen, Nelson Cowan, Dan Dennett, Josh Dever, John Dilworth, Bill Domhoff, Denise Durance, Dillon Emerick, Mark Engelbert, Kevin Falvey, Bill Faw, Carrie Figdor, Maggie Friend, Kirk Gable, Jim Garson, Brian Glenney, Alvin Goldman, Bob Gordon, Mike Gordon, Chris Hill, Jakob Hohwy, Changbing Huang, David Hunter, Russ Hurlburt, Jonathan Ichikawa, Manyul Im, Tony Jack,

Michael Jacovides, Brian Keeley, Sean Kelly, David Kirchner, Bryan Lee, Steven Lehar, Felipe Leon, Dom Lopes, Jessica Ludescher, Pete Mandik, Justin McDaniel, Tori McGeer, Stuart McKelvie, Pat Missin, Christopher Mole, Jennifer Nagel, Eddy Nahmias, Shaun Nichols, Alva Noë, Gualtiero Piccinini, Bill Prinzmetal, Erich Reck, Richard Reis, Teed Rockwell, Larry Rosenblum, David Rosenthal, Frank Russo, Josh Rust, Colleen Ryan, Sandy Ryan, Wade Savage, Brian Scholl, John Schwenkler, Susanna Siegel, Charles Siewert, Carol Slater, Declan Smithies, Maja Spener, Tom Stoneham, Nigel Thomas, Arnold Trehub, Penny Vinden, Glenn Vogel, Gary Watson, Gideon Yaffe, Jeff Yim, Chuck Young, Yifeng Zhou, and Aaron Zimmerman. I also thank the many readers of my blog who commented on these issues, mostly by first name or pseudonymously, and the many formal and informal "introspective observers" (to use Titchener's phrase; see chapter 5) who reported on their experience. Let me also apologize to those of you in that last group for not believing most of your reports—not that I necessarily *disbelieved* them either—and to the many people whose help I have unjustly forgotten.

I thank my son Davy for discussing philosophy with me on evening walks. I thank my daughter Kate for showing me the meditative powers of play sand. My greatest debt is to my wife, Pauline, who not only commented in detail on the entire manuscript, but also suffers through and supports my long hours and academic obsessions, though I cannot adequately justify them to her or even to myself.

Most of the chapters of this book are descendants of previously published work. I gratefully acknowledge the publishers for permission to use them here.

Chapter 1 descends from "Why Did We Think We Dreamed in Black and White?" *Studies in History and Philosophy of Science* 33 (2002): 649–660. Chapter 2 descends from "Do Things Look Flat?" *Philosophy and Phenomenological Research* 72 (2006): 589–599. Chapter 3 descends from "How Well Do We Know Our Own Conscious Experience? The Case of Visual Imagery," *Journal of Consciousness Studies* 9 (2002, no. 5–6): 35–53. Chapter 4 descends from "How Well Do We Know Our Own Conscious Experience? The Case of Human Echolocation" (with Michael S. Gordon), *Philosophical Topics* 28 (2000): 235–246. Chapter 5 descends from "Introspective Training Apprehensively Defended: Reflections on Titchener's Lab Manual," *Journal of Consciousness Studies* 11 (2004, no. 7–8): 58–76. Chapter 6 descends from "Do You Have Constant Tactile Experience of Your Feet in Your Shoes? Or Is Experience Limited to What's in Attention?" *Journal of Consciousness Studies* 14 (2007, no. 3): 5–35. Chapter 7 descends from "The Unreliability of Naive Introspection," *Philosophical Review* 117 (2008): 245–273.

1 Recoloring the Dreamworld

If you took all the girls I knew when I was single
And brought 'em all together for one night
I know they'd never match my sweet imagination
Everything looks worse [1973 version] / better [1981 version] in black and white
—Paul Simon, "Kodachrome"[1]

i

In 1951, Calvin S. Hall announced in *Scientific American* that 29 percent of dreams have at least some color in them. He called such dreams "technicolored," explicitly likening them to the technicolor movies that were increasingly prevalent at the time and implicitly contrasting them with lower-tech black-and-white movies and dreams. Some of Hall's contemporaries might have thought he was overestimating the occurrence of color in dreams. In 1958, Fernando Tapia and colleagues found that only about 9 percent of their non-psychiatric hospital patients reported dreaming in color (versus 12 percent of "neurotic" men and 21 percent of neurotic women). In 1953, a large majority of Manfred de Martino's undergraduate respondents said either that they never saw colors in their dreams or that they saw them less than once a month. In 1942, Warren Middleton reported that only 10 percent of his students said they saw colors in their dreams frequently or very frequently, and 71 percent said they rarely or never did (19 percent said they saw colors in their dreams "occasionally").[2] A widely shared opinion was that dreams were predominantly black-and-white phenomena, comparable to black-and-white movies, with an occasional splash of color here and there.

Scientific opinion changed dramatically in the 1960s, beginning with a report by Edwin Kahn and colleagues in 1962. Kahn and colleagues asserted that people awakened during rapid-eye-movement (REM) sleep attributed color to 83 percent of their dreams. In 1963, Ralph Berger, using a similar technique, found that color dreaming was reported after 71 percent of REM awakenings. In 1968, John Herman and colleagues reported 69 percent. In 1970, Frederick Snyder suggested that all dreams may contain color, even if the colors are not always remembered. Table 1.1 summarizes all the English-language studies I could find that report either the percentage of people claiming to dream in color or the percentage of dreams experimental subjects described as containing color. (The table excludes discussions

Table 1.1
Scientific studies of the incidence of color in dreams (English-speaking countries only).[a]

Author	Year	Method	Percentage of people reporting color dreams[b]	Percentage of people's dreams said to contain color
Middleton	1933	Questionnaire[c]	26	—
Husband	1935	Questionnaire	41	—
Middleton	1942	Questionnaire	29	—
Doust	1951	Questionnaire	19	—
Hall	1951	Dream reports[d]	—	29[e]
De Martino	1953	Questionnaire	17	—
Tapia, Werboff, Winokur	1958	Questionnaire	9	—
Kahn et al.	1962	REM awakenings[f]	94	83
Berger	1963	REM awakenings	100	71
Schecter et al.	1965	Dream reports	—	62
Suinn	1966	Dream reports	81	~41
Herman, Roffwarg, Tauber	1968	REM awakenings	—	69
Snyder	1970	REM awakenings	—	77
Padgham	1975	REM awakenings	100	50
Jankowski, Dee, Cartwright	1977	REM awakenings	89	62
Frayn	1991	Questionnaire	74	74
Rechtschaffen, Buchignani	1992	REM awakenings	—	80

Table 1.1 (continued)

Author	Year	Method	Percentage of people reporting color dreams[b]	Percentage of people's dreams said to contain color
Schwitzgebel, version 1	2003	Questionnaire	81	—
Schwitzgebel, version 2	2003	Questionnaire	100	—
Murzyn	2008	Questionnaire	92	—
Murzyn	2008	Dream reports	100	Older people: 72 younger: 89

a. For estimates of color incidence in non-Anglophone countries, see note 8.

b. These percentages exclude people saying they don't recall and include people who report a mix of color and black-and-white dreams. I am counting people who say they "occasionally" dream in color as reporting color dreaming, but not those who report color dreaming only "rarely."

c. The "questionnaire" method involves asking during normal waking hours for generalizations about dream content.

d. The "dream reports" method involves analyzing reports about the characteristics of individual dreams—dreams usually (but not always; see Hall 1947) recorded directly upon waking.

e. Hall's student Robert Fortier, also in 1951, published a dissertation suggesting that a majority of respondents report experiencing at least one color in at least five percent of their dreams.

f. The association between REM sleep and dreaming first became widely known in 1953 with a report in *Science* by Eugene Asersinsky and Nathaniel Kleitman.

based on personal experience or experience interpreting dream reports in psychotherapy, which are listed in note 3.) Two of the studies are my own. Schwitzgebel 2003, version 1 was as precise as possible a replication of Middleton's 1942 study, using Middleton's question "Do you see colors in your dreams?" and his response options "very frequently," "frequently," "occasionally," "rarely," and "never." Schwitzgebel 2003, version 2, given to different respondents, asked "Do you dream in color or black-and-white?" The response options were "color" (selected by 62 percent), "black-and-white" (0 percent), "both" (23 percent), "neither" (0 percent), and "don't know" (15 percent). The thesis of this chapter is that the last of those response options is, unfortunately, the best. I don't know, and you probably don't know, whether we dream in color or not. Although I have found in conversation that most people answer confidently when asked about the coloration or non-coloration of their dreams, that confidence is misplaced.

Before the rise of scientific psychology in the late nineteenth century, scholars interested in dreaming generally stated or assumed that dreams contain color. For example, Aristotle specifically includes colors among the remnants that sense impressions may leave in the organs and which thus appear to us in sleep (4th c. BCE/1996, 459a23–462a31). Epicurus says that our impressions in dreams have color and shape (3rd c. BCE/1926, *Letter to Herodotus*, 50–51). Descartes in his famous *Meditations* (1641/1984)—the same meditation in which he finds it impossible to doubt that he thinks and exists—describes a piece of wax as seeming to change color, and wants to grant that such an appearance could come to him in sleep. Indeed, the skeptical idea that ordinary waking experience is not qualitatively different from dream experience (also familiar from Descartes) requires that dreams be pervasively colored, since our ordinary waking experience is pervasively colored—at least presumably so. (I will raise some doubts about this, however, in chapters 6 and 7.) More explicitly, in *The Passions of the Soul*, Descartes asserts that "everything the soul perceives by means of the nerves [i.e., sensations] may also be represented to it through the fortuitous course of the spirits [i.e., in dreaming]" (1649/1985, §26). In general, I have not found in my wanderings through the pre-scientific literature on dreaming any assertion that dreams lack color. Commonly, dreams were likened to paintings or tapestries—typically colored media.

Early scientific psychologists were divided. The prominent psychophysicist Gustav Fechner writes "I also never dream in color, but all my experiences in dreams appear to me as though proceeding in a kind of twilight or night." (1860, volume 2, p. 470, my translation) Freud, in contrast, frequently reports color in his *Interpretation of Dreams* (1900/1931) without any special comment, apparently taking its presence for granted. (By my count, 50 percent of the long dream reports—those over 15 lines of text—in *Interpretation of Dreams* explicitly mention colors other than black, white, or gray.) Mary Calkins (1893), in a long and detailed description of the phenomenology of dreaming, describes dreams as consisting of reproduced and recombined images, never once mentioning any lack of color in those images, though in a 1900 paper a research assistant of Calkins reports color in fewer than half of her dreams (Andrews and Calkins 1900). In 1898, Edward Titchener describes "flashes of color" as a primary cause of dreams, but by 1912 his opinion too appears to have shifted—mentioning (evidently on the basis of a dinner conversation) that some people see only shades of gray in their dreams (Titchener 1912a). A few years later, Titchener's former student Madison Bentley, waking people randomly at night, reports about four times as many grays as chromatic colors in his participants' dream descriptions (Bentley 1915). By the 1930s, Warren Middleton and Richard Husband were finding that the majority of people denied dreaming in color.

So there appears to be an arc of opinion: before scientific psychology, a consensus or assumption that dreams are colored; divided opinion into the early twentieth century; a consensus that dreams typically have little color from about 1930 to 1960; and then a sudden overturning of that consensus in the 1960s.[4] Why?

ii

The early to middle years of the twentieth century were, of course, the heyday of black-and-white media. Black-and-white photography was first made public in the 1830s and became increasingly popular through the early twentieth century. Although color photography was invented in the 1860s, color photos did not become easily obtainable by the public until the 1940s. Motion pictures, invented around 1900, were from very early on occasionally hand-painted with colors, and two-color filming was sometimes used in the 1920s (for example in the 1925 version of *Ben Hur*). Nonetheless, motion pictures were overwhelmingly black-and-white until the late 1930s, when a few technicolored movies, including *Gone with the Wind* and *The Wizard of Oz*, drew huge crowds. It was not until the 1950s that color movies became commonplace, and as late as 1960 a black-and-white film, *The Apartment*, won the Academy Award for best picture. Black-and-white television became widespread after World War II; color television did not become popular until the late 1960s.

It can't be chance that this flourishing of black-and-white media coincided with the opinion that dreams are mostly black-and-white. In 2006, to further confirm the relationship between available media and opinion about dreams, I collected cross-cultural data with Changbing Huang and Yifeng Zhou, taking advantage of the fact that different groups in China had very different access to technology at that time. Huang, Zhou, and I examined three groups of Chinese students of different socioeconomic status and consequently different levels of exposure to black-and-white and color media: low-status rural high school students, high-status students at an elite urban university, and intermediate-status students at a non-elite urban university. We gave each group the same questionnaire that Middle-

Table 1.2
Reported color dreaming and media exposure in replications of Middleton's 1942 study. Adapted from Schwitzgebel, Huang, and Zhou 2006.

	Percentage reporting seeing colors in dreams at least occasionally	Percentage reporting access to color film media before age 11
Middleton (U.S.A.), 1942	29	0 (inferred)
Low-status rural Chinese, 2006	29	19
Intermediate-status urban Chinese, 2006	39	47
High-status urban Chinese, 2006	52	76
Schwitzgebel (U.S.A.), 2003	81	100 (inferred)

ton gave to his American students in 1942 and that I gave to mine in 2003, supplemented (at the end) with questions about the respondent's current and past media exposure. As Table 1.2 shows, the percentage of students reporting seeing colors in their dreams corresponds nicely with their subgroup's media history across the five replications of Middleton's study.[5,6]

One possible explanation of all this is that a ubiquity of black-and-white images in film media changes people's dreams. Although Aristotle, Epicurus, Freud, and their contemporaries dreamed in color, the average American in 1950 dreamed mostly in black-and-white. And now that color media again dominate, our dreams are returning to color.

But is this plausible? It does seem plausible that black-and-white media would affect people's dreams in various ways. After seeing a black-and-white film about Frankenstein's monster, one might have a nightmare in which his black-and-white figure appears as one's tormentor. And perhaps, since most romantic movies seen by people living in English-speaking countries in 1950 were black-and-white, some of those people dreaming of themselves as romantic heroes would paint their dreamworld that way. However, most of our dreams are not so directly modeled on motion pictures. Every day a person sees her house and family in full color. It would be odd to suppose that whether she dreams about them in color depends on what she sees in the cinema or on the television screen. Despite their cultural importance, photography, film, and television seem unlikely to have so profound an effect on our cognition as to regularly transform our dreams of all the things we normally see in color to black-and-white. If so, then, although people's *opinions* about their dreams changed dramatically, their dreams remained approximately the same.

One person's plausibility is another's tendentious guess, I suppose, so let me buttress this assertion with two more concrete pieces of evidence. One is the consistency of the use of color terms in dream reports since the 1940s. Calvin Hall and Robert Van de Castle (1966) collected hundreds of dream reports from 1947 to 1950. In these reports, about 0.19 percent of all words—about one word in 500—is a color term other than "black," "white," or "gray." Although that may seem like low rate of color-term use, it is virtually identical to the rates of color-term use I found in four sources of dream reports from the end of the twentieth century—rates ranging from 0.19 to 0.23 percent.[7] It is also somewhat higher than the color-term rates of approximately 0.02–0.14 percent in samples of English drawn from various other sources.[8] Nor is there any notable difference in the use of "black," "white," and "gray" between the two eras. Those achromatic terms constituted 0.09 percent of words in Hall and Van de Castle's report and 0.13 percent of the words in the modern dream reports (pooled together)—if anything, a trend in the wrong direction. So if Hall and Van de Castle's respondents were dreaming in less color than people 50 years later, that fact is not reflected in their use of color terms when describing those dreams.

A second piece of evidence that seems to support the idea that it is mainly opinions about dreams that have changed rather than dreams themselves is a finding from the Chinese study mentioned above. It turns out that in those data there is only a weak relationship between *individual-level* exposure to color or black-and-white media within each Chinese subgroup and reported black-and-white or color dreaming. The effects were mostly at the group level.[9] What this means is that respondents' opinions about color dreaming depended more on what sort of media exposure was characteristic of their group overall than on what they themselves had been exposed to, contrary to what one might expect if individual exposure to media was directly affecting dream experience. These results suggest that whatever is affecting people's reports is something shared at the group level—something, I suspect, like cultural attitude, or the availability of certain metaphors, or certain ways of thinking and talking about one's dream life.

The profound changes in opinion about the coloration of dreams, then, do not appear to correspond to equally profound changes in the dreams themselves. It follows that at least some people must be pretty badly mistaken about their dreams. If dreams really are mostly in color, then most of the 91 percent of Tapia's respondents who claimed not to dream in color must have been wrong, and Tapia must have been wrong when he believed them. If dreams really are mostly black-and-white, then most of us now must be wrong. Or maybe dreams are neither color nor black-and-white (a possibility I will explore in section v) and nearly everyone is wrong.

iii

One might attempt to defend the view that dreams are mostly black-and-white as follows: The failure of Aristotle, Descartes, and others to notice this feature of dreams was due to the lack of black-and-white film media in their time. Absent those media, it may have been natural to assume that since the things dreamed about are colored in real life (family, locations, etc.), they are colored in dreams. Once black-and-white media gained prominence early in the twentieth century, people came to recognize that their dream images resembled the images in those media. Now that black-and-white media are losing importance, most people have returned to mistakenly assuming that their dreams are thoroughly colored, though an observant few maintain that their dreams are mostly black-and-white. People may even mistakenly attribute color to black-and-white dream objects in the course of a dream, just as in a dream I might judge something to have the layout of my house when in fact it does not resemble my house at all. Slightly differently, one might simply *know* that an object is red without experiencing a red dream image, just as one might know in a dream that someone is one's sister even if she looks nothing like one's real sister.

A weakness in this argument is that it isn't clear that pre-twentieth-century media were generally colored. Black-and-white ink sketches and prints were common in some periods, as were monochromatic representations of people and animals on pottery and as sculpture. If dreams were black-and-white, they could as easily have been likened to those media as to colored paintings and tapestries. To this objection, the defender of black-and-white dreaming might counter that if dreams really are in color they could in 1950 just as easily have been likened to color media. Paintings and tapestries did not cease to exist. However, I think the suggested parity fails. Black-and-white movies had other advantages over the competing media of the time that may have compelled comparison to dreams. They integrated visuality with movement and narrative as had no other medium previously—except perhaps theater, if that's a medium. (Why wasn't it more common, I wonder, to describe dreams as like plays on the mind's stage? Not even Shakespeare, who writes so much about dreams and plays, ever seems to make that comparison.) Another problem for the friend of black-and-white dreaming is the implication that people who still report black-and-white dreaming are the ones who are most observant of their dreams. Recent evidence suggests that this isn't so. Michael Schredl and colleagues (2008) and Eva Murzyn (2008) have found that people reporting relatively high percentages of black-and-white dreams also report recalling fewer dreams and recall the dreams they do report less well. Schredl and colleagues interpret this as evidence that reports of black-and-white dreaming may simply reflect errors of memory, while Murzyn takes the reports of black-and-white dreams at face value, but neither Murzyn nor Schredl and colleagues find any special acumen among people reporting black-and-white dreams.

More appealing, perhaps, is the idea that dreams—at least, most people's dreams, most of the time, even 60 years ago—really are in color, and that the 1950s view that they were not was due to an infelicitous but natural analogy between dreams and the flourishing black-and-white media of the day. As paintings and tapestries yielded to photographs and movies, people naturally updated the media to which dreams were likened, and since these media were black-and-white, so also, it came to seem, were dreams. One of Middleton's 1942 respondents even claims that nearly all his dreams appear in sepia, a tint used in many old black-and-white photographs. (The respondent's own explanation: "Maybe it's because I'm partial to brown.") In the future, perhaps the media will integrate visual, auditory, and tactile elements, coming closer to giving us a full fictional sensory experience. People have often told me that tactile experiences are weak or rare in their dreams—they don't feel the impact of their feet on the sidewalk or the breeze against their arms, nor even in a nightmare do they feel the pain of the knife in the belly. Maybe this is why feeling a pinch is sometimes thought to indicate wakefulness. Perhaps if the media continue to improve, dreams will come to seem ever more vibrant with sensory detail—even if they really aren't, or even if they always were.

iv

Let me confess to a few difficulties for my thesis. First, there are some misalignments between features of the dominant media and features of people's dream reports. For example, paintings and tapestries don't represent motion well (despite some attempts). This has led me to wonder whether, when those analogies dominated, some scholars doubted that dream images moved. I can find no evidence of such doubts. Also, radio was a lively and pervasive medium for fiction in the early twentieth century. However, as far as I know, dreams were never likened to radio broadcasts. Now, perhaps dreams have some obvious features, such as visuality and motion, about which it is difficult to go wrong. But there are temporal misalignments too. Decades after the end of silent films, which came in the 1920s, Peter Knapp (1953) and Ángel Garma (1961) describe dreams as mostly soundless, more like silent movies than like "talkies." (The first sentence of Garma's article "Colour in Dreams" is "Dreams are like old silent films, without sound or technicolor.") Were Knapp and Garma old men clinging to an ossified concept of dreams from their child-hood? Not Knapp, at least: His publishing career ran from the late 1940s into the 1990s. Given the limited literature on the sensory aspects of dreams, it is difficult to assess exactly how unusual the "silent movies" view was—though presumably Calvin Hall (1951) would at least have mentioned it in his *Scientific American* article had he thought it true.

Second, and relatedly, the story of the previous section can't very well explain the *sudden* transition of opinion from the very low estimates of color dreaming in the late 1950s (e.g., Tapia's 1958 estimate that 9 percent of people dream in color) to the very high estimates of the early 1960s (e.g., Kahn's 1962 estimate of 94 percent). As I noted at the beginning of section ii, the transition from black-and-white to color media was much more gradual than that. If culturally salient metaphors are driving our opinions about dreaming, shouldn't the change in opinion be as slow as the change in the objects of metaphorical comparison?

Maybe the change in research methodology—from mostly question-naires in the 1940s and the 1950s to mostly REM awakenings in the 1960s—is partly explanatory. Maybe, for example, REM awakening is a more accurate method of assessing dream content. Then perhaps the ques-tionnaire studies assessed only casual opinion about dreams, which was influenced by media analogies, whereas the REM-awakening studies assessed the dreams themselves—dreams which contained color and always had—and once scientists had this better method in hand, their opinions changed rapidly.

Questionnaire studies from the 1960s would help us assess this sugges-tion if any such studies existed. If popular opinion lagged behind scientific opinion, scientists collecting REM reports might have been tapping into something other than just popular opinion about coloration—perhaps the truth about dreams. Unfortunately, the next English-language questionnaire study wasn't published until 1991. In research based on individual dream reports after natural awakening, there does appear to be a gradual rather than a sudden shift—from Hall's 1951 estimate that 29 percent of dreams contain color to Suinn's 1966 estimate of 41 percent to Schredl and colleagues' and Murzyn's 2008 estimates of 72 percent or more. That gradual shift is consistent with the view that, at least for this methodology, the change in dream reports tracks (perhaps with some delay, especially for the older people in Murzyn's study) the gradual change in the media.

To help improve my sense of popular opinion in the 1960s, I looked up "dreams" in the *Reader's Guide to Periodical Literature* and read every article on that subject (21 in all) published between 1955 and 1975 in the *New York Times Magazine*, in *Reader's Digest*, in the *Saturday Evening Post*, and in *Time* (magazines I chose for their wide circulation and general-interest news content). Unfortunately, I found only a few passing remarks about the coloration of dreams: two early articles (1959 and 1961) describing dreams as mostly monochromatic, a 1965 article on psychic dreams that describes the colors of two dream objects but makes no general comments about the coloration of dreams, a 1967 article briefly stating that dreams can be either color or black-and-white but not saying which is more common, and a 1971 article claiming that people who dream in color have more satisfying emotional lives. A ProQuest search of the *New York Times* and the *Los Angeles Times* from 1955 to 1969 yielded only two artists' claims (1962 and 1963) that they dreamed in color and a Nicaraguan poet's assertion (1969) that blue "is the color of dreams."

If immediately upon discovering the association of REM sleep and dreaming in 1953 REM-awakening researchers had asked their subjects about coloration, what would they have found? Would they have found that most people report—presumably to their own surprise—color dreams? If not, the change in scientific opinion from the 1950s to the 1960s could not have been simply the result of improved method. Here are two reasons to suspect that people would have reported mostly black-and-white dreams if REM-awakened in the 1950s: First, the closest early method to REM awakening was random midnight awakening, and Bentley (1915), using that method, got many more reports of gray than of colors. Second, dream researchers in the 1940s and the 1950s must often have spontaneously awoken from REM sleep and reflected on their dreams, thus executing an informal home version of the REM-awakening method with themselves as subjects; and presumably when they did so they judged the just-ended dreams to be mostly black-and-white.

v

Although the view that our dreams have color may seem more plausible to us today than the view that they are black-and-white, we should also consider the possibility that our dreams are neither color *nor* black-and-white, and that applying either of these categories is misleading. Consider, as an analogy, a novel. Though novels are surely not in black-and-white (though the words on the printed page may be), it also seems a little strange to say that they are in color. Novels, of course, attribute color ("she strode into the room in a dazzling red dress") and refer to objects that normally have particular colors ("she promptly chopped a carrot"). Perhaps it makes sense to say that such fictional claims are "in color" or partly so. However, most elements of most scenes in novels do not have determinate colors in that way. When the heroine slides into her 1966 Mustang and rumbles away, the scene could be imagined with any of a variety of colors. Her skin might be dark brown or light; the Mustang might be red, black, or green; the sky might be blue, gray, dusky, or star-spangled. And even though we know that the heroine's dress is red, it could be any of a variety of shades, as long as they are suitably dazzling. It is a bit odd to say that the sentence describing her departure is "in color" when the color of so much of it is underdetermined. And, correspondingly, it is a bit odd to say that the novel as a whole is in color, though perhaps one could say that if one were careful enough in circumscribing the implications of the phrase "in color."

One might more naturally say that the *images* that a novel evokes in (most of) its readers are in color (I imagine the Mustang as green and the sky as dusky), but even that may not be quite right. Can't one just imagine the character driving away, without imagining the colors of the car, the road, and the sky? If one is reading the novel quickly, one may not have time to piece together a completely colored scene in one's imagination. Stephen Kosslyn (1980) argues (based on the experiential reports of multiple subjects) that it takes considerable time to fill in the details of complex images. If that is so, then when one is reading quickly much must remain sketchy and underspecified, and a novel will not play before one's mind with all the detail of a color movie.

If you find yourself disinclined to think that novels or the images they evoke are properly described as being either in black-and-white or in color, you may also find yourself hesitant to apply the terms "black-and-white" and "color" to dreams. Maybe dream objects and dream events are similar to fictional objects and events, or to the images evoked by fiction, in having, typically, a certain indeterminacy of color—neither cerise nor taupe nor burnt umber, nor gray either. If so, the analogy between dreams and black-and-white movies might not be as inapt as I have been suggesting. Many of the objects in black-and-white movies are, after all, also indeterminate in color, though they appear on the screen as gray. Although our heroine is eating a bell pepper the screen image of which is gray, it does not follow that she is eating a gray bell pepper. The color of the bell pepper isn't specified by the medium. Black-and-white movies, then, may be like novels and dreams in leaving the colors of most of their objects indeterminate—something that color film cannot (or at least cannot easily) do. Thus, it is possible—*if* dreams are mostly indeterminate in color—that those folks from the 1950s were on to something that we have since forgotten, even if they went too far in saying that dreams were literally black-and-white.

vi

I am tempted by both of the contrasting views mentioned above—on the one hand the view that dreams are richly colored, perhaps as richly as ordinary vision (assuming that ordinary vision is richly colored), and on the other hand the view that most dream objects have only indeterminate color. But which view, if either, is right?

If neuroscience were more advanced, we could look to it. If we knew, for example, exactly what sort of brain activity co-occurred with the conscious experience of color, we could see whether people showed this sort of brain activity while dreaming. But as things are, neuroscientists disagree about the neurological basis of color experience (see Gegenfurtner and Kiper 2003; Solomon and Lennie 2007; Wade et al. 2008; Conway 2009), and neuropsychological research on visual brain activity during REM sleep has not yet even attempted to focus on narrow issues, such as the activity of color cells (Braun et al. 1998; Wehrle et al. 2005; Hong et al. 2009).[10]

We might take seriously the low rates at which people, in some recent questionnaires and dream reports, describe their dreams as "neither" color nor black-and-white when explicitly given that option (0 percent in Schwitzgebel 2003; 0–17 percent in Schwitzgebel, Huang, and Zhou 2006; 0–4 percent in Murzyn 2008). But if we are willing to suppose that in 1950 the majority of people could have been radically mistaken about the coloration of their dreams because they over-analogized to film media, it seems we should also take seriously the possibility that the majority of people today could be mistaken in saying their dreams are in color, being still under the sway of that analogy. Indeed, the idea that dreams must be *either* color or black-and-white—that there is no other possibility—may be even more deeply ingrained in the media metaphors we use in thinking about dreams than was black-and-whiteness in 1950. In 1950 the film media were not all black-and-white, but they were all, or virtually all, either black-and-white *or* color. And so of course were paintings and tapestries. If we allow ourselves to be guided by such analogies, the idea that dream experience could be neither color nor black-and-white might seem incoherent or impossible to understand. Now, perhaps the idea of imagery or dream experience that leaves its colors unspecified without thereby being grayscale or monochromatic *is* somehow incoherent, but it isn't obvious why this should be so, or that people's general avoidance of the "neither" option in surveys like mine and Murzyn's should be particularly telling on the matter.

Maybe if we could establish that dream experience was qualitatively identical to waking perceptual experience—what Descartes seems to have assumed and what Jonathan Ichikawa (2009) calls the "percepts" view— then, from the assumption that waking visual experience is mostly in color, it would follow that dream experience too is mostly in color. However, this argument seems to invert the order of explanation. Until we determine whether dreams are rich in color or whether they leave the colors of most objects unspecified, it seems premature to commit to the view that dream experience and waking perception are experientially identical. Perhaps some piece of evidence for the qualitative identity of perceptual experience and dream experience is so compelling, independent of any assumptions about coloration, that we can draw out the richness of dream color as a separate conclusion? I don't see that compelling argument. (I don't accept, for example, that qualitative identity follows from the fact that we sometimes mistakenly think we are awake.)

It might seem odd to appeal to such indirect forms of evidence. If dreams are richly colored, the subjective experience (or "phenomenology") of dreaming is radically different than if dreams leave the color of most of their objects unspecified. Shouldn't we then simply be able to reflect directly on the phenomenology of dreaming to decide the question? The experiential difference between the two cases is so vast that it seems— doesn't it?—that a moment's thought should make it obvious which view is correct. Can't we guard against cavalier assumptions about similarity to media and against loose ways of talking, and just go sleep on it? When we wake, shouldn't the answer be plain?

Here I find myself quite thick. Although many mornings I remember a dream or two—and sometimes they seem to have been quite vivid—I can't tell you whether those dreams are in color. The historical swings in opinion about black-and-white vs. color dreaming suggest that I am not singularly inept, and that incompetence in assessing the coloration, or lack of it, of our dream life is fairly widespread, despite the considerable confidence people often exhibit when questioned on the matter. We don't know the phenomenology of dreaming nearly as well as we think we do.

You might think that the mistakes I say people make, or have historically made, aren't so terribly large. After all, it is sometimes difficult to remember which classic movies are in color and which are black-and-white, and such amnesia doesn't constitute a serious epistemic failure. However, confusion about the coloration of dreams is substantially deeper than an innocuous mistake about a particular Jimmy Stewart film. It is more like being confused about—or, worse, confidently persisting in the wrong opinion about—whether *all* the movies one sees are in color or *all* are in black-and-white, or whether there is some mix, despite seeing movies every night.

vii

This fundamental fact about the experience of dreaming, then, eludes me—eludes many of us, and I suspect it eludes you. To determine the coloration or non-coloration of the dreamworld proves surprisingly difficult—pending, at least, substantially more sophisticated psychological or neuroscientific research. I conclude this chapter with a question that will bring us to the heart of this book: Is dreaming, in this respect, *particularly* elusive, or are we equally in the dark about other aspects of the stream of experience—our emotions, our waking imagery, our ongoing visual phenomenology?

It could well be that dreaming is particularly or uniquely elusive. We have a powerful tendency to forget dreams. Unless we fix upon them with special attention, they evaporate almost instantly when we wake. We don't forget outward events—especially emotionally powerful ones—as easily. Dream reports would thus appear to be good candidates for distorted reconstruction. Yet if I am right—and this is what I will argue for in the rest of this book—our profound ignorance of our dreams is accompanied by nearly equally profound ignorance of most of the rest of our subjective experience.

2 Do Things Look Flat?

When we set before our Eyes a round Globe, of any uniform color, v.g. Gold, Alabaster, or Jet, 'tis certain, that the Idea thereby imprinted in our Mind, is of a flat Circle variously shadow'd, with several degrees of Light and Brightness coming to our Eyes.

—John Locke, *An Essay Concerning Human Understanding* (1690/1975, p. 145, italics suppressed)

i

I have a penny on my desk, and I'm viewing it obliquely. Does it look circular? Or, instead, do I only *know* or *judge* that the penny is circular, while the figure it presents to my sight—its actual visual appearance—is an ellipse? I gaze out my window and see a row of streetlights. Do they look as if they shrink as they recede into the distance, or do they all look the same size? Get out a penny, open the blinds, try it yourself. What do you think?

Many philosophers, from Malebranche (1674/1997)[1] though David Armstrong (1955), Roderick Chisholm (1957), and John Austin (1962), to Michael Tye (2000), Alva Noë (2004), and Sean Kelly (2008), have said this: There is a sense in which the obliquely viewed penny looks elliptical and the distant streetlights look smaller, and there is a sense in which they don't. Tye says that the coin looks like an object that really is round and also that the coin looks "elliptical from here." He says the streetlights look the same "objective size" but also that the nearer ones look "larger from here." Noë uses similar terminology and furthermore emphasizes that it's just what it *is* for a coin to look circular that it presents varying elliptical appearances depending on the angle of view. According to Noë, our visual experience always has, simultaneously, two "aspects": a perspectival aspect (corresponding to the coin's elliptical appearance) and an aspect reflecting our experience of the constancy of the objects we see (corresponding to our experience of the coin as genuinely circular, regardless of viewing angle). Kelly argues, contra Noë, that we don't experience the circularity and ellipticality *simultaneously* but rather flip between the different ways of experiencing the coin, much as we flip, in a "Gestalt shift," between different ways of seeing an ambiguous figure such as a Necker cube or Wittgenstein's duck-rabbit—with circularity being the primary and ordinary experience. All agree with the apparently commonsensical view that the penny both looks circular (in one sense) and has an elliptical "apparent shape" that we experience at least sometimes.

The view is attractive. Maybe you feel tugged both ways by the questions in the opening paragraph, as I do. A dual-aspect view—whether simultaneous like Tye's and Noë's or involving a shift from one way of seeing to the other like Kelly's—embraces both sides of the ambivalence. You get your ellipse and your circle too. But philosophers are not unanimous on this point. John Locke (1690/1975), Bertrand Russell (1914/1926, 1914/1986), and C. D. Broad (1925), for example, seem to embrace a just-the-ellipse view.[2] A. J. Ayer (1940) and Charles Siewert (2006) say they see only the circle and that there is no elliptical aspect to their experience.[3] Maybe Locke, Russell, Broad, Ayer, and Siewert are mistaken. Indeed, someone must be mistaken, if we assume that everyone is speaking the same language, not just talking at cross-purposes, and that they have basically the same type of visual experience. Such disagreements, as well as disagreements within the dual-aspect camp, seem to reveal a difficulty in the introspective task.

Who is right, then? (There *is* a fact about who, if anyone, is right in this matter, isn't there?)

ii

At least since Descartes, philosophers have tended to embrace the view that nothing is so obvious, so immune to doubt, or so easy to know as one's own ongoing conscious experience. Descartes says, or seems to say (in his second *Meditation*, 1641/1984), that although it is possible to doubt anything at all about the outside world (since you might be dreaming or deceived by a demon) it isn't possible to doubt what your *sensory experiences* are, which seem to be produced by that outside world. Similarly, H. H. Price writes:

When I see a tomato there is much that I can doubt. I can doubt whether it is a tomato that I am seeing, and not a cleverly painted piece of wax. I can doubt whether there is any material thing there at all. Perhaps what I took for a tomato was really a reflection; perhaps I am even the victim of some hallucination. One thing however I cannot doubt: that there exists a red patch of a round and somewhat bulgy shape, standing out from a background of other colour-patches, and having a certain visual depth, and this whole field of colour is directly present to my consciousness. (1932, p. 3)

Although one may doubt anything at all about the external world, the basic facts about one's own current sensory experience are immediately obvious, unchallengeable, and beyond all doubt—including, according to Price, the experience of depth and shape in a tomato, or for that matter a penny (ibid., pp. 55–56, 207).

I don't share their confidence. What exactly is my sensory experience as I stare at a penny? My first and recurring inclination is to say that the penny looks just plain circular, in a three-dimensional space—not elliptical at all, in any sense or by any effort I can muster. However, I also find that if I dip my head lower to view the penny from flatter angle, I begin to see how one might think it looks elliptical. Closing one eye helps too. I open my eye again, sit up straight, and find myself confused. Am I still experiencing the ellipse? Maybe not. But neither can I say that I noticed any Gestalt shift. The lampposts puzzle me, too, in a somewhat different way—in that case I feel more pulled toward the idea that they look like they shrink into the distance. How could the penny seem to me so convincingly nothing-but-circular most of the time, while the lampposts seem to shrink? If there is perspectival distortion in the one case, why not in the other? Could it be, simply, that my visual experience is disorganized, so that there is no simple relationship between viewing angle and apparent shape, between viewing distance and apparent size?

Maybe my terms and concepts are muddled. What is it for something to "look elliptical"? Is my confusion, and is the philosophical dispute (that is, the dispute between Locke and Siewert, between them and Noë, between Kelly and pretty much everyone else) entirely linguistic, or purely theoretical, while the visual experience itself is utterly obvious?

Or am I simply a poor introspector? Maybe the fact that my own phenomenology in this case doesn't seem obvious to me reveals my introspective ineptitude. I mean that remark not at all ironically or disingenuously. And yet I am not sure I should trust other philosophers' introspections either. Nor am I hopeful (as Kelly is, for example) that psychological experimentation will soon yield cleanly interpretable results in matters of this sort.

I wish I could find my way through this morass. I can't. So I aim to drag you down into it with me.

iii

There are several ways to transform a circle into an ellipse, but the most natural in this context is to project it obliquely onto a two-dimensional plane—presumably a plane perpendicular to the line of sight. Suppose that is how the geometrical transformation is supposed to proceed in the case of the coin: The coin "looks elliptical" or has an elliptical "apparent shape" because projecting it along the line of sight onto a plane perpendicular to that line produces an elliptical figure. Plausible enough?

It is tempting, then, to generalize: The apparent shape of any normal object is determined by its two-dimensional projection onto a plane perpendicular to the line of sight. It's the shape that would perfectly occlude the object if pasted onto a flat interposing screen, the figure it would leave in a photograph. (In conversations, I sometimes hear, as though it obviously settled the matter, "Well, of course the penny looks elliptical. If you took a photo, that's the shape you would see on the print.") Most of the philosophers I have mentioned appear to either invite or explicitly embrace the idea that perspectival shape is the same as shape projected on an intervening plane. Tye, for example, writes that the coin looks "elliptical from here" because "it has a shape that would be occluded by an ellipse placed in a plane perpendicular to the line of sight" (2000, p. 79). Noë writes that "perspectival size" and "perspectival shape" correspond to the "patch one must fill in on a plane perpendicular to the line of sight in order to perfectly occlude the object from view" (2004, pp. 81–82).

Price is an interesting exception. He claims that the degree of perspectival distortion varies with distance—that we experience nearby objects in their true shapes and sizes (hence the "bulgy" red patch when examining a tomato), whereas more distant objects look progressively flatter and more distorted. An obliquely viewed penny at arm's length might, then, look circular, whereas a coliseum viewed at the same angle from a mountain looks elliptical. A matchbox on one's desk looks fully three-dimensional; a tower seen across the quad appears somewhat flattened, though not entirely flat; the mountains in the distance look almost as though painted on a wall (1932, pp. 218–221).[4] In certain moods I find myself tempted by Price's idea that nearby things appear in all their three-dimensional glory, whereas the far distance is a painted backdrop. But how about the middle distance? If the tower's square corner doesn't look as if it bends at a ninety degree angle but also doesn't look entirely flat, how does it look? Does it look as if it bends at an angle of a hundred and thirty-five degrees? Only with an extra burst of sympathy and the prop of the theoretical appeal of a gradual progression toward flatness, can I see any attractiveness in that view.

If we accept, contra Price, but apparently with Locke, Tye, Noë, and others, that the perspectival apparent shape of an object is defined by the projection it would make on a plane perpendicular to the line of sight, it follows that my hat viewed from the top also looks circular or elliptical, that the orange before me looks circular, that the obliquely viewed book on my desk appears (roughly) hexagonal—in short, that everything looks or appears (in the relevant perspectival sense of "looks" or "appears") two-dimensional, *flat*. The peculiarity of this view can be missed when the object in question, like a penny, is already something approximately flat.

I don't know whether most of the philosophers who claim that the coin in some sense presents an elliptical "apparent shape" would also accept the view that everything (in that same sense) looks flat; I suspect some would not. Yet it isn't evident how exactly they can justify resisting this conclusion. Can something's apparent shape be defined by its two-dimensional projection without its presenting any sort of flat appearance? Perhaps one should say it is neither flat *nor* non-flat, because depth is simply unrepresented—but then the word "elliptical," with its planar character, is misleading; it would be better to say simply that it has a certain angular extent (Reid 1764/1997, IV.9).[5]

The geometry of planar projection defies intuitive phenomenology. To account for the streetlights smalling off into the distance, we can have the projecting lines converge upon the eye, rendering more distant objects smaller in the projective plane—no problem there; that seems natural enough. But a peculiar result follows from the fact that lines coming from the side will intersect the plane obliquely: The planar projections of objects off the central line of sight will be considerably larger than their straight-ahead counterparts—weirdly larger, if projective size is supposed to be isomorphic to apparent size. They will be stretched especially in the direction of deviation from the center. (See figure 2.1.) Note the considerably larger shadow the right sphere casts in the plane. The rays crossing the plane spread obliquely over a larger area. For the same reason, winter is colder than summer. Also for this reason, traditional cameras cannot accurately capture panoramic views. But objects off the central line of sight don't really look substantially larger and horizontally stretched, do they? That certainly isn't a position I recall any philosopher or psychologist espousing in print. Yet it appears to follow straightforwardly from defining apparent size and shape by the geometry of planar projection.

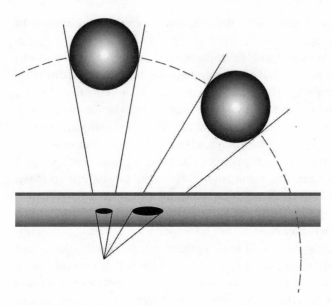

Figure 2.1

Note the larger appearance of the oblique projection in the plane, due mostly to horizontal stretching. A second factor increasing the relative size of the obliquely projected figure in the plane is that as the plane approaches the spheres, the sphere off to the side becomes disproportionately closer to the plane. This second distortion can be reduced by backing the plane away from the spheres, closer to the point of convergence, but the only way to eliminate the effect entirely would be to put the plane at the point of convergence—which would reduce the projections to points rather than two dimensional figures. (The latter infelicity may be avoidable through the use of limits, and I don't think it is as fundamental a problem as is the relative size and shape distortion due to the oblique angle.) Drafted by Glenn Vogel.

A natural way to avoid the distortion would be to project objects not onto a plane but rather onto a sphere centered at the eye. (Imagine bending the plane back on all sides until it forms a sphere centered around the convergence point.) Using spherical rather than planar projection would also capture the idea, which one sometimes encounters (e.g., on page 78 of Tye 2000), that apparent size is proportional to visual angle subtended. But now we have lost our ellipse. The projection of a circular region onto a spherical surface isn't elliptical: The ellipse is a planar figure. The resulting projection is a *concave* ellipse-like figure (or convex, depending on the assumed perspective). Is this, then, the coin's *real* apparent shape, to speak most accurately? Does the world look concave? I can almost (but only almost) warm up to the idea—it seems better to me than saying the world looks flat. The psychologist Steven Lehar, who considers the geometry of apparent size and shape more explicitly do than most writers on this topic, seems to conclude that there is a sense in which flat surfaces look concave (2003, p. 399). However, holding a large, flat object one foot from my face tends to dispel my attraction to that view.

This flawed geometry is a serious, perhaps fatal difficulty for any view committed to the elliptical appearance of the tilted coin, even if ellipticality is only one aspect of the coin's appearance. Nor is the difficulty new, though it has only rarely been noticed by philosophers. Leonardo da Vinci emphasizes the distortions of planar projection in his treatise on painting: Proportionality on a flat, painted surface is not the same, he says, as proportionality in appearance to the eye. A ball drawn at a height must be elongated to appear round, and objects drawn in very near perspective will appear monstrously foreshortened on the painting surface unless that surface is viewed from an angle that also foreshortens the appearance of the painted surface in just the same way (1519/1989, pp. 59–61). Perhaps, then, one might suggest, we are like Leonardo's correctly situated viewer, and some mechanism compensates for the distortions in planar projection so that the obliquely viewed sphere doesn't look larger than the sphere directly ahead despite its larger appearance in the plane. But then the geometry of visual appearance is no longer the geometry of the projective plane after all. What is it, then? That question is only pushed back, not answered.

Could it be that there is an ellipse upon the retina? Well, first, of course, the retina is not flat, but curved, so the figure there is not an ellipse but a convex ellipsoid—a figure not even approximately flat if the object in view occupies a large visual angle. Just as important, we shouldn't take it for granted that how things appear on the retina is how things *look*, phenomenologically. For starters, the retinal image is upside-down, has a hole in it where the optic nerve enters, and is not one but two—one for each eye, slightly different.

There appears to be no plausible geometry of flattism—no means of transforming the outward circle into the inward ellipse that doesn't, when generalized, lead to absurdities.

iv

Is it simply obvious and undeniable that the coin appears or looks (in some sense) elliptical, in a way that no geometrical cavils can touch? That seems to be the majority view, both among scholars and among the ordinary people I have quizzed on the topic. No elliptical appearance is obvious to me, but maybe I'm being obtuse or willfully blind. Quite possibly so!

However, I'll tell you what I suspect. I suspect that our inclination to regard the apparent shape of the coin as an ellipse and the more distant lightposts as smaller—our inclination to attribute to visual appearances or visual experience what I will henceforth call *projective distortions*—is due to over-analogizing visual experience to flat media such as paintings or snapshots. Noë himself suggests that theorists have often over-analogized visual experience to snapshots, mistakenly attributing to visual experience photographically rich detail from the center far into the periphery. (I will return to this point in chapter 7.) What I am suggesting is that the mainstream community in philosophy of perception, including Noë, over-analogizes to pictures in a different way, taking visual experience or "apparent shape" to be, in some sense, flat like a picture: The coin "looks" elliptical because that's how one would *paint* it.

We over-analogize the mind quite often, I suspect, casting what is difficult and recondite in terms of better-known outward media and technologies, then misattributing features of those technologies back into the mind. If you're a connectionist (emphasizing the value of a certain sort of non-classical computation) or a fan of John Searle (1984), you may think that in the 1970s and the 1980s many philosophers and cognitive psychologists over-analogized thought to classical computation. (Earlier materialist philosophers analogized thought to clockwork or hydraulics.) In chapter 1, I suggested that Americans in the 1950s over-analogized dreams to movies.

v

I am not sure how to establish what I have just suggested. Maybe it can't be established. But here is a conjecture that, if true, may support the idea: Theorists writing in cultural contexts where vision isn't typically analogized to two-dimensional projective media will be substantially less likely to attribute projective distortions to visual experience—especially planar projective distortions—than will theorists writing in contexts where flat media metaphors dominate. Two historical periods are especially relevant to this hypothesis: ancient Greece, where the dominant analogy for visual perception was impressing a signet upon wax, and introspective psychology around 1900, where the dominant analogy (for *binocular* vision) was the stereoscope.

If a signet is correctly applied, the impression on wax will accurately match, in complement, the entire shape of the signet, with a part-for-part correspondence that doesn't vary with the circumstances of application. Unlike photographs or paintings, wax impressions don't reflect different parts of their subject, or take on a different arrangement of shapes, with variations in perspective (though, of course, we may *see* a wax impression from different perspectives, or a signet may happen to be engraved with a perspectivally represented scene). Now, perhaps this absence of perspective is a weakness in the wax-signet analogy: Clearly, perception—vision especially—is perspectival. Furthermore, vision, painting, and photography are similarly perspectival in at least the following respect: A picture will portray (and omit) almost exactly the same parts of its subject that a viewer would see (and not see) from that side. In this respect at least, the picture analogy is superior to the wax-signet analogy for vision. But of course it doesn't follow from this alone that things look flat.

Aristotle famously employs the signet analogy for perception in *De Anima* (4th c. BCE/1936, 424a, 435a) and *De Memoria* (4th c. BCE/1906, 450a, though in the latter passage he also employs the picture analogy). He writes, for example, that "sense is that which is receptive of the form of sensible objects without the matter, just as the wax receives the impression of the signet ring without the iron or the gold" (424a). In neither of these works, nor in the related works I have reviewed, does Aristotle attribute projective distortions to visual appearances.[6] Epicurus embraces the signet analogy (see *Letter to Herodotus*, ca. 300 BCE/1926, 49, and the description of his view in Plutarch's *Brutus*, ca. 100 CE/1918, XXXVII), and he emphasizes that our impressions are the same shape as the objects perceived—that is, apparently, not projectively distorted.[7] Sextus Empiricus, though critical of the signet analogy in some places (e.g., *Against the Logicians*, 2nd c. CE/2005, I.228, 250–251, 372, II.400; *Outlines of Skepticism*, 2nd c. CE/1994, II.70), appears to employ it uncritically in others (*AL* I.293; *OS* I.49) and never (that I can find) analogizes perception to having a picture in the mind. Sextus is a particularly telling case, I think, because he repeatedly emphasizes variation and distortion in sensory appearances, offering extensive catalogs at, e.g., *OS* I.44–52, 100–127 and *AL* I.192–209, 414. For example, Sextus notes that things look different after one has stared at the sun, or when one presses the side of one's eye, that mirrors can change the appearance of things, that oars look bent in water, that what appears in motion or at rest depends on whether one is on the ship or the shore, and so on. Sextus is the greatest of the Greek skeptics—or at least the one with the largest body of extant work—and his skeptical arguments require that he emphasize how sensory appearances vary with differences in situation; that is one of his most famous and central points.

And yet I can discover no unambiguous example of two-dimensional projective distortion. It is difficult to imagine that Sextus would have left phenomena of this sort off his lists of perspectival variation had they occurred to him.

Before considering two potentially ambiguous passages in Sextus (and two others in Plato), I must emphasize the distinction between illusion and projective distortion. The two are very different: One can reject all varieties of flattism and yet hold that we may on some occasions see a round object as elliptical or a distant object as smaller than it is. In fact, the latter might be quite common: Young children systematically underestimate the sizes of distant objects. Adults' judgments are more accurate, but whether that is because we no longer suffer the illusion or whether instead we compensate for it in our judgments about objective size isn't clear (Gilinsky 1951; Epstein et al. 1961; Leibowitz et al. 1967; Higashiyama and Shimono 1994; Granrud 2009). If there is a persistent size illusion with distance, cognitively compensated for, that may explain why I feel readier to acknowledge the appearance of shrinking streetlights than elliptical-looking coins: There would still be some truth in the thought that the streetlights look smaller—not because any sort of flattism is true, but rather because the visual system tends to misjudge the size of distant objects. It wouldn't follow that the coin looks elliptical or a rectangular table trapezoidal. But *is* there a persistent illusion of smallness in distant things? I find it interestingly difficult to distinguish veridical perception from perception of known illusions adequately compensated for in judgment.[8] Regardless, however, *everyone* has to permit some illusion, no matter their attitude about projective distortion. In fact, it probably is best to think of projective distortion, if it exists, as veridical rather than illusory: As Noë emphasizes, the coin's elliptical appearance at an angle underwrites our knowledge of its objective circularity; the distant streetlight's looking about half the height of the near one underwrites our knowledge that it is in fact the same size and about twice as far away. On this view, perspectival distortions are not misleading illusions but accurate representations of perspectival properties from a particular point of view.

Although I can't quite extricate myself from that tangle of issues, this much seems clear: Since everyone must allow for the existence of illusion, we cannot automatically assume that whenever an author says that something appears the wrong size or shape, he embraces the existence of perspectival distortion in the relevant sense. Sextus writes that a colonnade appears to narrow when viewed from one end but appears symmetrical when viewed from the middle,[9] and that from a distance a square tower may look round or a large thing small (OS I.118). Someone who finds flattism a natural and obvious position might be tempted to see projective distortion in these claims, but I believe the examples are more naturally read as cases of illusion. If Sextus were speaking here of projective distortion, he would have to say that the colonnade narrows at *both* ends when viewed from the middle, rather than contrasting, as he does, the narrowing and the symmetricality. Illusions in the perception of columns were well known to the ancient Greeks, and were famously employed in the design of the Parthenon; there is no reason not to think this is what Sextus had in mind. Likewise, just as we can misperceive a square tower in the distance as round, Sextus seems to be saying, we can misjudge its size. No planar projection need be involved; he needn't be accepting flattism. Epicurus makes a similar claim about distant towers (reported by Sextus in *AL* I.208–209), which presumably influenced Sextus's own claim; and Epicurus attributes both the roundness and the smallness, not to planar projection (how could something square in that way become round, anyhow?) but rather to the wearing off and smoothing of the edges of effused images from the distant tower in the course of their travel to the eye. (For a related but slightly different explanation, see figure 9 of Euclid's *Optics*, ca. 300 BCE/1945.)

Plato is another interesting case. His use of analogy is unusual in the ancient Greek context: Although he employs the wax signet analogy for memory (in the *Theaetetus*, 4th c. BCE/1961, esp. 191c–194d) he does not appear to use it for perception, and he does, in at least one place, liken visual appearances to paintings (*Republic*, 4th c. BCE/1961, X.597e–598c, where he says that the painter imitates the appearance of the couch); so the ancient Greeks aren't entirely univocal in their choice of analogies. Plato also, in the *Protagoras*, says that "the same magnitudes seem greater to the eye from near at hand than they do from a distance" (4th c. BCE/1961, 356c, p. 347), but this passing remark is too brief to reveal whether Plato has misperception or projective distortion in mind. In the *Sophist* (4th c. BCE/1961, 235e–236a), a "stranger" suggests that the tops of colossal statues look too small unless artists render them disproportionately large. But this can't be a matter of projective distortion: If the artists were to try to compensate fully for projective distortion, that would require *radical* enlargement of the tops of a colossal statues; and of course there is no need to compensate for ordinary projective distortion anyway, since a proportionate colossus *should*, in the relevant sense, "look smaller" at the top if it is also to look objectively proportionate. Again, the remark appears to concern illusion and the Greeks' Parthenonesque tricks of design to please the eye.

In the ancient Greek literature I have reviewed, I've found only a few explicit comparisons of visual perception, or even visual imagery, to sketches or paintings. And I've found *no* clear case of any ancient Greek's attributing projective distortions to visual appearances. I have found a few remarks, discussed above, that might be interpreted either way, though even these pertain mainly to size distortion. No elliptical coins, no flat-looking globes.

Am I setting the bar too high? What, one might wonder, would count as an unambiguous attribution of perspectival distortion? Well, although there are no examples in ancient Greece, there are several in ancient Italy and Egypt. Lucretius writes that "though a colonnade runs on straight-set lines all the way, and stands resting on equal columns from end to end, yet when its whole length is seen from the top end, little by little it contracts to the pointed head of a narrow cone" (*De Rerum Natura* 1st c. BCE/1910, IV ca. l. 430). Both the extreme decrease in size and the fact that no one would be genuinely tempted to think she was looking at a cone seem to me to invite the idea that Lucretius does not intend to be discussing an ordinary case of illusion—though it complicates the interpretation that this case is discussed alongside cases of illusion (as well as dreams) as cases that might "spoil our trust in the senses." Another ancient Italian, Philodemus, asserts that "for the most part distance decreases magnitudes, which are many times greater than their appearance" (1st c. BCE/1978, §15). Again, the magnitude of the distortion and the generality of the remark invite the thought that Philodemus is not discussing the ordinary mistakes of illusion.

The ancient Egyptian geometer Euclid writes that "if the line falling from the eye to the center of the circle is not at right angles to the plane of the circle nor equal to the radius and does not enclose equal angles, the diameters with which it makes unequal angles will appear unequal" (*Optics*, ca. 300 BCE/1945, figure 35). In other words, the obliquely viewed circle will appear to the eye to have the unequal diameters (longer, say, from side to side than from top to bottom) characteristic of an ellipse. Indeed, throughout the *Optics* Euclid characterizes apparent size and shape in terms of visual angle (e.g., figure 5). His angular geometry, like the geometry of projection onto a sphere, does not imply the stretching of objects off the central line of sight (though I don't think it's straightforward how depth is experienced on Euclid's view). Ptolemy, following Euclid in Egypt centuries later, espouses similar views in his own *Optics* (2nd c. CE/1996).

These cases do not, I think, falsify my conjecture but rather confirm it: The ancient Italians and Egyptians seem much less enamored of the wax signet analogy. The ancient Egyptian Plotinus, for example, regularly vilifies the analogy in his *Enneads* (3rd c. CE/1966–1988, e.g., at III.6.2 and throughout IV.5–6). But neither does comparison to flat media seem to be common in these literatures. Fittingly, then, the perspectival distortions that Lucretius, Euclid, and Ptolemy attribute to visual experience do not show a planar character. Lucretius describes the apparent shape of his colonnade as a cone, and Euclid and Ptolemy use an angular geometry.[10]

(If you read English translations of the Greek classics with my hypothesis in mind, you may notice many occurrences of the word "picture" in discussions of visual imagery—in discussions, that is, not of visual sensations but of visual imaginings. In most of the cases I have examined, it appears to be the translator bringing in the analogy; the original Greek texts do not explicitly suggest it. Such translations may arise because calling images "pictures" almost doesn't seem metaphorical to contemporary English speakers. Is this because images *are* flat?)

vi

The stereoscope, invented by Charles Wheatstone in the 1830s and popular in nineteenth-century parlors, served as the preferred analogy for binocular vision among some of the early introspective psychologists, including Hermann von Helmholtz (1856/1909/1962), Ernst Mach (1886/1959), Wilhelm Wundt (1896/1897), and Edward Titchener (1901–1905, 1910). A stereoscope holds two photographs, taken from slightly different perspectives, and presents one to each eye. If the perceiver succeeds in "fusing" the two pictures, she experiences a lively three-dimensional effect. Although stereoscopes are perspectival, whereas signet impressions are not, the stereoscopic image is not a simple two-dimensional projection.

In accord with my conjecture in section iv, the psychologists favoring stereoscopy as an analogy for sight also tend to avoid saying (except in cases of outright illusion) that "apparent size" varies with distance or that the circle viewed obliquely "looks" elliptical—though Helmholtz is a notable exception. Conversely, authors who are less enamored of stereoscopy (e.g., Dewey 1886), or who seem generally to prefer the picture analogy (e.g., James 1890/1981), more frequently attribute projective distortions to experience.

Psychologists analogizing vision to stereoscopy tend to emphasize the difference between monocular and binocular vision. Mach, for example, in presenting a sketch of what he describes as a moment of his visual experience, emphasizes that a flat picture can only adequately represent monocular vision; "stereoscopic" vision, he says, can't be represented by a single plane drawing (1886/1959, pp. 18–19). (Noë, though he reproduces the sketch, does not mention this aspect of Mach's presentation.) Would Mach, then, have been willing to say that a circle viewed at an angle looks like an ellipse monocularly but not binocularly? To contemporary sensibilities this may seem strange. It seems—to me at least—that monocular vision does not differ that much from binocular vision, though Brian O'Shaughnessy (2003) and Oliver Sacks (2006) appear to disagree with me on this point.[11] Binocular disparity, as late-nineteenth-century psychologists well knew, is only one among many depth cues. The world doesn't, I think, go flat and then puff out as I open and close one eye. But of course in stereoscopy the difference between monocular and binocular views is essential.

vii

Psychologists fond of the stereoscope analogy also seem readier than others to find *doubling* in visual experience, like the doubling, perhaps, of an unfused image in a stereoscope. For example, Titchener writes:

[T]he field of vision . . . shows a good deal of doubling: the tip of the cigar in your mouth splits into two, the edge of the open door wavers into two, the ropes of the swing, the telegraph pole, the stem of another, nearer tree, all are doubled. So long, that is, as the eyes are at rest, only certain objects in the field are seen single; the rest are seen double. (1910, p. 309)

That most people fail to notice this, Titchener remarks, is "one of the curiosities of binocular vision." Similarly, Helmholtz writes:

When a person's attention is directed for the first time to the double images in binocular vision, he is usually greatly astonished to think that he had never noticed them before, especially when he reflects that the only objects he has ever seen single were those few that happened at the moment to be about as far from his eyes as the point of fixation. The great majority of objects, comprising all those that were farther or nearer than this point, were all seen double. (1856/1909/1962, volume 3, pp. 6–7)

Now, I must confess that I find quite remarkable—almost unbelievable— the idea that most of what I see, most of the time, is doubled. However, P. L. Panum (1858) suggests that we shouldn't be too surprised by people's ignorance on this point. First, Panum says, double images are generally indefinite [*unbestimmt*] and foggy [*nebelhaft*], partly because they usually arise from objects that are not at the focal distance to which the eyes are at that moment accommodated. And second, since the eyes generally converge upon whatever object we are attending to, through their convergence making it appear single, it is generally only unattended and thus quickly forgotten objects that appear double.[12]

Holding my finger about four inches before my nose and focusing my eyes in the distance, I find that the finger does in some sense look doubled. With a little more effort, if I focus on my finger 12 inches in front of my face, I can see objects in the distance as doubled. (It helps if the object is a small light source and the environment is relatively dark; it also helps if I open and shut one eye first.) But is this how things seem most of the time? As I took my morning stroll today, I repeatedly considered this question. I held my finger a foot in front of my face and focused on it, considering how the houses in the distance or the car parked on my left looked. I can only say that I was struck by the singleness of everything, contra Titchener, Helmholtz, and Panum. This singleness was sometimes blurry; but blurriness is not much like doubling, except perhaps when both are very minor or when the target object is unadorned and amorphous.

It could be that I am different from most people. I was diagnosed with amblyopia ("lazy eye") as a child, and even now I have, I think, an unusually dominant left eye, so I find it natural to close my right eye in bright sunlight and very difficult to freely fuse "Magic Eye" autostereograms. Thus, my visual experience may depend less on binocular cues than is usual, and consequently I may differ from the majority in my experience of double images and visual depth. When I presented the ideas of this section to my undergraduate seminar in 2007, I was surprised to find that all eight students reported seeing many of the things around them as double, and one student remarked that for years he had been aware of the pervasive doubling of things away from the point of focus. On the other hand, Stephen Palmer, in his influential textbook *Vision Science*, suggests that we don't ordinarily experience binocular disparity as doubleness, but rather as depth, except when we specifically attend to that disparity (1999, p. 209; see also Lee and Dobbins 2006). The issue has not been systematically explored by contemporary psychologists.

It would be in keeping with the general theme of this chapter and the preceding one if I could link the rise and (partial) decline of the view that most objects are seen double with the rise and decline of the popularity of stereoscopes. And indeed there does seem to be some relationship.

Nevertheless, the view that experience is pervasively doubled antedates the invention of the stereoscope by a millennium and a half, going back at least to Ptolemy; so the media analogy is at best a partial explanation. Also operative here, I think, is the theory of the *horopter*—a term (invented by François de Aguilón in 1613) for the region of space from which rays radiating to each eye will fall on corresponding parts of the retina, with the distance of that region depending on the degree of convergence of the eyes. (Ptolemy's version of this theory, in *Optics* II.27–44, does not specifically invoke the retina. Other important pre-stereoscope advocates of pervasive doubling are Reid (1764/1997 VI.13), Purkinje (1819/2001, pp. 102–104), and Müller (1837–1840, volume 2, pp. 376–387). For a good recent discussion of the horopter—though one that is virtually silent on the issue of doubling—see Schreiber et al. 2008.) Unfortunately, I see no straightforward way to assess whether the geometrical beauty of the horopter theory, and perhaps the invention of the stereoscope, enabled the discovery of the pervasive doubling of visual experience, or whether they instead misled researchers into attributing a doubling that is, at most, present only in unusual cases or when the fact of disparity is attended to.

Is the question really so difficult, though? Shouldn't the difference between a pervasively doubled and a pervasively singular visual field be so huge and obvious that—despite Panum's cautions—it would be almost impossible for a careful observer to get it wrong? It might be tempting to attribute disagreements on the matter entirely to terminological differences, if only the terminology weren't so seemingly straightforward. Who can't, simply by putting her finger before her nose, grasp the relevant sense of "appearing double"? Do people, then, though outwardly similar, just visually experience the world in radically different ways?

viii

Of course we can tell by looking that an obliquely viewed coin would project as an ellipse upon an intervening plane. But we can also tell that it would project as a circle onto the ceiling, would project as two ellipses onto two planes at slightly different angles (one for each eye, say), would project as a concave ellipsoid on the exterior of a sphere, and would be likely to make a particular impression in wax. Surely the coin looks different from different perspectives, despite its objective constancy. (Similarly, perhaps, the shadowed part of a wall looks different from the sunlit part, even though we can tell by looking that it is painted a single color; and a person sounds different far away than she does nearby even though we know by hearing that she is speaking no less loudly.) But whether the differences in the coin's appearance as I move my head are well captured by saying it "looks elliptical"—that's another question.

David Hume writes:

Tis commonly allowed by philosophers, that all bodies, which discover themselves to the eye, appear as if painted on a plain surface. (1740/1978, p. 56)

And G. E. Moore, after holding up an envelope, says:

Those of you on that side of the room will have seen a rhomboidal figure, while those in front of me will have seen a figure more nearly rectangular. (1953, p. 33)

It isn't as obvious to me as it has been to many others that there is any sense in which such remarks are true. But I'm not sure how to go about resolving this question. Staring longer at the penny only leaves me more perplexed.

3 Galton's Other Folly

There was a time when I could visualize the obverse, and then the reverse. Now I see them simultaneously. This is not as though the Zahir were crystal, because it is not a matter of one face being superimposed upon another; rather, it is as though my eyesight were spherical, with the Zahir in the center.

—Jorge Luis Borges, "The Zahir" (1949/1962)

i

Francis Galton was one of the great intellectual pioneers of the Victorian era. He explored Africa, introduced the pressure-system weather map, invented the statistical concepts of correlation and regression, and published influential works on heredity, fingerprints, and genius. His interest in quantification was sometimes whimsical—for example, he invented a way to measure boredom at meetings of the Royal Geographic Society (by counting fidgets), and he worked on a "beauty map" of Britain that was based on counting the number of "attractive, indifferent, or repellent" girls seen in the streets. Like many pioneers, he sometimes misjudged the new territory, most notoriously and problematically in his advocacy of eugenics (a term he coined). Prefigurings of twentieth century racist and classist eugenics can be seen in Galton's cavalier assumptions about how much human variation, including between the races, is due to heredity and in his readiness to forbid the reproduction of "degenerate" and "unfit" people including criminals and paupers. (He himself was independently wealthy.) "Folly" may be too gentle a word.

Galton's other folly, in my view, was one of the contributions for which he is most praised: his cataloguing of human differences in visual imagery on the basis of self-report and anecdote (1880, 1883/1907). I will argue in this chapter that the differences in people's reports about their imagery fail to reflect whatever real differences there might be in their underlying imagery experience. For 130 years, the study of imagery has been burdened with excessive optimism about subjective report, inherited partly from Galton.

ii

Close your eyes and form a visual image. (Are your eyes closed? No, I can tell, you're peeking!) Imagine—as Galton (1880) suggests in his first classic study of imagery, which I will discuss in more detail shortly—your break-fast table as you sat down to it this morning. Or imagine the front of your house as viewed from the street. Assuming that you can form such imagery (some people say they can't[1]), consider this: How well do you know, right now, that imagery experience? You know, I assume, *that* you have an image, and you know some aspects of its content—that it is your house, say, from a particular point of view. But that really isn't to say very much about your imagery experience.

Consider these further questions: How much of the scene can you vividly visualize at once? Can you keep the image of the chimney vividly in mind at the same time that you vividly imagine your front door, or does the image of the chimney fade as you begin to think about the door? How much detail does your image have? How stable is it? If you can't visually imagine the entire front of your house in rich detail all at once, what happens to the aspects of the image that are relatively less detailed? If the chimney is still experienced as part of your imagery when your image-making energies are focused on the front door, how exactly is it experi-enced? Does it have determinate shape, determinate color? In general, do the objects in your image have color before you think to assign color to them, or do some of the colors remain indeterminate, at least for a while (as, in chapter 1, I suggested may be the case for many dream objects)? If there is indeterminacy of color, how is that indeterminacy experienced? As gray? Does your visual image have depth in the same way your sensory visual experience does (*if* it does—see chapter 2), or is your imagery somehow flatter, more like a sketch or a picture? How much is your visual imagery like the experience of seeing a picture, or having phosphenes (the spots of color many people report when they press on their eyes[2]), or afterimages, or dreams, or daydreams? Do you experience the image as located somewhere in egocentric space—inside your head, or before your eyes, or in front of your forehead—or does it make no sense to attempt to assign it a position in this way?

Most of the people I have interviewed about their imagery, when faced with such a series of questions, stumble or feel uncertain at some point.

The questions seem hard—at least some of them do (different ones, I've found, to different people). They seem like questions one might get wrong, even when reflecting calmly and patiently. And if the questions are hard, so that people can in fact easily err—well, on the face of it that would seem to conflict with many philosophers' optimistic views about the infallibility or practical accuracy of our knowledge of our ongoing stream of experience. It would seem to conflict, for example, with Descartes' (1637/1985, 1641/1984) claim, and Locke's (1690/1975), and Price's (1932, as quoted in chapter 2), and Sydney Shoemaker's (1963), and David Chalmers's (2003), that it isn't possible to doubt or be mistaken about one's own experiences, at least to the extent that your judgments pertain entirely to your ongoing phenomenology (that is, your subjective experience or consciousness). It also calls into doubt, I think, the wisdom of psychologists' (including Galton's) widespread trust in the general accuracy of people's reports about features of their stream of experience. Now, I don't want to reject such optimistic assessments of our self-knowledge too hastily. This whole book is aimed at undermining such optimism, and I will return repeatedly to optimists' possible responses, qualifications, and countermoves. But here I merely want to note the surface plausibility of the following inference: *If* people can easily err about their own ongoing conscious experience of imagery, then there is at least one major type of conscious experience about which people can easily go wrong; and that would seem to problematize broad claims about the impossibility, or the rarity, or the necessarily pathological origins of mistakes about one's own currently ongoing stream of experience.

Of course, not every reader faced with these questions will feel the same uncertainty that I feel and that most of my interviewees seem to feel. If you are one of those confident readers, then I suspect you will not sympathize with my critique of the optimism of Galton and others. The sense of doubt I hope to evoke in this section is what gives force to the rest of this chapter. It is what lends plausibility to the thought that there may be widespread error in the cases I'll soon be describing. If you don't feel such doubt, you probably will find some alternative explanation of the phenomena to be discussed more appealing. If while reading the opening two paragraphs of this section you didn't attempt to form an image and answer the questions, I urge you to do so now and to frankly assess, as well as one can in such circumstances, the difficulty of the questions and the potential for error.

Suppose you do feel some uncertainty or see some room for error. You may still know your experience perfectly well. Possible error doesn't entail actual error or even, always, a failure of knowledge. Or your feeling of uncertainty might be a poor index of the likelihood of error. Furthermore, it could be that any uncertainty you feel flows not from some shortcoming in your epistemic relationship to your imagery experience but from the tangle of concepts I have invoked in my questions. Your confusion might, that is, be like the confusion I would feel if someone asked me whether a particular shade of red I'm looking at is scarlet, maroon, vermillion, or magenta. I know perfectly well what shade I'm looking at, but my command of the sub-vocabulary of redness is too weak for me to confidently apply such labels. Or maybe it's like the confusion I might feel if my accountant (as a practical joke) were to ask me if I had stopped cheating on my taxes yet. I don't recall ever cheating on my taxes, and ordinarily I would say that I know this fact about myself; but I'm not *certain* that I've never cheated (perhaps I cheated in a small way that I have since forgotten), so the question leaves me flustered. It builds in a false presupposition that I can't decisively reject. Such sources of doubt are artifactual, are incidental to how the questions are posed, and don't reflect the sort of potentiality for error that I have in mind.

Granted, then, some of the expressions I have used may strike you as strange (for example, "image-making energies"), and some of the questions may have problematic presuppositions (for example, that an image is the kind of thing to which it makes sense to attribute stability or instability). That probably is unavoidable. (Why unavoidable? I suspect it's because our limited understanding of our imagery hobbles our thought and talk about it, but to put any weight on that suspicion here would be to assume what I hope to conclude.) So feel free to set aside the questions that seem problematic to you. Or better, recast them in your own terms. Return to them at leisure, when they aren't crowded among a dozen others. Don't worry about keeping to a shared, stable vocabulary; instead try to consider only your knowledge of the experience itself, broadly considered. For me, even when I try all this, the feeling of difficulty and uncertainty remains.

There may be a level of detail beyond which it isn't appropriate to ask questions. One can imagine a striped tiger without imagining it as having a determinate number of stripes (Price 1941; Dennett 1969; Block 1981)— at least, maybe one can: George Berkeley would disagree (see the next section). It would, then, be perverse to insist on a precise answer about the number of stripes and to take any resulting uncertainty as a sign of intro-spective ineptitude. But I hope my questions aren't like that. They concern, for example, *whether* the imagined tiger (or chimney) has a determinate number of stripes (or bricks)—which is a substantial, or at least middle-sized, feature of the imagery experience, namely how detailed or "sketchy" it is. (Of course it might be indeterminate whether an image is indeterminate, but advocating higher-order indeterminacy is quite different from accepting the more ordinary view that images often *do* have some indeterminacy.[3])

iii

The history of psychology and philosophy has seen three major debates about imagery, which I want to address briefly before returning to Galton. The most recent of these occurred in the 1980s (when it was often called "the imagery debate") and concerned underlying cognitive structure—that is, whether imagery is underwritten by language-like symbolic structures (Pylyshyn 1973, 2002) or whether, instead, it requires some more irreducibly pictorial (or "quasi-pictorial") cognitive structure (Kosslyn 1980, 1994). Whether this debate turns on any disagreement about the actual conscious experience of imagery isn't clear. Maybe theoreticians in both camps could entirely agree about imagery experience while continuing to disagree about cognitive architecture.[4] However, the two other major historical debates about imagery seem to involve—or to *be*—disagreements about conscious experience or phenomenology.

The "imageless thought" controversy of the early twentieth century concerned (as one might guess from its label) the possibility of conscious thought without imagery, where "imagery" was construed to include not only visual imagery but also auditory imagery (e.g., sentences in "inner speech" or silent tunes in one's head), kinesthetic imagery (e.g., imagining the feeling of waving one's arms), and imagery in any other modality. Psychologists working at Würzburg under Oswald Külpe, such as Narziss Ach (1905) and Karl Bühler (1907), asserted that one could have conscious thoughts that involved nothing imagistic whatsoever. Titchener (1909) rejected that view, as did (probably) Wundt (1907, 1908b).[5] Titchener claims that he regularly entertains visual images of all sorts of "unpicturable notions," including the notion of *meaning*—which he normally sees as "the blue-grey tip of a kind of scoop, which has a bit of yellow about it (probably a part of the handle), and which is just digging into a dark mass of what appears to be plastic material" (1909, pp. 18–19). Of course, Titchener allows that other people may more often think with auditory images, such as the sound of spoken words. Külpe, in contrast, records thoughts such as "with Darwin, chance is considered as an explanation of purpose" with no trace of any image, including of the word "Darwin" (Bühler 1907, pp. 318–319; translated from Humphrey 1951). Even Aristotle (4th c. BCE/1936, 431a) appears to take a stand, saying "the soul never thinks without an image" (if we may translate "φαντάσματος" as meaning "image" in the relevant sense).

Before the "imageless thought" controversy, there was a debate between Locke and Berkeley about abstract ideas. Locke seems to have felt that he could form an image of a triangle that is "neither oblique, nor rectangle, neither equilateral, equicrural, nor scalenon; but all and none of these at once" (1690/1975, p. 596).[6] In response, Berkeley writes: "If any man has the faculty of framing in his mind such an idea of a triangle as is here described, it is in vain to pretend to dispute him out of it, nor would I go about it. All I desire is that the reader would fully and certainly inform himself whether he has such an idea or no." (1710/1965, p. 12). Only with tongue in cheek does Berkeley grant the possibility of such a faculty; the whole point of his discussion is to demonstrate the impossibility of such "abstract ideas." Locke, he thinks, is wrong about his own experience.

Is it clear who is right in the dispute about "abstract ideas"? My own inclination favors Locke, though I have to admit that abstraction and indeterminacy seem to me supportable only up to a point: Would Locke allow that we can visually imagine a circle and a triangle side by side without imagining which one is on which side? That is, could we imagine its remaining indeterminate or unspecified whether the circle is on the right and the triangle is on the left or vice versa while nonetheless visually imagining the two as next to each other? That gives me pause. On the other hand, I doubt that images are always as perfectly determinate as Berkeley seems to insist. Russell Hurlburt offers what strikes me as a plausible example of an indeterminate image:

Susan, a college student, was critical of her roommate Helen's relationships with boys. Susan reported having [when a random beeper went off to cue her to think about her stream of inner experience] an image of Helen, seen from the waist up sitting on their couch with a boy. Helen in the image was wearing only a bra. Helen and the couch and the bra were seen clearly in the image, but the boy's face was unelaborated or indistinct. (Hurlburt and Schwitzgebel 2007, p. 106)

Contrast Berkeley (1710/1965, p. 8): "Likewise, the idea of a man that I frame to myself must be either of a white, or a black, or a tawny, a straight, or a crooked, a tall, or a low, or a middle-sized man." Might images be capable of indeterminacy, but only to a limited degree—as perhaps ink-and-paper sketches (or quavery, shifting, animated sketches) are? I find that view appealing, but I worry that I'm being captured by media meta-phors in the manner I criticize in chapters 1 and 2.

Or perhaps Locke and Berkeley just had very different sorts of imagery, so that each is right about his own experience and wrong only in general-izing to other people. (Locke does say it requires "some pains and skill" to form a general idea like that of his triangle; maybe Berkeley lacked the skill or wasn't inspired to take the pains.) Perhaps Titchener never thought without imagery, whereas Külpe did so regularly. Or maybe there is some confusion of words, so that although all the parties have basically the same experience they somehow end up talking past one another. I must say, however, that the uncertainty I myself feel in the face of questions like those with which I began this chapter warms me to the idea that Locke or Berkeley or Külpe or Titchener may indeed be simply mistaken about his experience—perhaps blinded in part by theory, preconception, or analogy.

iv

Since people differ substantially in their perceptual and cognitive abilities, they probably also differ in their visual imagery. However, the imagery reports of apparently normal people differ so much that one might reason-ably question the veracity of those reports. For most traits (barring defect, injury, or prodigy), human variation keeps within certain limits of normal-ity. As the ancient Chinese philosopher Mencius says, "When someone makes a shoe for a foot he has not seen, I am sure he will not produce a basket." (4th c. BCE/1970, 6A7)

In the 1870s, Galton, as I have mentioned, asked his subjects to visualize their breakfast tables. He instructed them to describe various features of the resulting imagery, as follows:

1. *Illumination.*—Is the image dim or fairly clear? Is its brightness comparable to that of the actual scene?

2. *Definition.*—Are all the objects pretty well defined at the same time, or is the place of sharpest definition at any one moment more contracted than it is in the real scene?

3. *Coloring.*—Are the colors of the china, of the toast, breadcrust, mustard, meat, parsley, or whatever may have been on the table, quite distinct and natural? (1880, p. 302)

This may have been the very first psychological questionnaire; I'm aware of none earlier. Any resemblance to the questions with which I began section ii is, of course, not coincidental.

Galton had several hundred men and boys complete his questionnaire, and he supplemented this research with anecdotal reports from a variety of sources. This classic collection of narrative reports about imagery, to my knowledge, remains unmatched (probably partly because of scientists' preference, which Galton himself largely shared, for easily quantifiable and replicable measures), so I will treat it as representing the scope of opinion, even if it is dated. (If the scope of opinion has changed substantially since then, that may also support my suspicions, unless there has been a corresponding change in the actual distribution of imagery.)

What, then, do Galton's respondents say? Well, they say very different things. Some claim to have no imagery whatsoever. Others claim to have imagery as vivid and detailed as ordinary vision or even more so. Though the bulk of respondents express more intermediate views, both extremes seem to be well represented among (apparently) normal respondents. Here are some quotes from respondents at the high end: "The image that arises in my mind is perfectly clear. . . . I can see in my mind's eye just as well as if I was beholding the scene with my real eye." (1880, p. 310) "All clear and bright; all the objects seem to me well defined at the same time." (ibid., p. 305) "The mental image appears to correspond in all respects with reality. I think it is as clear as the actual scene." (ibid., p. 305) Some respondents say they can visualize an object from more than one angle at once, like Borges's character in "The Zahir." One respondent says: "My mental field of vision is larger than the normal one. In the former I appear to see everything from some commanding point of view, which at once embraces every object and all sides of every object." (1880, p. 314) Galton also says that he knows "many cases of persons mentally reading off scores when playing the pianoforte, or manuscript when they are making speeches. One statesman has assured me that a certain hesitation in utterance which he has at times is due to his being plagued by the image of the manuscript speech with its original erasures and corrections. He cannot lay the ghost, and he puzzles in trying to decipher it." (1883/1907, p. 67) (Titchener evidently made similar claims—see Sommer 1978, pp. 44–45.) Other respondents say the following: "My powers are zero. To my consciousness there is almost no association of memory with objective visual impressions. I recollect the breakfast table, but do not see it." (1880, p. 306) "No power of visualizing." (ibid., p. 306) "My impressions are in all respects so dim, vague and transient, that I doubt whether they can reasonably be called images." (ibid., p. 306) William James (who in his classic *Principles of Psychology* leans heavily on Galton's treatment of imagery) claims that his own powers of visual imagery are so weak that he "can seldom call to mind even a single letter of the alphabet in purely retinal terms. I must trace the letter by running my mental eye over its contour in order that the image of it shall have any distinctness at all." (1890/1981, p. 708)

One of Galton's subjects, a scientist, criticizes Galton's questionnaire itself:

These questions presuppose assent to some sort of a proposition regarding the "mind's eye" and the "images" which it sees. . . . This points to some initial fallacy. . . . It is only by a figure of speech that I can describe my recollection of a scene as a "mental image" which I can "see" with my "mind's eye." . . . I do not see it . . . any more than a man sees the thousand lines of Sophocles which under due pressure he is ready to repeat. (1880, p. 302, ellipses Galton's)

In fact, Galton says that "the great majority of men of science" with whom he interacted at the start of his investigations "protested that mental imagery was unknown to them, and they looked on me as fanciful and fantastic in supposing that the words 'mental imagery' really expressed what I believed everybody supposed them to mean" (ibid.). Failing to find such skepticism among non-scientists—finding, instead, a general willingness to declare their imagery distinct and full of detail, even in the face of feigned skepticism from him—Galton concludes that, contrary to what one might have expected, scientists tend to "have feeble powers of visual representation" relative to non-scientists (1880, p. 304). (In recent studies, however, Isaac and Marks (1994) and Brewer and Schommer-Aikins (2006) have failed to replicate Galton's result, finding that undergraduate science majors and practicing scientists report imagery about as vivid as that reported by non-scientists. This may reflect a change in culture, a difference in subject pools, or perhaps a theory-driven misinterpretation or distortion by Galton of his own data, as suggested by Brewer and Schommer-Aikins and contemplated by Burbridge (1994).)

Although Galton and James assume that the above-mentioned self-reports accurately reflect a surprising variation in the quantity and quality of visual imagery, I am inclined to view the reports suspiciously. You might not share such suspicion, but you may grant that before we accept the existence of such wide variability in the imagery of normal people we should ask whether people who report high and low imagery powers differ significantly in their success on cognitive tasks that plausibly are aided by the use of visual imagery. In this vein, James Angell (1910), discussing the imagery literature of the time, emphasizes the importance of looking for correlations between what he calls "objective methods" of measuring imagery, in which success or failure on a task depends on the nature of a subject's imagery, and "subjective methods" of self-report. If the correlation between subjective and objective methods is poor, Angell suggests, the differences in subjective report might be differences in report only, not reflecting real differences in imagery experience. And furthermore, if differences in imagery ability are as vast as they would seem to be from the reports of Galton's respondents, we should presumably expect vast corresponding differences in performance on cognitive tasks involving imagery—differences comparable to that between a prodigy and a normal person or between a normal person and one with severe disabilities. For example, we might expect Galton's erasure-plagued statesman to show stupendous memory of the look and layout of his manuscript. Antecedently, it seems plausible to doubt that such differences will be prevalent in normal populations—but let's look at the data.

(Established prodigies do, by the way, sometimes claim to have detailed imagery of the sort that could explain their special talents (see, e.g., Luria 1965/1968; Coltheart and Glick 1974; Grandin 1995; Sacks 1995). Temple Grandin, famous for her self-description of life with Asperger's Syndrome, claims that she can visually imagine and design entire slaughterhouses in her head—and that consequently, once the imagination is complete, she can transfer the design quickly and effortlessly to paper as no ordinary architect could do. In such cases, the subjective reports have at least prima facie plausibility—although it is also possible that some prodigies are confabulating details of their imagery to explain what they know to be unusual performances.)

v

In the past hundred years, many researchers have, as Angell advised, compared subjective and objective measures of visual imagery. The results are discouraging.

Research has focused mainly on three subjective measures, all of which are more readily quantifiable descendants of Galton's original questionnaire: Betts's (1909) Questionnaire upon Mental Imagery (and Sheehan's (1967) shortened version of that questionnaire), Gordon's (1949) Test of Visual Imagery Control, and Marks's (1973) Vividness of Visual Imagery Questionnaire (VVIQ). The early returns were very bad. Through the 1970s, attempts to correlate these subjective measures with anything objective failed so regularly that most prominent reviewers, including Ernest (1977) and Richardson (1980), denied the existence of any relationship between objective and subjective measures of imagery. Even Allan Paivio, otherwise a great defender of the importance of visual imagery, concluded that "self-report measures of imagery tend to be uncorrelated with objective performance tests" (1986, p. 117). Self-reports and objective measures did not line up.

More recent reviews have been slightly more optimistic. The most thorough treatment is Stuart McKelvie's (1995) review and meta-analysis of the literature on Marks's VVIQ, the most extensively studied of all the visual imagery questionnaires. The VVIQ prompts subjects to form visual images (such as of a relative and of a rising sun), then asks them to rate the vividness of those images on a scale from 1 ("perfectly clear and as vivid as normal vision") to 5 ("no image at all, you only 'know' that you are thinking of the object"). McKelvie finds strong relationships between the VVIQ and tests of hypnotic suggestibility, tests involving the Gestalt completion of incomplete figures (e.g., the speed at which someone would recognize a fragmentary stimulus as a "circle"), and tests of motor and physiological control; he finds spotty relationships between the VVIQ and tests of visual memory; and he finds no relationship between the VVIQ and tests of visual creativity (for people of normal IQ[7]) or tests of ability at spatial transformation or "mental rotation." (A mental rotation task might involve judging whether the line drawings of two three-dimensional objects are such that one object would be a simple rotation of the other. Another type of spatial transformation task might involve something like judging how a sheet of paper will look when folded along indicated lines.) McKelvie concludes, primarily on the basis of this pattern of results, that "on balance . . . the evidence favors the construct validity of the VVIQ, with a more definitive conclusion awaiting further research" (p. 93).

Suppose we accept McKelvie's tentatively positive assessment. Though that might cheer us a bit, it would still seem to follow that researchers generally have failed to find the dramatic performance differences that seem implied by the wide disparity of narrative reports in Galton, and consequently that the reports of Galton's subjects remain to a significant extent unjustified.[8]

However, I believe that McKelvie's conclusion is too sanguine. First, it's a bit odd to suggest that further research is needed to establish the VVIQ's validity. McKelvie's bibliography contains more than 250 publications, many of them reports of multiple VVIQ studies. The VVIQ is not a complex instrument: It has only sixteen questions, and it fits on one page. If there is any hope of establishing its validity as a measure of imagery vividness, shouldn't several hundred studies be sufficient? Also, it appears that the four kinds of tasks at which psychologists historically expected good visualizers to excel were visual memory, visual creativity, mental rotation, and other sorts of spatial transformation tasks such as mental folding. McKelvie finds no relationship between the VVIQ and any but the first of these—and even there, the relationship is at best partial and disorganized. The three tasks McKelvie reports as showing the most robust relationship between objective performance and the VVIQ have not been studied nearly as thoroughly, and are tasks whose connection with visual imagery seems prima facie more tenuous: hypnotizability, motor and physiological control, and Gestalt figure completion. Furthermore, more recent research has called into doubt the robustness of two of these three relationships: Crawford and Allen (1996), Kogon et al. (1998), Sebastiani et al. (2003), and Gemignani et al. (2006) find no relationship between the VVIQ and hypnotic suggestibility (though Santarcangelo et al. (2005) find a relationship), and Eton et al. (1998) find no relationship between the VVIQ and motor control. Although McKelvie describes the Gestalt completion findings as derived from four different studies, in fact all four of these studies are reported by a single author in a single six-page journal article (Wallace 1990). The result does not appear to have been replicated across time or laboratories. And although reports of correlations between the VVIQ and performance on various cognitive tasks presumably involving visual imagery have continued to appear since 1995, so too, perhaps even more often, have studies reporting no significant correlation between the VVIQ and visual or imagery-related tasks.[9]

There is reason to expect *some* positive findings even if the VVIQ doesn't accurately measure visual imagery. For one thing, as Paul Meehl (1990) has emphasized, psychological variables tend to correlate, sometimes robustly, for a variety of reasons apart from those hypothesized by the experimenter. For example, low (vivid) VVIQ scores and good performance on a cognitive task might both be influenced by some feature of one's social background or one's personality: Upper-middle-class Caucasians or extroverts (completely hypothetically), or people who tend to give excessively positive self-descriptions (somewhat less hypothetically—see Allbutt et al. 2008) might tend both to say they have vivid imagery and to do well on certain laboratory tasks, independent of any actual difference in imagery.

Reactivity between the measures also seems highly likely (and doesn't, it seems to me, receive nearly enough skeptical attention from psychologists in the imagery literature or in most other psychological subliteratures). Suppose you are a participant in an experiment on mental imagery—say, an undergraduate, volunteering to participate in some studies to fulfill psychology course requirements. First, you are given the VVIQ—that is, you're asked how vivid your visual imagery is. Then you are given a test of your visual memory—for example, a test of how many objects you can correctly recall after staring for a couple of minutes at a complex visual display. If I were taking part in such an experiment and I had rated myself as an especially good visualizer when given the VVIQ, I might, when presented with the memory test, think something like this: "Damn! This experimenter is trying to see whether my imaging ability is really as good as I said it was! It'll be embarrassing if I bomb. I'd better try especially hard." Conversely, if I had said I was a poor visualizer, I might not put too much energy into the memory task, so as to confirm my self-report or what I take to be the experimenter's hypothesis. Reactivity can work the other way, too, if the VVIQ is given second. Say I do poorly on the memory task or some other task, and then I'm given the VVIQ. I may be inclined to think of myself as a poor visualizer in part *because* I know I did poorly on the first task. In general, participants are not passive innocents. Any time you give them two different tests, you should *expect* their knowledge of the first test to affect their performance on the second. Exactly how subjects will react to the second test in light of the first may be difficult to predict, but the probability of such reactivity should lead us to anticipate that, even if the VVIQ fails utterly as a measure of imagery vividness, some researchers should find correlations between the VVIQ and performance on cognitive tasks. To the extent that there is a pattern in the relationship between the VVIQ and memory performance, the tendency is for the correlations to be higher in free recall tasks than in recognition tasks, as McKelvie (1995) has noted. Free recall tasks (like trying to list items in a remembered display) generally require more effort and energy from the subject than recognition tests (like "did you see this, yes or no?") and so may show more reactivity between the measures, as well as more mediation by differences in personality or motivation.

Psychologists have also tended to find that the experimenter's expectations often influence the outcome of experiments, sometimes through subtle or non-verbal communications between the experimenter and the subject (Rosnow and Rosenthal 1997). Margaret Intons-Peterson (1983) found such experimenter effects in imagery studies, using advanced undergraduates as her experimenters. She led some experimenters to expect subjects to do better on a mental rotation task under one condition and other experimenters to expect the reverse pattern of performance. The experimenters then read instructions to subjects from a typewritten sheet. All stimuli and responses were presented and recorded by computer, minimizing the most overt sources of experimenter influence on results. Despite these precautions, Intons-Peterson found that subjects' responses tended to conform to the experimenters' (presumably) subtly communicated expectations. It is also widely recognized in psychology that positive findings, whether they arise spuriously or from the experimenters' hypothesized causes, are more likely to be pursued and published than negative findings—the "file drawer effect." Paul Chara (1992) emphasizes the importance of this source of distortion in imagery research.

For all these reasons, then, we ought to expect some reports of a relationship between subjective measures of visual imagery, like Galton's questionnaire or the VVIQ (or Betts's 1909 QMI or Gordon's 1949 TVIC), and performance on cognitive tasks. The question is, what do the positive findings look like? Are there mostly positive relationships between the subjective reports of imagery and skills that would theoretically be aided by imagery? Are there mostly weaker or negative relationships with skills that would presumably not be aided by imagery? Or—as we should expect if there is in fact no substantial relationship between subjective measures of imagery and actual patterns of imagery use in cognitive tasks—are the positive findings a disorganized smattering, with frequent failures of replication? The evidence I've just reviewed suggests the latter.

vi

Eidetic imagery—sometimes popularly (but in the view of many theoreticians inaccurately) called "photographic memory"—has also been widely studied with the aim of finding correlations between subjective imagery report and performance on cognitive tests. Eidetic imagery is imagery of previous but now absent visual stimulation (such as of a witnessed scene or a viewed page) that is in some respects like an afterimage, but with two crucial differences: Whereas most long-lasting afterimages have colors complementary to the colors of the objects perceived (e.g., a red object will normally leave a green afterimage), eidetic images retain normal color, and whereas afterimages follow the eye's movement, eidetic images are motionless and scannable. Eidetic images may also be more under voluntary control than are afterimages (Jaensch 1930; Haber and Haber 1964).[10] Eidetic imagery is measured primarily by subjective report (though some researchers, following Haber and Haber 1964, also check that direction of gaze corresponds with the relative location of the details being reported) and is attributed primarily to children. Often, eidetic images are described as very detailed (e.g., Allport 1924; Jaensch 1930; though see Leask et al. 1969). Unlike "photographic memory" as the phrase is commonly used, eidetic imagery is defined purely phenomenologically, in terms of the imagery experience resembling (in certain ways) looking at a photograph. One might expect—and researchers did expect—that people with imagery experiences of that sort would tend to have excellent visual memories; but that would be an empirical question, not something true by definition.

Early researchers on eidetic imagery sometimes claimed to find a variety of differences between "eidetikers" and non-eidetikers in personality, perception, and cognition—including, of course, visual memory—but the methodology was often obscure and was inconsistent between laboratories. (For critical reviews, see Allport 1928, Klüver 1933, and Gray and Gummerman 1975.) For example, Gray and Gummerman state that frequency estimates of eidetic imagery among children span the full range from 0 percent to 100 percent, depending in part on the methodology of the study. Later, more careful research, begun and inspired by Ralph Haber and his colleagues in the 1960s, resolved some of these methodological inconsistencies, but at the price of most of the positive results—so much so that in 1979 Haber was forced to concede that "extensive research has failed to demonstrate consistent correlates between the presence of eidetic imagery and any cognitive, intellectual, neurological, or emotional measure" (p. 583). Soon thereafter, mainstream psychologists largely abandoned the study of differences between people who report eidetic imagery and people who do not.[11]

vii

Back to our main question: Are people, as Galton assumed, accurate judges of their own imagery experiences? I have offered some grounds for pessimism: the ease with which most people can be brought to confusion or uncertainty about substantial features of their imagery experiences when confronted with questions like those in section ii, the incredible diversity of imagery reports (even among apparently normal people without unusual skills or deficits), and the apparent lack of any systematic relationship between differences in imagery report and differences in performance on any sort of objective cognitive test (especially tests that psychologists have historically thought likely to be enhanced by imagery, including tests of visual memory, mental rotation tasks, and tests of ability at other sorts of spatial transformation).

Of course, all this evidence is indirect. It is not possible—at least, it is not possible right now, with neuropsychology in its current state—to measure people's imagery directly. (I'm not sure that advanced neuroscience will ever definitively settle questions about imagery and other aspects of the stream of consciousness. I don't dismiss the possibility, but in chapter 6 I will offer one reason for doubting that neuroscience will be a panacea.) So the argument I offer here has limited force: I recommend pessimism only as the most plausible interpretation of the evidence. There is ample room for the determined optimist to stage a response. This is, I find, true in general for claims about the accuracy or inaccuracy of judgments about conscious experience—the claims at the heart of this book. The indirectness of the evidence makes fertile ground for disagreement. Let's consider a few avenues for the optimist, focusing on gaps in my last argument, the one that turns on the lack of relationship between subjective report and objective performance. I will address the first three of these potential responses quickly. I will dwell on the fourth a bit more, since it easily generalizes into a concern for every chapter of this book.

First, it could be that quantified versions of Galton's questionnaire like the VVIQ, and other related measures, don't really capture the aspects of imagery relevant to performance on cognitive tests. Akhter Ahsen (1985, 1986, 1987), for example, suggests that vividness is often irrelevant or even detrimental to cognitive tasks. The view has some plausibility: In rotating an imagined figure, for instance, to see if it matches another figure on the page, what would seem to matter is its gross morphology, not its vividness. Of course, not all imagery questionnaires center on vividness. Gordon's (1949) Test of Visual Imagery Control, which has also been studied extensively, simply asks respondents *whether* they form certain visual images, such as an image of a car crashing through a house. It correlates no better than the VVIQ with cognitive performance measures. (For recent studies, mostly negative, see Antonietti, Bologna, and Lupi 1997; González, Campos, and Pérez 1997; Lequerica et al. 2002; MacIntyre et al. 2002; Burton and Fogarty 2003; Guillot et al. 2007.) This objection also doesn't address non-imagers or people with imagery as feeble and apparently useless as James claims his to be. Of course it could be that there are systemic difficulties with *all* the major visual imagery questionnaires, but someone who wishes to mount this sort of argument at least owes us a story about why a century of trying hasn't yielded anything demonstrably better.

Or it could be that visual imagery is useless in most of the cognitive tasks we have been examining. There would be no reason, then, to expect subjective measures, even if accurate, to correlate with the cognitive tests. An extreme version of this view would treat imagery as completely cognitively epiphenomenal: Although some people have powerful, vivid, lifelike imagery and others have very little imagery at all, the actual mechanisms they deploy to manage cognitive tasks and to solve problems are the same. The cost of this position is that it seems to posit a major faculty with a fairly obvious range of purposes but in fact with little purpose at all, and little effect on behavior apart from the power to generate reports. The strangeness of this view is compounded if one treats subjective reports of imagery with the uncritical credulity of Galton and James, since people will often claim to have used their imagery to solve a problem. To the extent that an advocate of this line of response mitigates extreme epiphenomenalism by allowing visual imagery to serve *some* important cognitive functions, it becomes mysterious why correlations haven't been found between measures like the VVIQ and success on any but a suspiciously desultory sprinkle of tasks.

Or it could be that both self-reported good and poor visualizers use imagery, but only good visualizers experience that imagery consciously. This position is a variant of the previous one, except that what is epiphenomenal is not the imagery itself but the conscious experience of it. People seem ordinarily to think of imagery as consciously experienced, as part of the flow of phenomenology, but perhaps a suitably functional approach can give some sense to the idea of an unconscious image (as in Paivio 1971). However, unless conscious experience is epiphenomenal, people whose imagery is mostly conscious ought to perform somewhat differently on cognitive tasks than people whose imagery is largely unconscious, and thus it remains strange that such differences have not been found. Maybe consciousness *is* epiphenomenal, or at least largely so, but such a view faces the challenge of explaining why whatever biological or functional facts permit some cognitive processes but not others to be conscious seem to have so few other ramifications.[12] Locating the top of the scale also creates challenges for this view. To fully credit subjects' reports, we would have to take reports of extremely detailed and vivid imagery as the benchmark of fully conscious imagery and assume that every subject has imagery (perhaps partly unconscious) at roughly that level of detail. Otherwise, one must either grant that there are substantial differences in the degree of detail in subjects' imagery after all, thus rekindling the original problem of explaining the lack of correlation between subjective report and cognitive test, or one must grant that the subjects at the top of the scale have overestimated their imagery, which would mean granting just the sort of error for which I am arguing. But if everyone's imagery has the level of detail described in the grandest self-assessments, it is surprising that we don't all perform substantially better on mental rotation tasks, visual memory tasks, and the like.

viii

Even if Galton's (and others') uncritical acceptance of such reports is folly—or, to put the point more politely, even if people's differences in self-report generally fail to reflect whatever underlying differences there might be in their imagery—we may still know our imagery perfectly well. Perhaps the problem is mostly one of verbal expression.

Galton asks his respondents "Is the image dim or fairly clear? Is its brightness comparable to that of the actual scene?" (1880, p. 302) Marks tops the VVIQ scale with the phrase "perfectly clear and as vivid as normal vision" (1973, p. 24). What do such phrases mean? In interpreting them, at least two problems arise. (For similar concerns, see Richardson 1980 and Cornoldi 1995.) First, it isn't entirely obvious what it is for an image to be "clear" or "vivid." Is the question whether the images are detailed? Sharply contoured? Salient? Full of saturated color? Lively? Forceful? Some or all of these? Respondents may understand the question very differently. Second, there is the problem of comparing clarity across different types of experience. When I visit the optometrist and she asks if what I see through one lens is as clear as what I see through another, I understand the question. Since I am comparing two sensory visual experiences, what it is to be "clear" remains the same across the cases. But if I am asked to compare the clarity of my vision without glasses against the clarity of an orchestra heard through a wall, the matter isn't so straightforward. Although visual imagery and visual sensation presumably have some phenomenological commonalities, they also seem to differ significantly, which makes it unclear what the criteria are for saying that a visual image is as clear and vivid as normal vision. (Exactly how sensation and imagery differ phenomenologically is, as one might expect, a matter of dispute. Hume notoriously suggests that images differ from sensory experiences mainly in being fainter (1740/1978, pp. 1–2), whereas most scholars seem to hold that imagery experiences differ from sensory experiences in kind, not just intensity. Titchener describes images as also having a "textural difference from sensation . . . more filmy, more transparent, more vaporous" (1910/1915, p. 199). McGinn says that, in comparison with percepts, images are indeterminate, "gappy, coarse, discrete" (2004, p. 25). Thomas (2010) argues that imagery differs from sense experience only in degree, but along three dimensions: vividness, stimulus constrainedness, and amenability to voluntary control. These views doesn't exhaust the alternatives, of course.) Thus, respondents interpreting "vividness" differently or using different standards for the comparison of clarity may have similar imagery experiences, which they apprehend accurately and yet describe differently.

Consider also Galton's skeptical scientist who finds a fallacy in supposing the existence of a "mind's eye" that "sees" images. If we take "see" literally, the scientist is surely right: There is no homunculus who literally sees your images. Yet there also seems to be a looser or metaphorical sense in which it is permissible to say that we see our visual imagery. Perhaps, then, the difference between the scientists' and non-scientists' responses to Galton's questions reflects neither differences in their imagery (as Galton supposes) nor epistemic failure (as I suggest) but only differences in how strictly they interpret the word "see."

These verbal difficulties are mostly what we might call *between-subjects* difficulties. *Within-subjects* measures—that is, measures that compare different instances of imagery within individuals over time—should avoid at least some of these problems, as long as the subject interprets the questionnaire items consistently over time. When someone reports that one of her images is different from another, that report, even if it isn't comparable with the reports of other subjects, may reflect a real difference between those two instances of her imagery, and thus possibly a real cognitive difference. Unfortunately, few researchers have explored such within-subjects differences in imagery (exceptions include Bower (1972) and Walczyk (1995)[13]), and the methodological difficulties are daunting. For example, if a subject rates an image as vivid and then remembers it better than she remembers an image rated as less vivid, there are many possible explanations for this relationship, only one of which is that the memory performance shows that she had accurately discerned the phenomenological vividness of the image.

I accept that the lack of clear reporting standards accounts for some of the variation in reports; in fact, I believe it is hugely problematic. However, I don't think that can be the whole story. Although the standards of "vividness" may be particularly murky, especially across different experience types, other questions involve no such problematic language, unless even the term "image" is problematic. (And if the term "image" *is* so problematic that its use invalidates all imagery questionnaires, I doubt that the optimist about introspective accuracy can find much consolation in that fact.) Gordon's Test of Visual Imagery Control, as I have mentioned, simply asks respondents whether they can form visual imagery of particular situations, such as a car crashing through a house. And although Galton's skeptical scientist may be a mere quibbler over words, if a respondent *can* form an image of his breakfast table it would be perverse to deny that fact—the fact Galton clearly is after—on the basis of concerns about how the question is phrased. Are we to suppose that all Galton's imageless scientists were so perverse? Likewise, the disputes between Locke and Berkeley and those between Titchener and Külpe don't *seem* to be disputes merely over the use of words. There are substantive phenomenological issues in the vicinity—issues the resolution of which, I find, is not entirely obvious, judging by my own experience. Barring a compelling reason to suppose otherwise, I recommend taking the disputes at face value, rather than recasting them as miscommunication. And if they are genuine disputes, and if we assume that the disputants did not differ radically in their imagistic phenomenology, then some of the parties must have been quite badly wrong about their own experience.

ix

It is extreme, of course, to suppose that there is absolutely no correlation between what people say or think about their visual imagery and their actual experienced visual phenomenology. In particular, I see nothing that inclines me to doubt that people, when they report visually imagining something, have at least a bit of a handle on what it is, roughly, that they are visually imagining. (Though I wonder: Why not doubt even this? Is it my own and others' seemingly unshakeable confidence about such matters? Could that confidence be misplaced?) However, regarding more general features of imagery experience—structural or presentational features, we might say—such as its vividness, its degree of indeterminacy, its color saturation, its spatial location or flatness, its picturelikeness, the evidence is discouraging. If there is any relationship between our subjective judgments about such matters and our actual phenomenology, for some reason it remains scientifically unproven.

The explanation to which I am drawn is that our judgments about our experience just aren't in fact very well aligned with the experiences we actually have: We tend, simply, to get it wrong, to be captured by our own assumptions, our metaphors—by what it seems appealing to say in the face of strange questions. This is, I think, a natural interpretation of the experimental and historical evidence. And it harmonizes well, I think, with the introspective and anecdotal considerations offered in the first few sections of this chapter. I find in my own case—and so also apparently do many (but not all) other people, when I have interviewed them about such matters—that it isn't entirely obvious how vivid and detailed my visual imagery is, how determinate or indeterminate, how narrowly it confines itself to my scope of attention, how richly colored, and so on. I feel in myself, and I think you may feel in yourself, the potential for error, the liability to be swept up by a theory, or a picture, or a set of background assumptions. I find the introspection of visual imagery difficult, if I set about it conscientiously. Thus, I don't think we should be surprised if people—including, perhaps, you and me—can go badly awry.

4 Human Echolocation

(with Michael S. Gordon)

[B]at sonar, though clearly a form of perception, is not similar in its operation to any sense that we possess, and there is no reason to suppose that it is subjectively like anything we can experience or imagine.

—Thomas Nagel, "What Is It Like to Be a Bat?" (1974, p. 438)[1]

i

Hold this book open before you and read this sentence aloud. Can you *hear* where the book is? Can you hear that it has a certain size, shape, and texture? Pull the book away and continue to speak. Can you hear the emptiness of the space before you? If you close your eyes and speak, can you hear that there is a wall a few feet to your left, or a large desk at hand level?

Michael Gordon (co-author of this chapter and hereafter Mike), a psychology professor who studies sensation and perception, has convinced me that I can and often do hear such things—that I am more bat-like in this way than I had previously supposed, more bat-like than Nagel, in the epigraph, takes us to be. We suspect that you, if you aren't substantially impaired, are also somewhat bat-like in this way.

Unless you are already acquainted with the relevant literature, you probably doubt that you can hear silent objects and their properties, or at least that you can hear them very much. By the end of this chapter, Mike and I hope that you will have come to regard such doubts as a naive mistake, in fact a twofold mistake—a mistake not only about your perceptual capacities (that is, about your ability to respond to inputs in a certain way), but also about your stream of conscious experience, your everyday auditory phenomenology, including the phenomenology you (probably) think you had, or didn't have, when you tried the experiment described in the first sentences of this chapter. Mike and I will argue that people typically know the auditory phenomenology produced by silent objects only poorly. Thus, this chapter provides another case supporting the central contention of this book, that people are, in general, poor judges of their own stream of experience.[2]

ii

First, let's look at the basic experimental research on human echolocation. As Mike and I will be using the term, "echolocation" refers to the ability to detect features of the environment, especially features of objects that generally do not themselves produce sound, using the acoustic changes in sounds from other sources as they reflect off or are otherwise mediated by those environmental features or objects.[3] When a bat detects the presence of a (silent) wall by gauging how sounds reflect from it, it is echolocating. Likewise, if a bat can learn about an insect using information about how sound is transformed in passing through the insect, that too is echolocation. In echolocation, one detects properties of objects not by detecting waves that emanate directly from those objects as sound *sources*, but rather by detecting how those objects act as sound *reflectors* and sound *modifiers*.

Many species of bats, of course, and dolphins and whales, echolocate very accurately (Griffin 1958; Kellogg 1958; Evans 1973).[4] Blind people also often use echolocation while they walk—or even bicycle—through unfamiliar or changing environments, often tapping a cane or making clicking sounds with their mouths (Supa et al. 1944; Cotzin and Dallenbach 1950; McCarty and Worchel 1954; Rice 1967; Stoffregen and Pittinger 1995). The blind mobility instructor Daniel Kish offers a delightful retrospective account of life as blind child (2009), using echolocation to navigate by foot and bicycle, to play tag, and to climb trees. Videos demonstrating the tremendous echolocatory abilities of the blind, including bicycling and roller skating, can be found at www.worldaccessfortheblind.org. (See also Rosenblum 2010.)

A small body of empirical research shows that people with normal vision can also echolocate, at least a little bit, with brief training. For example, Michael Supa and colleagues (1944) asked both blind and normally sighted people to walk toward a large masonite board mounted at various distances from them. During their approach, participants signaled both the moment when they first detected the board and also when they were as close to the board as possible without touching it. Blind participants could detect the board several feet before contact and could move to within a few inches of its surface. After about thirty trials, sighted participants achieved similar accuracy. To confirm the auditory basis of this ability, Supa and colleagues reduced auditory input, first by having participants remove their shoes and walk toward the board in socks, then by giving them earstops, then finally by projecting noise directly into their ears. People's performance deteriorated proportionately with their induced deafness to the point where all participants collided with the board in every trial. Carol Ammons and colleagues (1953) and Lawrence Rosenblum and colleagues (2000) found similar results. Sighted but thoroughly blindfolded participants, after brief training, were able to stop just before walking into a large, sound-reflecting surface. Rosenblum and colleagues also found that sighted participants could use echolocation to discern the approximate distance of a wall that was positioned 3–12 feet in front of them. Blindfolded participants echolocated using self-generated sounds (such as saying the word "hello" repeatedly), and possibly ambient sound too, while either moving or standing still. Then, with the wall removed, they estimated its distance by walking to where they thought it had been. Although the task was easier while moving, even stationary participants had some ability to detect the 3-foot differences between wall positions.

Steven Hausfeld and colleagues (1982) asked blindfolded sighted participants to echolocate an object placed 25 centimeters before the face. They varied the texture and shape of the targets: fabric, Plexiglas, carpet, or wood, and circle, triangle, or square (all of equal surface area), or no target. After brief training, participants could distinguish—not dependably, but better than chance—between the shapes and between some of the textures. (See also Rice 1967. Mike and I also informally replicated this in my office, finding some people to be approximately at chance and others to be more than 50 percent accurate in shape detection.) Lawrence Rosenblum and Ryan Robart (2007) found that blindfolded participants could distinguish, at rates above chance, between triangles, squares, and circles, when noise-emitting speakers were positioned directly behind the shapes. Gordon (Mike) and Rosenblum (2004) found that people could judge the size of an aperture—specifically, whether they would be able to walk through it without turning their shoulders or ducking their heads—while blindfolded and hearing crowd noise from speakers behind the aperture.

How do people do this, exactly? The question has only begun to be studied. The most deflationary interpretation, perhaps, is that people simply notice differences in sound intensity: Their "hello" sounds louder when reflected back from a nearby wall than when uttered into empty space, and a smaller aperture permits less crowd noise to pass though. This is probably too simple an interpretation, though, given evidence from Rosenblum's laboratory showing dissociations between sound intensity and echolocatory judgments.[5] Daniel Ashmead and Robert Wall (1999) suggest that the most important cue for avoiding walls may be the accumulation of low-frequency sound, in particular. Other possible sources of information include the time delay between an emitted (or otherwise localizable) sound and the return of its reflection; differences in loudness, pitch, and timbre due to patterns in the efficiency of the reflection and transmission of different acoustic frequencies; and interference patterns in reflected sound.

This body of research demonstrates beyond a reasonable doubt, we think, that ordinary, sighted people at least *can* echolocate, in certain conditions, with a bit of training. People can detect the presence or absence, and to some extent the distance, and perhaps even the shape and texture, of silent objects by hearing how sound reflects off, transmits through, or reverberates from those objects. Of course, whether people *do* echolocate in their daily lives, and whether there is an auditory experience of echolocation—those questions, to which we now turn, are not resolved by the evidence just reviewed. We are not aware of any systematic research on those issues; so we will have to employ introspection, anecdote, and plausibility arguments.

iii

First, consider your experience walking down a long, tiled hallway in hard-soled shoes. With each step, a burst of noise radiates into the area around you. In hearing this sound, you hear not only the shoe striking the floor but also the reflections of that sound from surrounding surfaces. If the space were much different—if, say, you were taking a few steps across the tile of a bathroom floor—your auditory experience would be quite different. Similarly, there is an obvious echoic difference that makes you sound like Pavarotti in the shower and like yourself everywhere else. Hallways and showers sound different. They do so not because hallways and showers *produce* different sounds but because they *reflect* sound differently. In reacting to their acoustic differences, you are using echoic information.

If what we think to be a concert hall doesn't sound like a concert hall or what we think to be a shower doesn't sound like a shower, we will ordinarily notice the difference—or so, at least, it seems plausible to suppose. If you were in the shower embellishing a cadenza and suddenly, silently, the walls were removed so that your echoic environment became that of a concert hall, we expect you would be rather startled. More subtly, imagine stepping through a doorway into a familiar tile hallway, visually focusing to the left, being surprised by the sound of your footstep, then turning to your right and discovering a large piece of furniture where none was before. Echoic information would, in such a case, be guiding your visual attention. If such thought experiments are telling, then in moving through the world we are constantly using echoic information at least to supplement and confirm what we know primarily through sight, memory, and non-echoic aspects of hearing.

The Wenger Corporation has developed a "virtual room" that is able to artificially synthesize the acoustics of a variety of spaces, from an office to a symphony hall (which practicing musicians have found useful). If the acoustics of the virtual room are set to emulate an area much larger than the room's actual size, listeners quickly notice that something is amiss. Typically, people entering the room glance upward to see if the ceiling is especially high. If echoic information weren't regularly used to supplement other sensory information, people wouldn't do that, since people don't normally glance at the ceiling immediately upon entering a room.

Close your eyes and try to echolocate your hand while holding it in front of your face. Make hissing noises, or repeat a favorite syllable, while moving your hand closer to your mouth and farther away, right and left, up and down. Even better, recruit a friend to move her hand around in front of you. If you are like most of the people we've tried this with, you will find that you can tell something about where the hand is from the differences in the sound. The hand itself is silent, of course; you are echolocating. We're inclined to think that there is something it's like, phenomenologically speaking, to do this—not just something it's like to move your hand, to make noises, and to hear your own voice, but something it's like to get a sense of where the hand is from hearing the changes in reflected sound as it moves. You have an auditory experience of the hand's being very near or farther away, and as moving to the right or to the left. You hear, we think, the proximity of your silent hand.

Now try another test. Find an empty stretch of floor near a wall. Close your eyes and slowly walk toward the wall, repeating the word "hello." We venture that you will have little trouble stopping a few inches from the wall, and that you will notice substantial changes in the reflected sound of your voice. When you are a few inches away, it will *sound* to you like you're a few inches away. (If you are concerned that your judgment here will be inappropriately affected by your visual knowledge of where the wall is, have a friend move you an unknown distance from a wall. Analogous changes can also be made to the other tests suggested below.) Next, step from a small room into a larger one, noticing the sound as you walk; then enter a small room again. Just as an orange presents a different visual phenomenology than a grape, so, we think, a long hallway presents a different echoic phenomenology than a closet. Walking through a doorway, can you hear the frame approach your ear? Sitting at a desk sounds different from sitting in a wide open room, especially if you start talking. Slowly move this book or some other book toward one ear, bringing it within a few inches. You hear the approach of this silent object, don't you? If, unbeknownst to you and outside your visual field, a silent object were approaching your ear in that way, you would probably react unless you were very absorbed in or distracted by other things—more reason to think that echoic information constantly contributes to your general sense of your environment.

Now try one last test, one more pertinent to shape and texture. Closing your eyes and repeating a syllable, slowly move this book toward your face, noticing the changing sound of your reflected voice. Now do the same with something large and hollow—for example, a mixing bowl or a cardboard box. Now try it again with something soft like a wadded shirt. Don't the book, the hollow object, and the soft object sound quite different? Doesn't the box or bowl sound hollow? Holding the book about a foot from your face, play around with its orientation. Do the same with the box or bowl. Now consider again the opening questions of this chapter.

iv

Thomas Nagel, the philosopher quoted in the epigraph, says that the bat's sonar "is not similar in its operation to any sense that we possess." If the initial reactions of participants in Mike's experiments and reactions from our colleagues in philosophy and psychology are any guide, a significant proportion of the adult population will deny that they can detect, or have any conscious auditory experience of, the size, distance, shape, or texture of silent objects by attending to patterns of reflected sound. I have entertained tables full of philosophers at conference dinners by having them echolocate one another's hands, an activity that reliably produces giggles of surprise even among some of the more sober eminences.

You might think that the blind, whose abilities at echolocation are generally thought to be superior to those of normally sighted people, and who often actively use echolocation to avoid objects in novel environments, would be immune to such ignorance. Not so. For example, one of the two blind participants in a 1944 study by Michael Supa, Milton Cotzin, and Karl Dallenbach believed that his ability to avoid collisions was supported by cutaneous sensations in his forehead, and that sound was irrelevant and distracted him (pp. 144, 146). Although he was asked to attend carefully to what enabled him to avoid colliding with silent obstacles, it was only after a long series of experiments, with and without auditory information, and several resultant collisions, that he was convinced. Similarly, Philip Worchel and Karl Dallenbach (1947) report that a nearly blind participant believed that he detected the presence of objects by feeling pressure on his face. Like Supa's subject, he was disabused of this idea only after long experimentation. (That participant, it turned out, used his impoverished visual sense of light and dark more than he used tactile *or* echoic information.) Such opinions used to be so common among the blind—until Supa, Dallenbach, and their collaborators demonstrated otherwise—that the ability of the blind to avoid objects in novel and changing environments was widely regarded as a tactile or tactile-like "facial vision," perhaps underwritten by feeling air currents. (See Diderot 1749/1916; James 1890/1981; Hayes 1935; Supa et al. 1944. The negligible relevance of air currents is shown by participants' excellent performance when the ears are left clear and cloth is draped over the rest of the face and their poor performance when the ears are stopped and the face is left clear.) Presumably, if blind people experience auditory echoic phenomenology, and if they are—as people in general are widely assumed to be—accurate judges of their phenomenology, it should occur to them that they detect silent objects at least in part through audition. They should not make such large mistakes about the informational underpinnings of their object sense.

Modus tollens on that last conditional, of course, yields only a disjunction: *Either* blind people don't experience auditory echoic phenomenology (at least not enough to notice its pertinence when prompted to reflect on their remarkable ability to avoid unseen obstacles) *or* they aren't accurate judges of their phenomenology. And you might think the first disjunct considerably more probable than the second. In the journal article on which this chapter is based (Schwitzgebel and Gordon 2000), Mike and I argued that echoic information was unlikely to be experienced phenomenologically as pressure on the face; but now we aren't so sure. On the one hand, the cross-modal sensory transformation required seems peculiar: Other than in rare cases of synaesthesia, how often do people experience auditory input as tactile?[6] In general, background expectations don't seem enough to induce such a change: When you think your cell phone is set to "vibrate" and instead it plays your ringtone, you don't normally

(I assume) experience that ringtone as tactile vibration in your pocket. On the other hand, Mike has come to think that he sometimes experiences a feeling of pressure on his face when echoic information is highly salient, and Hiroshi Ono and colleagues (1986) found that even when people are aware of the actual informational basis of their abilities a substantial proportion (both blind and sighted) continue to report experiencing facial pressure. Even if so, we are inclined to think that facial pressure ordinarily does not *replace* auditory phenomenology as much as *accompany* it. Consequently, those who deny auditory echoic phenomenology are still mistaken about their experience.[7]

This much is straightforward: People often deny the existence of a capacity they demonstrably have: the capacity to detect the position and properties of silent objects by using echoic information. But that fact still leaves open the question most central to the theme of this book: Do people err about their sensory *experience* too, that is, do they err about not just about their abilities but also about their phenomenology? Mike and I are inclined to think they do. The phenomenology of echolocation is (often, at least) auditory, yet people tend to deny that they have such an auditory experience.

Mike and I are wrong in our central contention if one of two things is true: if either (a) echolocation does not typically have an auditory phenomenology, or (b) echolocation does typically have an auditory phenomenology and people generally know that it does. In support of the second of these possibilities one might suggest the following: Although people deny that they have auditory experience of silent objects when the question is posed abstractly, that's merely a theoretical mistake, not a mistake about their conscious experience. When the matter is put less abstractly— for example, when people are asked whether they can hear the difference between being in a shower and being in a concert hall, or whether they can hear the difference between speaking into a bowl and speaking into a blanket—people often grant that they can hear such differences. They just tend not to think of that as "echolocation"—perhaps because they think of echolocation as an exotic talent of bats and dolphins. It's like the case of timbre, perhaps. Without any background on the topic, someone might deny that he could hear the subtle differences in the overtone series that constitute changes in timbre. Though he knows that flutes and trumpets sound different, for example, he could easily be unaware that the physical basis of much of that difference is in the overtone series. He knows his experience of timbre perfectly well, just not under that label or guise. There is no *introspective* error in such a case.

Mike and I acknowledge that there is some merit in that objection. People are not, perhaps, *as badly* mistaken about their echolocatory phenomenology as it might seem from their tendency toward flat denials when asked abstractly. After all, they know at least that they can hear echoed shouts across canyons and the echoic difference between showers and concert halls. And yet they are, we think, nonetheless quite badly mistaken about their experience. Most people feel surprised—not just about their skills, but also about their auditory experience—when they discover that they can hear whether a hand or a wall is near their mouth or far away. The parallel does not hold for the person we have imagined as doubtful about timbre, who is *not* surprised that he can hear the difference—what we, but not he, would call the difference in timbre—between a flute and a trumpet. The doubter of timbre experience makes only a theoretical mistake or a mistake of labeling—a mistake that is repaired not by introspection but by learning acoustics—whereas the doubter of echolocation fails to appreciate an introspectively discoverable aspect of her experience.

Is it simply, then, that people are perfectly good at introspecting their echolocatory phenomenology when they consider specific, ongoing instances, such as the hand or bowl in front of the face, and wrong only in their generalizations? No; we think people will tend to be wrong in specific, ongoing instances too. The cases of the hand and the wall and the bowl, described in section iii, are cases meant to be especially striking. In less striking cases, such as the case with which Mike and I began this chapter, people will tend to be wrong about their current, ongoing auditory phenomenology. You *do* ordinarily hear silent things nearby, we think, at least crudely; they are part of a rough echoic experience of the space around you, an experience which, if you are typical, we doubt you appreciated at the beginning of this chapter. The echolocatory experience of distance, and other properties, is hard to discern in most cases, despite its pervasiveness. Though it sounds to you as if there is a wall a few feet to your left, and though this sensory knowledge helps guide your behavior, you may fail to discern this aspect of your experience even on careful introspection. One may not know that one is having such experience, under any label or guise, even when one pauses to patiently reflect on the possibility.

Consider, then, the other way to reject our thesis: Maybe people don't, in fact, generally have auditory experience of silent objects and their properties. The question isn't whether people in fact echolocate in their ordinary, daily lives. We addressed that issue as well as we could in section iii, with anecdotes and thought experiments about shower walls and the Wenger room. The question, rather, is whether, despite a certain level of sensory attunement to echoic properties, there might in fact be no echoic phenomenology. Maybe people hear only sound *sources*, that is, things that emit sound, as modified by environmental conditions, and then make *inferences* about silent objects, which remain unheard. Or perhaps people have some non-inferential, direct sensory knowledge, but without *any* experienced sense modality—as might be the case when one has the sense that one is being stared at without knowing how exactly one knows that fact (hearing? peripheral vision? ESP?).

Suppose the chair of the philosophy department is standing behind me talking, and someone tosses a blanket over his head. I will notice a sudden difference in his voice. But it doesn't seem right to say that I hear the blanket. Rather, I hear only the man's voice, and that it has suddenly changed, from which I infer that something is muffling it. Or if your footsteps are suddenly quieter, you may hear a difference in them that suggests that you have moved from tile to carpet; but perhaps it isn't quite right to say that you hear the tile or the carpet. As you approach the wall in an echolocation experiment, you have auditory experience of your own voice saying the word "hello," and you experience a certain change in the sound of your voice from which you can infer or otherwise learn of the presence of a wall, but (the objector might say) there is no auditory experience of the wall itself. Such cases may be analogous to your hearing a change in your dog's barking that indicates that the mail carrier has arrived without directly hearing the mail carrier.

Mike and I find it implausible to draw the sharp line, implicit in the view just sketched, between heard objects that produce sound and unheard objects that reflect or otherwise modify sound. People are embedded in massively complex acoustic environments with rich echoic and reverberatory properties, and our sensory systems wisely exploit that fact without, we think, troubling to limit our sensory experience to sound producers. We find it odd to suppose that we detect this large class of acoustic events yet omit them from our phenomenology. Certainly in vision we experience not just light sources but even more commonly objects that reflect light.

If I clap loudly, the steel bookcase to my left picks up some of the disturbance and rings for about half a second, as I can distinctly hear if I put my ear up next to it. It seems that in that case, at least, I hear the bookcase *as though* it were a sound source. Is it, then, a source, in the relevant phenomenological sense? My trashcan rings and reverberates less; my piano more. The reverberations and ringings are more distinctively associated with particular objects if I am very near them, and more generally diffused through the room as I back away. Where is the sharp distinction? And how do we draw the boundaries around a "source," anyway? If I cup my hands around my mouth to shout better, are my hands part of the sound source, or are they modifiers of it? If a car crashes through a building, which parts of the car and the building produce that horrible noise and which parts merely modify it? It seems to us that a full appreciation of the complexity of sound environments makes it unnatural to center one's theory on a robust and principled distinction between sound sources that people auditorily experience and non-sources that which people cannot auditorily experience. Partly for this reason, Mike and I, in arguing for a phenomenology of echolocation, are not arguing that the experience of hearing reflective and reverberant objects is different in kind from hearing sound sources; quite the opposite. They are of a piece, belonging to a unified auditory experience of our surroundings.

I will grant that I can't hear the blanket that is covering the department chair's head, or even (perhaps a weaker claim) *that* he has a blanket over his head. My echolocatory skills are not so finely tuned. I hear only that something soft has interposed. But perhaps someone with longer experience of such things—or a bat—could hear that he has a blanket over his head, as opposed to, say, a rubber mask. Just as while standing in a parking lot I may auditorily experience an approaching sound source like a car (or would it only be the engine and wheels that are the source?), so also as I step toward a wall—eyes open or eyes closed—I have an auditory experience of the wall's looming nearer. You too: You visually experience depth (or so I assume, though see chapter 2); you auditorily experience the distance of sound sources (for example, a voice may sound far away); and likewise you auditorily experience the distance of silent sound reflecting objects, such as the book near your ear or the bowl you are speaking into. Auditory experience of the presence or absence of, and the properties of, reflective and reverberant objects is pervasive. We think that people, hampered by a simplistic folk acoustics and insufficient appreciation of their auditory skills, are inclined to miss this fact when they casually introspect.

Another objection: Maybe even if *Mike and I* experience the world as echoically rich—at least when we explicitly reflect on it—that's only because our experience is not what it once was. We are no longer naive about echolocation, and thus perhaps we no longer hear in quite the same way. Theoretical knowledge about echolocation may create echolocatory experiences where none were before; it may create experiences that most people don't have and thus correctly deny. Mike and I may be erroneously assuming that others are like us, or like we are in our most echolocatory-reflective moments. If so, then introspective accuracy can be preserved. Every individual could be right about his or her own experience.

One reason we are reluctant to such an optimistic view is that it seems to us that upon noticing echoic properties in our experience—for example, in the hand-in-front-of-the-face demonstration, which was my own first experience with echolocation considered explicitly as such—we have the sense not of creating some new phenomenology but rather of recognizing something familiar, an aspect of experience that had always been there and was only then being made salient and properly considered for the first time. Another reason we are reluctant to accept the view that echolocation deniers are correct about their own experience is that they sometimes change their minds. They admit, sometimes, in conversations with us, to having been mistaken, not only about their capacities but also about their experience. Recall Supa's blind participant who regarded sound as "distracting." The experimenters don't provide a detailed phenomenological report (even though Supa's advisor and co-author Dallenbach had been a student of the great introspective psychologist Titchener), but we would guess that this man, like many of the sighted people we have informally interviewed, would have re-evaluated his auditory phenomenology by the end of the experiment. On the everyone-is-right view, people's confessions of error would themselves have to be mistaken. People's experience would have had to change radically in character, from nonechoic to echoic, in the course perhaps of a few minutes, while they failed to notice having undergone this change. This seems an odd pairing of moment-by-moment accuracy with serious ignorance of change over time. One might also wonder whether such a seemingly fundamental shift in experience is likely to be driven by the acquisition of a little high-level knowledge. Mike and I don't mean to deny that knowledge about echolocation can substantially alter one's auditory experience. Maybe our own auditory experience, now, does differ importantly from that of someone ignorant of human echolocation. All we mean to deny is that the change is so profound as to introduce pervasive echolocatory phenomenology where none was before. Unless there is such a profound change, the echolocation avowers and the echolocation deniers cannot both be right about their experience.

v

But now that the argument is complete and I read back on the preceding sections, I find myself somewhat uncomfortable with the confident tone.

I am not actually all that sure about my echoic phenomenology. (I can't speak here for Mike, who remains confident.) I recognize that this admission partly undercuts the argument of this chapter. But since my arguments in other chapters sometimes turn on confessional epistemology—on expressed feelings of confidence or uncertainty, which I hope the reader will share or recognize—I want to avoid conveying false confidence here.

The idea of a pervasive echoic phenomenology does tempt me, both introspectively and theoretically. But as I sit here in my office, as I tap on my keyboard and the hum of freeway traffic penetrates my window, I find myself not completely convinced that I really do have auditory experience of the wall to my left and the desk before me. I close my eyes and speak aloud. I feel fairly confident that I can hear that my voice isn't being reflected back by an object within 3 inches; but do I really hear, even crudely, the various silent things around me? When I went to Rosenblum's lab and tried out the Rosenblum-Robart shape detection experiment for myself, I did very well. In a short run of ten trials, I was correct on nine. Evidently, I could hear whether there was a triangle, a circle, or a square before me. So now I close my eyes, and saying "da da da da" I lean in close to my computer monitor. Can I hear that it's square? Even if I could rightly guess that it's square just from the hearing, is there some distinctive auditory phenomenology of squareness, analogous to the visual phenomenology of squareness that I experience with my eyes open?

Well, now you have as many tools to judge in your case as I have to judge in mine.

5 Titchener's Introspective Training Manual

The conformity of replies from so many different sources . . . and the evident effort made to give accurate answers, have convinced me that it is a much easier matter than I had anticipated to obtain trustworthy replies to psychological questions. Many persons, especially women and intelligent children, take pleasure in introspection, and strive their very best to explain their mental processes. I think that a delight in self-dissection must be a strong ingredient in the pleasure that many are said to take in confessing themselves to priests.

—Francis Galton, *Inquiries into the Human Faculty and Its Development* (1883/1907), p. 60

Such statements [as the foregoing, quoted] suggest that introspective exercises may be paralleled, as a form of polite recreation, with the word-puzzles in the magazines, and that the circular of questions is a royal road to the attainment of psychological truth. . . . [But] we get replies upon the introspective level of the average educated man. This level is low. . . . The ordinary observer, untrained in psychological method, can give an opinion as to the match of two colours upon a colour mixer, while he is wholly unable to follow the course of an after-image.

—Edward B. Titchener, *Experimental Psychology: A Manual of Laboratory Practice* (1901–1905), volume I, part 2, p. 389

i

We err, or at least are susceptible to confusion, about much of our stream of experience: our dreams (chapter 1), our imagery (chapter 3), our visual experience of depth (chapter 2), our auditory experience of echolocation (chapter 4). And more examples will come. In such matters our judgment is easily led astray. If I am right about this, a natural question is, can we get better? In the late nineteenth and the early twentieth century, at the peak of introspectionist psychology, many psychologists thought so—none more explicitly and insistently than Titchener, whose introspective training techniques are the topic of this chapter.

Experimental psychology arose as a distinct academic discipline in the second half of the nineteenth century. At its sociological center was Wilhelm Wundt (1832–1920), who founded the first formal psychology laboratory in 1879, who trained many of the next generation's leading psychologists, including Titchener, and who in 1881 launched one of the first psychology journals (*Philosophische Studien*).[1] Although the development of psychology as a rigorous empirical science had been urged and anticipated for more than a century (e.g., in Hume 1740/1978), what finally enabled it to flourish appears to have been the emergence of *quantitative introspective methods*, especially regarding sense experience. These methods were first developed a half-generation before Wundt by researchers such as Gustav Fechner (1801–1887) and Hermann von Helmholtz (1821–1894). Early psychologists' emphasis on introspection helped differentiate their new discipline from physiology (the formal background of many early and proto-psychologists, including Wundt and Helmholtz) by focusing it on the operations of the mind; at the same time, their quantitative experimental methods distinguished their work from previous work on the mind by philosophers such as Locke, Hume, and Kant. Although early psychological research—for example, the studies of test performance by Galton and Alfred Binet, of memory by Hermann Ebbinghaus, and of reaction time by Wundt himself—wasn't always introspective, non-introspective research was not at the programmatic center of nineteenth-century psychology. Wundt (1888, 1896/1897) describes psychology's subject matter as experiential processes and its central method as introspective self-observation, and William James, in his summary of the methods of psychology, writes that "introspective observation is what we have to rely on first and foremost and always" (1890/1981, p. 185).

The emphasis on quantification rendered scientific psychologists' claims more precise than their philosophical predecessors' had been, thus opening up a field of questions that seemed to invite the straightforward application of laboratory methods. Among the central questions were these: By how much must two sensory stimuli differ to produce an introspectively observable difference in experience? What is the threshold or "limen" of experience in various sensory modalities (e.g., what tone and light frequencies are audible and visible, and how weak a stimulus can still be consciously heard or seen)? What is the relationship between the experienced intensity of a sensation and the physical intensity of the stimulus producing it? (The Weber-Fechner law—a topic of early dispute and still occasionally a topic of dispute today—holds that the relationship is logarithmic.) Along what dimensions can sense experience vary? (Color experience, for example, was discovered to vary systematically in three dimensions: hue (e.g., red, green, yellow, blue), saturation (how intensely colored vs. how pastel or grayish), and lightness or brightness (distance along the dimension from black to white), with the combination of these three dimensions creating the "color spindle" or "color cone" still accepted by psychologists today.) One can see how quantifying questions of this sort invites the systematic research, the number-and-equation-filled journal articles, and the progressive consensus building that characterize scientific disciplines.

By the early twentieth century, however, it was becoming clear that on many issues consensus was elusive. For example, the dimensions of variation in emotional experience was a topic of hot and frequent disputes, with no resolution on the horizon (see, e.g., James 1890/1981; Wundt 1896/1897; Titchener 1908); so too was the existence or non-existence of "imageless thought" (which I briefly discuss in chapters 3 and 7) and the experience of attention (James 1890/1981; Pillsbury 1908; Titchener 1908). Although the most straightforward psychophysical questions about the relationship between external stimuli and sensory experience often yielded readily to the introspectivists' methods, experiences whose connection to sensory stimuli was more complex proved trickier.

By the 1910s, behaviorism, which focused simply on the relationship between outward stimuli and behavioral response, had declared war on introspective psychology, portraying it as bogged down in irresolvable disputes between introspective "experts." (See, e.g., Watson 1913.) In the 1920s and the 1930s, introspective studies were increasingly marginalized.[2] Although strict behaviorism declined in the 1960s and the 1970s, its main replacement, cognitivist functionalism (which treats functionally defined internal cognitive processes as central to psychological inquiry), generally continued to share behaviorism's disdain for introspective reports about conscious experience. Interest in consciousness has resurged in the last decade or two, but few psychologists have looked seriously at early introspective methods to see what methodological insights might be recovered from that period.

Titchener's 1600-page introspective training manual, *Experimental Psychology: A Manual of Laboratory Practice* (1901–1905), was perhaps the pinnacle of early introspective method. With separate parts for student and instructor, it presents and discusses a vast number of introspective exercises. It is peerless in its combination of depth, variety, concreteness, and attention to detail. Reading it, I feel—and I will attempt to convey in this chapter—both the potential promise of formal introspective training and, simultaneously, the daunting obstacles for any such program.

ii

Psychologists of Titchener's era often accepted as a condition of sound scientific method that introspective reports come from subjects—or, as Titchener preferred to say, "observers"—with substantial introspective training. (Galton—see the epigraph and chapter 3—was a notable exception.) In published research, it was standard to rely exclusively on observers with graduate training in psychology and thus presumably with at least several months, and often several or many years, of intensive experience with introspective methods. Wundt was reputed not to have admitted data from observers who hadn't performed at least 10,000 laboratory introspections (Boring 1953).

In his 1898 *Primer of Psychology*, Titchener likens the development of skill in introspection to the development of skill in physical measurement and chemical analysis (1898/1900, p. 25). Just as a chemist would never rely on an untrained assistant for any but the simplest measurements, a laboratory psychologist cannot rely on untrained introspectors for any but the crudest observations. In fact, Titchener argues soon afterward in his laboratory manual that quantitative introspection is considerably more difficult than similarly precise work in chemistry (1901–1905, II.2, cliii–clvii).[3] Consequently, "the average student, on entering the laboratory, is simply not competent" to participate as an introspective observer in demanding experiments (II.2.cliv; see also I.2.389). Difficulties include maintaining consistent attention, avoiding bias, knowing what to look for, and parsing the complexity of experience as it flows rapidly past (1898/1900, pp. 24–25; see also 1915, pp. 20–22). For example, without introspective training, Titchener asserts, it is difficult to compare the relative brightness of two different colors (I.1.13; I.2.31); to differentiate a very low tone sensation from a sensation of atonal noise (II.1.1; II.1.3); to make the quantitative assessment that two sensations are each an equal distance, in different directions, from a third (e.g., that one tone sounds as high in pitch above a reference tone as another tone sounds below it) (II.2.201–204; II.1.xxxii–xxxiv); or even just to follow the course of one's afterimages (see this chapter's epigraph). Experienced introspectors, Titchener says, are also more likely than untrained introspectors to maintain a consistent standard of judgment and to accurately report lapses of attention and interfering influences.[4]

Titchener turns on its head the standard argument against introspective training: that it introduces bias. Especially with respect to our own minds, Titchener believes, everyone is subject to bias and preconceptions. People do not generally approach psychology neutral between theses, even when those theses are dry, psychophysical ones—and when people do start out relatively open-minded, after a few introspections they are apt to speculate and form hypotheses. Titchener consequently rejects the ideal of an introspective account "furnished by a naive, commonsense, non-scientific observer, who has not yet adopted the special attitude of the psychologist" and thus supposedly takes a "neutral standpoint" (1912b, p. 489). Such a neutral standpoint is unattainable: "We can hardly, with the pressure of tradition and linguistic forms upon us, consider mental phenomena in a really naive way, with a truly blank prescientific impartiality." (ibid.)[5] In Titchener's view, avoiding bias requires not naiveté but expertise. Introspective practice and an "objective" frame of mind aid the observer in setting aside expectations to report mental phenomena accurately (I.2.xxv–xxvii; I.2.151; II.2.133–134; II.2.202). "The trained observer, psychologist or physicist or what not, can take the suggestion [i.e., the hypothesis toward which he might be biased] for what it's worth; he does not allow it to affect his observation. But the beginner is exceedingly liable to be led by interest into partiality." (1896/1906, p. 45; see also Müller 1904)

Although the intractable laboratory-vs.-laboratory disputes of his era suggest that Titchener may have overestimated the ability of trained introspectors to overcome bias, it doesn't follow that naive introspection is any better. I take the evidence presented in chapters 1–4 above to suggest that ordinary introspectors are often misled by preconceptions, theories, and culturally available metaphors. To see some of the other limitations of untrained introspection—and simultaneously (contra Titchener) to see some of the limitations of introspective training in Titchener's style—let us consider in detail three exercises from Titchener's laboratory manual.

iii

If two tones of frequency U (for the upper tone) and L (for the lower tone) are sounded together, it is sometimes possible simultaneously to hear a third tone, which is lower and generally quieter. This third tone is called a *difference tone*. Its pitch will resemble that of a tone of frequency U minus L.[6] For example, when two flutes simultaneously play the notes F_6 (fundamental frequency 1,396.9 hertz) and C_6 (1,046.5 hertz), listeners may also report hearing a note at about the pitch of F_4 (349.23 hertz) (Stickney and

Englert 1975). Combining sine waves in a sound editor program can produce similar effects. The standard view, and Titchener's, is that difference tones so generated do not exist in the environment but rather are a consequence of "non-linearities" in the human ear—that is, they result from the ear's failure to respond proportionately to all frequencies and energies of auditory input, distorting the signal somewhat as an overdriven amplifier does (Plomp 1976; Hall 1980/2002; Rossing et al. 1982/2002).[7] In addition to the (first) difference tone at U − L, a *second difference tone* (also called a *cubic difference tone*) may sometimes be heard at 2L − U, and more rarely other tones, including a *third difference tone* at 3L − U and disputably a *summation tone* at L + U. As a class, these are known as *combination tones*.

Titchener introduces his introspectors in training to combination tones in the seventh experiment series in the first volume of his laboratory training manual (I.1.39–46). He begins by directing their attention to a particularly salient difference tone produced by two Quincke's tubes with fundamental frequencies of approximately 1,584 and 1,980 hertz. (A Quincke's tube consists of a glass whistle connected to a resonator, producing a relatively pure tone; these two frequencies are approximately equivalent to the third G and B above middle C on the standard scale.) Titchener remarks that the difference tone's "moderate loudness" and its depth (two octaves below the lower primary tone or "generator") should make it "easily recognizable" to the student (I.1.41). He advises the student to produce the tone repeatedly until he "is entirely satisfied with his introspections." Titchener next recommends that the student listen for the difference tone of two Quincke's tubes of 1,584 and 2,376 hertz, which he describes as particularly loud and one octave below the lower generator. After these two introspections (expected to be easy) are rehearsed several times, the student is instructed to proceed up and down an octave's worth of musical intervals, then to practice hearing difference tones when one or both of the generating tones is quiet and when the duration of the tones is short. Titchener suggests that several comparison tones be produced and that the student be required to say which tone is closest in pitch to the difference tone he purports to hear (I.2.70). Finally, the student is instructed in similar procedures for the second and third difference tones and the summation tone. Titchener expects students to have only limited success in hearing the more difficult of these tones. Still, by the end of the experiment series—presumably conducted within one or a few sessions over the course of a week or less—the student should be able to discern combination tones that previously would have eluded him. He has, apparently, become something of an "introspective expert" in this limited domain.

If you would like to try a bit of the training yourself, I have produced a web adaptation of Titchener's difference tone training procedure. It is available from the "Difference Tone Training" link on my home page (http://faculty.ucr.edu/~eschwitz) and also from the free online journal *Psyche* (Schwitzgebel 2005). For understanding the issues, nothing beats actually hearing the stimuli.

Discerning combination tones is difficult. Titchener begins, therefore, with comparatively easy cases, proceeding to the more difficult ones only after the easier ones are mastered. Also, since there are good theoretical reasons to expect each difference tone to be heard at a particular pitch (reasons having to do with acoustics and the ear and confirmed by accomplished introspectors), the students' introspective reports can be verified—a good occasion for training. Many of Titchener's exercises share these features of scaled difficulty and corrective feedback; so do many ordinary non-introspective training procedures.

Let's back up a bit, though, and ask: Are students in this experiment really introspecting? When I try it, it seems to me that attempting to discern a combination tone doesn't differ at all from attempting to discern a faint tone of the ordinary sort. It seems just like listening for sounds in the external environment. As far as I can tell, the judgment need not be distinctively introspective in any way.[8]

One might hope to defend the view that the training is nonetheless introspective on the grounds that combination tones, being (in general opinion) an artifact of distortions in the ear, do not exist in the world in the same way that ordinary tones do, and thus that in attending to them one cannot be attending to the outside world. Since it sounds odd to say that one is attending to one's ear, it is easy to suppose that one must be attending to some part of one's experience, or introspecting. However, this argument would prove too much. If every sensory or perceptual judgment about something that doesn't exist outside the observer is an introspective judgment, then many of the perceptual mistakes we make due to illusion must likewise involve introspective judgments. Perhaps, indeed, we should regard combination tones as similar to double images, color adaptation effects, or the floating black spots experienced by people with a certain sort of eye damage—that is, as a kind of illusion, a product of our sensory apparatus not straightforwardly reflecting how things stand in the world beyond. If you hold your finger six inches before your nose and focus on something in the distance while continuing to attend to the finger and you consequently notice a doubling, are you necessarily introspecting—or could you just be looking, in a particular way, at your finger? I could see the argument going either way. (By the way, did the double image exist before you attended to it? See chapters 2 and 6.) But surely you needn't be introspecting if, with yellow-adapted eyes (perhaps unbeknownst to you), you mistakenly judge a white wall to be baby blue. The blueness is, in some sense, only in your own mind—but you do not introspect it. You are making an ordinary (mistaken) perceptual judgment about the color of the wall, not an introspective judgment about anything going on in your mind. The same holds, I'd suggest, in hearing difference tones.

To see how Titchener's procedure qualifies as introspective training we must take a different tack. Consider the naive introspector asked to describe his auditory experience of an interval sounded by a musical instrument. If he has a minimum of musical knowledge, he might be able to describe the interval as, for example, a major third, considerably above the middle of the scale, and indicate the instrument played if it is a familiar one. But his experience is vastly richer than those words suggest—or at least it's plausible to suppose that it is—influenced by harmonics, resonances, echoes, deficiencies in his ear, and sundry other acoustic and aural phe-nomena, including (presumably) combination tones. Some of these facts are indicated indirectly by his statement that it was a major third played upon (say) a piano; others are not. Auditory experience is far too complex for ordinary people to parse. Thus a new student entering Titchener's laboratory, asked to describe her auditory experience with care and in detail, would be baffled. To provide introspective reports of any value, she needs concepts and a vocabulary, a sense of what to look for, and practice in discerning these aspects of her experience as it occurs. Training in discerning combination tones is thus introspective training not because reporting such tones is necessarily an introspective act (involving a judg-ment about one's own mind) but because for the person antecedently interested in reaching introspective judgments about her auditory experi-ence the training provides a way of identifying and labeling one aspect of it. "Introspective training" need not always involve acts of introspection— just as athletic training need not always involve acts of athletic prowess—as long as the training improves the quality of introspective acts when they do occur.

Trained musicians and psychophysicists, therefore, although they don't generally conceive of themselves as "trained introspectors" in the Titch-enerian sense, and although they have ordinarily not undergone any general course of training and reflection on the methodology of introspec-tion, possess some tools for apprehending their conscious experience that others lack and that it's part of the Titchenerian introspective training procedure to provide. Indeed, to the extent that their aim *is* to apprehend their own experience—as opposed to, say, just improving (or mapping) their capacity to discriminate and label aspects of the publicly shared audible world—their project does resemble Titchener's and might profit from broader reflection on introspective methods and epistemology.

When an untrained observer at first can't discern a combination tone and then later, after training, in an acoustically identical situation, can do so, what exactly has happened? At one extreme, we might suppose that while on the second occasion she genuinely experiences the difference tone, on the first occasion the difference tone was in all respects so thoroughly absent from her experience that we couldn't even say that it contributed in some ineffable way to its richness. At the other extreme, we might hold that the auditory experience remains in all respects completely identical from one occasion to the other, the only difference consisting in a separable introspective process and judgment. Neither extreme seems to me especially inviting. Most philosophers and psychologists now take for granted that general knowledge can influence sensory experience, so that two people with the same sensory stimulation may nonetheless have different sensory experiences (e.g., Bruner and Postman 1949; Polanyi 1966; Hanson 1969; Lamme and Roelfsema 2000). If so, it seems likely that knowledge of combination tones and practice in discerning them will affect one's auditory experience, at least when one is deliberately listening for them. On the other hand, if we grant that auditory experience is rich, beyond the capacity of most observers fully to parse and articulate, and if we grant that combination tone sensations are not wholly *created* by the training procedure but can in some sense be discovered in experience, then despite the "top down" effect of general knowledge on sensory experience, a gap of ignorance still divides the naive introspector's auditory experience from his judgments about it; and if Titchener is right, introspective training can help reduce this gap.

Here is an issue, though, that Titchener did not, I think, sufficiently consider: When should we regard an introspector as sufficiently attentive and well trained that we may take at face value her claim not to hear a combination tone?[9] Besides the combination tones so far described, combination tones of 2U − L, 3L − 2U, 4L − 3U, 2U − 2L, and others are sometimes reported for various stimulus intensities and frequency ranges, as well as combination tones arising from the interaction of the harmonics of the fundamental tones. Let's say you deny hearing 3L − 2U in some context in which others do say they hear it, and let's suppose also that you are a fairly well trained expert by now and firm in your opinion. Is there any way to determine whether you are missing a tone that is a (perhaps subtle) part of your experience? To say that you couldn't possibly be missing it, even if it is ever so subtle, seems to attribute to you an implausible infallibility. On the other hand, it seems wrong simply to assume that you must be missing it. Could we simply measure activity in auditory regions of the brain to settle the question (assuming we can sufficiently improve the resolution of neuroimaging equipment)? To do that, we would have to know in considerable detail the relationship between neural activity and auditory experience—and that might require knowing, first, the answer to the very issue I have just raised. Perhaps it isn't hopeless, but I see no simple resolution.

The issue, of course, isn't limited to combination tones. Difficulties of this sort will emerge anywhere we admit the possibility of erroneously reporting the absence of experience (see also chapter 6), potentially creating a major stumbling block both for evaluating individual reports, whether in the course of training or as scientific evidence, and for evaluating the final success of training methods. Perhaps tellingly, Titchener seems to shift, either deliberately or in confusion, between speaking of unreported difference tones as absent and speaking of them as merely introspectively undetected (I.1.39–46; I.2.66–72).

iv

The fourth series of laboratory training experiments in Titchener's manual concerns afterimages. The fifteenth and last of these afterimage experiments begins with an observer sitting for 5 minutes in a dark room before a curtained window. When his partner gives a signal, the observer looks toward the window, the curtain is removed to reveal the upper two panes, and he stares fixedly for 20 seconds at the vertical bar separating the window panes. He then closes his eyes and with the room again darkened he reports the next few minutes' visual experience. The experiment is to be repeated, Titchener says, until the observer reports similar visual experiences on every trial (I.1.29–30).

What the observer sees is a sequence of shifting afterimages known as the "flight of colors." You can easily induce a flight of colors in yourself by staring for a few moments at an incandescent light bulb or by glancing at the sun and then closing your eyes; or you might attempt a closer replication of Titchener's experiment.

I will now quote at length from Titchener's discussion of this experiment in the instructor's part of the first volume. Notice the specificity of the report Titchener says his observers converge on, after their initial "mere chaos":

This experiment shows, in a striking way, the effects of practice. The report of a wholly unpracticed observer is a mere chaos. With attention, the uniformity of the phenomena soon becomes apparent; and presently the observers who at first gave radically different accounts of the after-image will reach agreement upon all essential points.

With an unclouded sky, or a sky thinly covered with clouds and presenting an even white surface, the flight of colors is as follows:

(a) A momentary positive and same-colored image.

(b) Interval of 5 or 6 sec.

(c) Positive image, fluctuating in color; sometimes with patches of red and green. After 1 or 2 sec., the image settles down to a sky *blue*, the vertical bar remaining dark.

(d) The blue passes, with or without interruption, into a *green*. The green is at first very vivid; it disappears and reappears five or six times, growing gradually paler; at last it is almost whitish.—These initial changes show a good deal of individual variation. Some [observers] now see

(e) A *yellow* image. This (or the whitish green preceding) is regularly followed by

(f) A deep *red* image. The black bar becomes luminous and slightly greenish, the light appearing at first as a crack in its length. This is the stage of transition from the positive to the negative image. The red undergoes several fluctuations. Then follows

(g) A deep *blue* image, with yellowish bright bar, more lasting than any of the preceding phases. The blue darkens, and the image gradually disappears, with or without passing into

(h) A dark *green* image. . . . Note the periodicity[10] of stages *c* to *h*:

B – G – Y – R – B – G

Whether Titchener is right that practiced observers eventually settle on similar descriptions of the flight of colors isn't clear. Titchener cites Helmholtz (1856/1909/1962) and Washburn (1899), who report roughly similar sequences of colors. However, Helmholtz's description is a rather bare statement that intense white light produces afterimages that proceed white-blue-green-red-blue. And Washburn was not really an independent source, having recently earned her Ph.D. under Titchener. One might wonder whether Titchener's explicit instruction that observers are to settle on a single sequence influenced his findings. It is also unclear what influences, including theories discussed in the laboratory, might incline observers to report one sequence rather than another.

By far the most detailed treatment of the flight of colors, complete with color plates depicting the afterimages, is a 1913 article by the psychologist Paul Homuth. Homuth is even more insistent about training than Titchener, claiming that expertise requires several months of intensive practice in observing afterimages. Homuth divides his images (which do not include a vertical bar) into four parts—the center, the border, the outer frame, and the extreme periphery—which undergo different color shifts. In his primary condition with bright white light, Homuth reports the center of the afterimage to be mainly blue, alternating with reddish-violet, magenta, or pinkish-violet, with the sequence concluding in brownish-yellow. The resemblance to Titchener's description is minimal at best.

William Berry (1922) reviews the literature on the flight of colors back to Aristotle and finds great variability of this sort among researchers. He concludes that there is no consistent sequence in the flight of colors, a point he later (1927) supports with a study with his own graduate-student observers. On the other hand, V. M. Robertson and G. A. Fry (1937) point out that earlier observations were conducted in a wide variety of conditions and might be expected to produce variable results even if there is consistency in the flight of colors in any one condition. They report consistency among their own observers, with results fairly similar to Titchener's, as do Weve (1925) and Barry and Bousfield (1934). The little recent research I have been able to find on the flight of colors does nothing to resolve the issue. The matter was less settled than dropped.[11]

But—you might wonder, as I do—how difficult could it be, really, to sketch, in broad outline, the flight of colors? What exactly is the challenge here? It may be difficult to articulate precisely what is going on in Homuth's four regions, or to describe accurately an exact shade, or to characterize (or even inarticulately appreciate) the complexities in an afterimage with shifting, ragged borders. But to label the general approximate color range of an afterimage if that same general color persists over several seconds seems rather easy, doesn't it? When I have tried to replicate Titchener's windowpane exercise, the color of the resulting afterimages usually seems to me to be very obvious. For example, this morning (May 6, 2009) I tried the exercise again. It seemed to me that my afterimage evolved, over the course of about a minute, from white or off-white (with a dark bar in the middle) to a kind of lavender and then to brilliant red, finally fading into blackish blue, with the bar becoming lighter near the end. Could I be wrong about this? Might the image really have been, for some of this period, vivid green (as required in Titchener's sequence), though I thought it was lavender or brilliant red? I find this rather difficult to imagine. I don't feel the same kind of uncertainty here that I felt about my imagery experience at the beginning of chapter 3 (when I considered how stable the image was, how flat, and so on) or about my echoic experience at the end of chapter 4. Nor does it seem likely to me that others would err in a similar situation.

This feeling of confidence, this feeling of the ease of the introspective task, is of course just an intuitive assessment. I can imagine Titchener rejecting that assessment. There are features of the retina we all share, he says, that explain the evolution of afterimages (I.2.49), so the flight of colors should be the same in all normal perceivers (assuming the retina to be properly whitewashed with light). Consequently, my flight must have had a green phase—or if not my flight (since I may somehow have done the experiment wrong), then at least the flights of Titchener's own students, despite the novices' divergent reports. Furthermore, Titchener might say, if it is difficult even for novices to go grossly wrong about the flight of colors, and if his students do in fact move from diverse to convergent reports, then it would seem to follow that his training procedure somehow *regularizes* the flight of colors; but that strains against the natural idea that the flight of colors is driven by relatively early (e.g., retinal) features of the visual system. So if I or some other insufficiently trained observer detect no period of "vivid [green] . . . growing gradually paler" in some properly induced flight, then perhaps the best conclusion to draw, and the conclusion that Titchener presumably would draw, is that we're just wrong, any intuitive sense of certainty notwithstanding. Why should we think, anyway, that our intuitive sense of certainty or uncertainty about such matters is particularly trustworthy?

This argument, I confess, leaves me cold. I just can't bring myself to doubt that experience of lavender followed by brilliant red. There was no green. But am I guilty here of the same unjustified blasé confidence that I so readily attribute to others? Or does my judgment instead reflect instead some reasonable attunement to what is and what is not relatively dubious?

v

The compelling visual illusions that one generally sees in books and other demonstrations tend to mask the introspective difficulties that arise for weak or non-obvious illusions. Confronted with Poggendorff's illusion (figure 5.1, from I.1.165 in Titchener's laboratory manual), most people

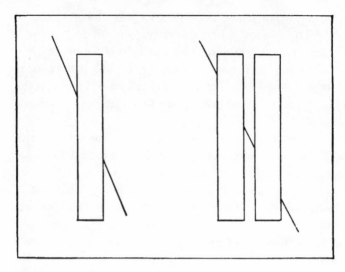

Figure 5.1
Poggendorff's illusion, from I.1.165 in Titchener's laboratory manual.

feel unambivalently comfortable in reporting that, in some sense, the partially occluded line we may know to be straight "looks" crooked. If we accustom ourselves only to such easy cases—the "best" illusions—it may seem inconceivable that one would have to look hard to find an illusion, that one might be talented or inept at the introspection of illusions, and that the criteria of illusoriness and visual appearance are evasive.

Carefully examine figure 5.2, which is from page I.1.154 of Titchener's manual. Titchener invites his students to consider the following questions, which I ask you also to consider:

How does the figure A strike you at first sight? Fixate on some point on [the line segment] *be*. What is the appearance of the figure? Move the eye slowly from *b* to *e*, and back again. Does the figure change its perspective? Move the eye from *b* to *c*, and back again. Is there any change? Is there any uniformity of perspective, according as you move in the directions *bc*, *ba*, *ef*, *ed*, or in the opposite directions?

How does the figure B strike you at first sight? Fixate, first, a point upon *bd*, and then a point upon *ac*, *ad* or *cd*. Is there any difference of perspective? Move the eye slowly in the direction *ba* or *bc*; and then in the direction *ab* or *cb*. What happens in the two cases? What secondary modifications of the appearance of the figure are conditioned upon the shift of perspective? How many perspective illusions, in all, is the figure capable of producing? (I.1.154)

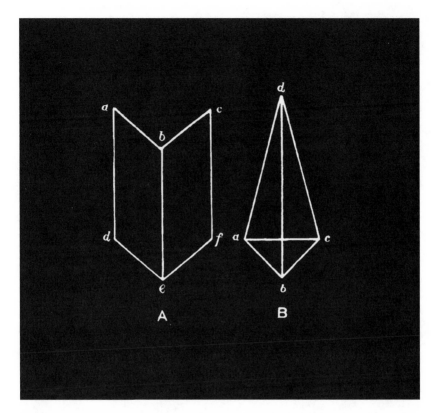

Figure 5.2
From page I.1.154 of Titchener's manual.

If you are like me, these directions are rather difficult to follow—perhaps surprisingly so. It is difficult, in part, because it is difficult to control one's attention and the movement of one's eyes, resisting the temptation, for example, to glance at point *c* as one is supposed to be moving one's fixation slowly along *ab*. Since controlling attention and eye movement is crucial to many introspective tasks, such practice is part of Titchener's introspective training. (For references, see note 4.)

In the instructor's part of the book, Titchener says that in both figures the central line is usually seen as closer to the observer but that fixation on any point on a line tends to bring that line forward, with consequent modifications of perceived transparency and orientation (I.2.310–311).[12] Also, he says, moving one's eyes along a line tends to bring forward the initial vertex rather than the terminal one. Although my own intro-

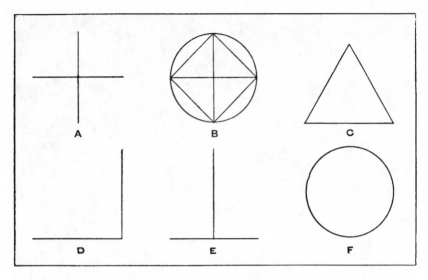

Figure 5.3
From page I.1.160 of Titchener's manual.

spections of the experiences produced by figure 5.2 were initially rather disorganized, I find them now mostly to conform to the pattern Titchener describes. But I am not sure whether I am now judging my experience of the figures more accurately or whether accepting Titchener's generalization has altered my experience.

Consider another figure, one in which perspectival Gestalt shifts are less salient: figure 5.3 (from I.1.160). Titchener asks his students to view the objects in this figure serially, first with both eyes, then with one eye at a time. He asks: "Is there any illusion of extent [i.e., in the apparent length of the lines]? Is there any other illusion? Look very carefully, in both cases, and do not be satisfied with your first discovery." (All the figures are perfectly regular on the printed page.) Faced with this task, I feel considerable uncertainty about how the shapes in the figure really look to me. Maybe you will feel the same way. In figure A, does the vertical line look longer, shorter, or the same length as the horizontal? With your right eye closed, does the right horizontal limb look longer, shorter, or the same length as the left? Of course, you can quickly toss out a response, confident that no one will prove you wrong (if such a proof is even possible); but approaching these questions conscientiously, I at least am unsure of myself. If you share this feeling, perhaps you will also share the sense that finding yourself in this difficulty is, in a way, peculiar. How could it be hard to reach a judgment about how things appear to you? Although judgments about how things *are* understandably carry some risk, judgments about how things *look to you right now* seem insulated in a particular way. Could you really go wrong in such a judgment? And if you couldn't go wrong, where does the difficulty lie?

Some readers will not feel any difficulty or have any sense that they could be mistaken. If that feeling arises from general temperament or philosophical conviction, this chapter, indeed this whole book, will probably seem to them misconceived. Other readers, however, may have approached the task too casually. Consider, in more detail, figure A within figure 5.3. Examine it both binocularly and monocularly. On first glance, I have found, most viewers report no illusion: The two lines look to be equal in length and to bisect each other perfectly at right angles. Nevertheless, figures of this sort are standardly presented as examples of the "horizontal-vertical" illusion (e.g., Robinson 1972, p. 97; Coren and Girgus 1978, p. 29).[13] Experts in visual illusion appear to agree that, in some sense, the vertical line in figure A *does* look longer to normal perceivers. Now, maybe something about the arrangement of this particular figure, with other shapes and a frame nearby, compromises this illusion, but Titchener appears not to have thought so (I.2.309, I.2.315). Examine figure E and figure D, which may show the illusion more obviously, and then return to figure A. Are you still confident that the lines look to be of the same length? With one eye closed, the horizontal-vertical illusion purportedly is reduced or vanishes (I.2.315; see also Prinzmetal and Gettleman 1993). Titchener also claims that in monocular vision the outer horizontal limb (on the side away from the nose) looks longer than the inner, and that in binocular vision the upper vertical limb looks longer than the lower (I.2.315).[14] Is it obvious to you which of these illusions is present or absent in your own experience?

Part of the difficulty here—if I have managed to persuade you that there is a difficulty—may be that what it is for two lines to "look" to be of the same length isn't clear. Clearly, it can't be a matter of one's *overall* judgment about the length of the lines, since one can judge that two lines look to be of different lengths even when one knows them to be equal in length. Is it a judgment about what your assessment of the lines would be if you were to depend only on immediate visual cues? I doubt that visual cues operate separately from general knowledge in the way presupposed by such an approach. And in any case, the necessary judgment would seem to be a difficult hypothetical one, requiring us to ascertain the bases of and the influences on our assessments—which we seem to be rather poor at, generally speaking, for reasons famously reviewed in Nisbett and Wilson 1977, Nisbett and Ross 1980, and Wilson 2002.

Do two lines look to be of the same length if they extend equal lengths across what we might think of as the television screen of visual experience? Many psychologists and philosophers now think that there is no one locus of visual experience, where everything comes together as on a screen, but rather a sequence of processes, some in parallel, that may yield differing results. (Such a perspective is engagingly explored in Dennett 1991.) Empirical evidence suggests that different parts of the visual system are differently subject to illusion. One influential series of experiments studied the Ebbinghaus (or Titchener Circles) Illusion, in which people will say that a circle surrounded by larger circles looks smaller than a circle of the same size surrounded by smaller circles (Agliotti et al. 1995; Haffenden and Goodale 1998; Clark 2001; Glover 2002; Smeets and Brenner 2006; Goodale et al. 2008). The experimenters found that the part of the visual system that guides reaching, as measured by the distance between the fingers during grasp, is largely unaffected by the illusion. One question, though, is whether grasp aperture is a good measure of illusion, conceived of as a feature of visual experience. Maybe it's a better measure of one's assessment of how things stand in the world. (One's visual experience and one's assessment of how things stand in the world may of course come apart, as in cases of known illusion.) Or maybe part of the illusion is that one's grasp aperture is different in the two cases, so that two grasps of the same aperture may correspond to different experienced sizes. Furthermore, even if we decide that there is something like a single television screen of visual experience (flat or otherwise; see chapter 2), it isn't clear whether how things look should be judged by their appearance on that screen. Does an oar half in water "look" straight, or bent (Ayer 1940; Austin 1962)? Does a cat behind a picket fence "look" like several cat slices (Noë 2004)? Presumably there is an illusion in figure 5.3A if and only if the lines look to be of different lengths. But now I'm not sure exactly what this means or how we can come to a dependable judgment about it.

One way to approach the question of whether there are illusions in figure 5.3, even for people who claim to see none, would be to present a variety of similar figures in which the lines differ in length. The subject might then be required to state which figures are skewed in which direction, and the researcher could check for a tendency to err one way or another. (Künnapas (1955) did this for figures like D and E.) Alternatively, the subject might be given the opportunity to adjust the lines until they seem equal length. (Gardner and Long (1960a,b) did this for figures like D and E.) However, this approach too is dogged by difficulties. Such judgments either replace judgments about how long the lines *look* with judgments about how long the lines *are* or blur the two sorts of judgment together. This might be acceptable if the participants are sufficiently naive, but someone aware of the possibility of illusion might treat the two questions differently. Furthermore, the presentation of multiple figures in sequence, or the ability to control the length of the lines, significantly alters the cognitive situation. Gardner and Long found that as small a variation as whether the horizontal line is fixed and the vertical adjustable or vice versa had a pronounced effect on the magnitude of error. Therefore, it is conceivable that people may consistently err on such tests and yet experience no corresponding illusions in figure 5.3.

If someone reports no horizontal-vertical illusion in figure 5.3A, should we conclude that she genuinely does not experience such an illusion? Or might one line look longer than the other despite the observer's being an insufficiently capable introspector to discover that fact about her visual experience? I can't see how we might easily resolve that issue. To insist on the former seems unrealistically to deny the possibility of inaccuracy in assessing the complex stream of visual experience. To insist on the latter risks opening the door to a world of illusions that no one reports and that never deceive us.

Perhaps we can imagine an observer who, when presented with a variety of figures like those in figure 5.3, reports experiencing several small illusions in one direction or another for each of the figures, though most observers report no such illusions; and perhaps it turns out that both this observer and those who deny the illusions, when given behavioral tests like those described two paragraphs above, err slightly but similarly in the directions predicted from the reports of the first observer. It might then be plausible to suggest that all the observers experienced illusion in the original figures—that the lines actually looked to them, in *some* relevant sense of "looked," to be of different lengths despite their contrary report—and thus that the first introspector has a talent for discovering non-obvious illusions that others misreport. Maybe such a talent could be nurtured with proper training. This is, I think, what Titchener hoped and believed. But whether things would turn out so neatly is anyone's guess. Neither Titchener's trainees nor anyone else I'm aware of has been tested systematically.

vi

Probably no part of early introspective methodology was more thoroughly and durably overthrown than the emphasis on introspective training. No recent research employs observers that Wundt or Titchener would regard as well trained. Yet if accurate introspection is difficult, one might expect training to produce substantial benefits. It is plausible that a trained introspector would at least, as Titchener says, employ more stable standards of judgment, better maintain consistent attention, know better what to look for, and deploy more sophisticated concepts for describing complex experiences. Maybe, too, a trained introspector will better follow the course of an afterimage, more dependably spot subtle visual illusions, and more accurately detect combination tones. Yet the effects of classical introspective training were never tested adequately. Just when introspective psychology seemed to be on the brink of becoming rigorously self-conscious about evaluating its training methods—Müller (1904) and Wundt (1907) come to mind in addition to Titchener—it perished amid squabbles and at the eager hands of behaviorism.

Proving the value of introspective training would never have been straightforward, as I hope the examples of this chapter illustrate. It is challenging to evaluate the accuracy of introspective reports not only when the relationship between stimulus and experience is likely to be complex and highly variable (as with emotional experience and abstract thought) but even sometimes when the relationship between stimulus and experience appears to be comparatively simple and dependable (as with combination tones, afterimages, and visual illusions). To what extent does introspective training alter the target experience? When is someone expert enough that we should accept her denials of subtle experience? With how much skepticism should we view reports (by novices or by experts) that conflict with the most straightforward interpretations of non-introspective evidence? Might attempts to verify introspective reports problematically change the target experience? How much weight should simple assertions of confidence receive, and might practiced introspectors' confidence be better calibrated? Such questions may not be unanswerable. The right conjunction of evidence might confirm the value of reports by trained introspectors. In view of the dubious quality of introspective judgments by untrained subjects and by philosophers and psychologists across history, some more formal training regimens may be worth at least a try. I would wager on mixed results.

6 Do You Have Constant Tactile Experience of Your Feet in Your Shoes? And Some Pessimistic Thoughts about Theories of Consciousness

[U]p to this moment I have been focusing my attention on the philosophical problem of describing consciousness, and I have not been paying any attention to the feeling of the chair against my back, the tightness of my shoes, or the slight headache I have from drinking too much wine last night. Nonetheless, all of these phenomena are part of my conscious awareness.

—John Searle, *The Rediscovery of the Mind* (1992, pp. 137–138)

[T]here is no conscious perception without attention.

—Arien Mack and Irvin Rock, *Inattentional Blindness* (1998, p. 14, italics suppressed)

i

Do you have constant tactile experience of your feet in your shoes? Constant auditory experience of the hum of traffic in the background? Constant visual experience of the frames of your eyeglasses? Or, when you aren't attending to such matters, do they drop out of consciousness, so that they are in no way part of your stream of experience, your phenomenology? Is consciousness *abundant*, the stream of experience bristling with phenomenology in a wide variety of modalities simultaneously (visual, auditory, tactile, olfactory, imagistic, proprioceptive, emotional), or is it *sparse*, limited to one or a few things at a time?[1]

Suppose you have driven to work by the same route a thousand times. Today, you are absorbed in remembering an unpleasant interaction with your department head. Traffic is light, no dangerous situation occurs, and you drive habitually. You arrive at your usual parking area and seem to "wake up"—"Ah, I'm at work already!"—with virtually no memory of having driven there. Did you have visual experience while you were driving? You responded to events on the road, stopped at red lights, and stayed in your lane. Visual input obviously had some influence on your behavior. But perhaps visual input can influence behavior without the involvement of consciousness. Many psychologists, including Marcel (1980), Merikle et al. (2001), and Snodgrass et al. (2004),[2] believe that a very brief visual display, quickly masked and not consciously experienced, can shape one's later responses, for example in deciphering or choosing words that accord with the masked display. In popular imagination—if not perhaps in actuality (see Bornstein 1989 and Trappey 1996)—a single frame of the phrase "Drink Coke" inserted into a film may have no effect on your visual experience yet propel you to the soda machine at intermission. Although absent-minded driving isn't exactly like either of these cases, might you still have had no sensory experience of the road as you drove, or only very intermittent experience? The mere fact of behavioral responsiveness doesn't settle the question, at least not without further argument.

Ordinary people's intuitions differ. Researchers disagree. William James (1890/1981) and John Searle (1992), for example, endorse the abundant view, according to which the stream of experience involves both a center of attention and a broad periphery of consciously experienced but unattended objects and background feelings. Julian Jaynes (1976), Daniel Dennett (1969, 1991[3]), and Arien Mack and Irvin Rock (1998) endorse the sparse view, according to which consciousness is limited to only one or a few objects, modalities, topics, or fields at a time, and the unattended hum of traffic in the background is no part, not even a peripheral part, of your experience when you are sufficiently absorbed in other things.

Who is right? I hope you will agree that this is a substantive question—even if the answer seems obvious—and that it is central to our understanding of consciousness. There is a huge difference between thinking that phenomenology abundantly outruns attention and thinking it doesn't.

ii

You might wonder what I mean by "consciousness." So far in this book I have given no formal definition of the term; I have leaned on examples and on intuitive understanding. The definitional issue arises acutely here, though, and for this reason: If you think it *is* obvious whether experience is sparse or abundant, you may think that those who seem to disagree with you—being, presumably, smart and sane philosophers and psychologists—must really just be using *terms* differently, must mean something different by "consciousness." There could be no disagreement in substance, really, about such an obvious issue.

I myself don't find it obvious which view is right (or whether instead some intermediate view is right). Consequently, I think we should expect disagreements in substance. One aim of this chapter is to convince you of the difficulty—the virtual intractability, even—of the sparse-vs.-abundant issue, with (I hope) the side effect of undermining the view that all disputes in this area must be merely terminological. Both sides, I think, generally mean the same thing by "consciousness" or "experience"; they merely disagree about how broadly it spreads; and both sides have maneuvers available to explain away opponents' contrary intuitions. To anticipate a bit: Advocates of the sparse view can suggest that advocates of abundance mistake the ready availability of experience in any modality for the actual presence of experience in each modality all the time. It doesn't follow from the fact that I can now call to mind how my feet feel in my shoes that two seconds ago I was experiencing the tightness of my shoes. It doesn't follow from the fact that I can suddenly notice that the clock tower has already chimed twice that I consciously experienced those chimes when they occurred rather than nonconsciously processing them and storing them in short-term memory. On the other side, advocates of abundance can remind advocates of sparseness that unremembered does not necessarily mean unexperienced, and they can emphasize that on their view unattended experience may often be vague, inarticulate, indistinct, or largely unactionable, yet be experience nonetheless. You may think one side or the other has the better of such arguments, but the very existence of such arguments suggests that adherents can attach to both sides.

The most obvious way to quiet the worry that the sparse-vs.-abundant dispute is entirely terminological would be to define "consciousness" clearly enough to prevent terminological misalignment, then observe that the disagreement persists. Unfortunately, I can't do this. The two best avenues for formal definition are closed. We can't define "consciousness" *analytically*, because consciousness is a foundationally simple concept not divisible into component parts. It isn't like "bachelor" (marriageable but unmarried man) or "quadrilateral" (closed planar figure with four straight sides). Nor can we define consciousness *functionally* by appeal to the role it plays in a system (a "heart" is an organ that pumps blood; "currency" is whatever physical tokens serve as the medium of economic exchange), since the functional role of consciousness, if any, is still very much in dispute. (The dispute may even be fundamentally irresolvable—see my preface and the end of this chapter.) It may be helpful to define "consciousness" by synonymy: By "conscious experience" or "consciousness" I mean whatever it is by virtue of which (in Nagel's 1974 terminology) there is "something it's like" to be you, or a bat, and (presumably) nothing it's like to be a rock or toy robot; I mean "subjective experience"; I mean "phenomenology" as the term is used in recent Anglophone philosophy of mind; I mean Ned Block's (1995b) "phenomenal consciousness," or David Chalmers's (1996) "qualia." But definition by synonymy will work only if we mean the same thing by the synonyms, and it may not be clear that we do.

The best approach, I think, is to clarify by example and contrast: By "furniture" I mean tables, chairs, dressers, beds, and things like that, not plates, doors, or toys; by "square" I mean these sorts of things (here imagine some examples drawn on a page) and not these others. With diverse enough positive and negative instances, hopefully the listener gets the idea. So, then, by "conscious experience" I mean sensations of attended objects, words uttered silently to oneself, deliberately formed visual images, thrills of emotion, and things like that (including when they occur in dreams[4]), and *not* immune-system response, dendritic growth, early visual processing, unreportable subliminal processing, or things like that. Now, while I hope someone initially confused by the terminology will latch on to the right concept from such a list, the list as I have constructed it has a serious problem: To avoid begging the question in favor of sparseness or abundance, I have omitted the kinds of cases that adherents of the two sides would tend to dispute, such as unattended peripheral stimuli. Consequently, a variety of concepts might satisfy the positive and negative instances, and I can't be sure that we will all latch onto the same one. However, I think there is only one intuitively obvious, pre-theoretical concept that embraces all the positive instances and none of the negative instances and leaves it an empirical question, neither true nor false by definition, whether conscious experience greatly outruns attention and reportability. That concept is phenomenal consciousness in the sense that makes dualism tempting and the mind-body problem interesting. I may be wrong. Maybe there is more than one intuitively obvious concept meeting these criteria. That would complicate the argument of the chapter. But all I really need for my goals in this chapter is that by the end—after I have discussed the methodological and introspective difficulties—it seems plausible to you that people's radical disagreements about abundance are often substantive and not *merely* terminological.

iii

Those who see consciousness as abundant, such as James and Searle, generally provide little positive argument. They tend simply to state the position and expect the reader to agree. For example, James writes:

The next thing to be noticed is this, that every one of the bodily changes, whatsoever it be, is felt, acutely or obscurely, the moment it occurs. . . . Our whole cubic capacity is sensibly alive; and each morsel of it contributes its pulsations of feeling, dim or sharp, pleasant, painful, or dubious, to that sense of personality that every one of us unfailingly carries with him. (1890/1981, pp. 1066–1067)

James does not defend this view other than by its intuitive appeal, either here or (as far as I'm aware) anywhere else in his work.[5] Siewert (1998), arguing specifically for the abundance of visual experience, prepares the ground somewhat more carefully, clarifying what is at issue and what the abundant view is *not* committed to. He emphasizes that every detail needn't be appreciated sharply or separately—an important qualification. But when it comes time for defense of abundance, so clarified and qualified, Siewert gives us no more than James or Searle. It is as though he implicitly assumes that the only potential source of disagreement is misunderstanding, which, once cleared up, leaves the abundance of visual experience simply evident to reflection.

The trouble with this, of course, is that not everyone believes that consciousness is abundant, even when the view is stated clearly. We don't all share James's and Searle's intuitions on the matter. Some people believe that the shirt on one's back and the shoes on one's feet aren't experienced— even vaguely, inarticulately, or peripherally—at every moment of the day; they believe that one's visual phenomenology may lapse entirely from time to time. This is not obviously preposterous. Others find themselves torn, or uncertain, or inclined to see one sensory modality as abundantly ever-present and another as experienced only sparsely and sporadically. And, of course, even if there were a broad intuitive consensus favoring the abundant view, that consensus might be mistaken. Surely, then, it would be good to defend abundance on the basis of something more than its natural charm.

Some advocates of the sparse view similarly rely principally on folk intuition. David Armstrong (1981), for example, appears to think it is simply evident that we lack visual experience in the absent-minded driving case. And Julian Jaynes writes: "We are constantly reacting to things without being conscious of them at the time. Sitting against a tree, I am always reacting to the tree and to the ground and to my own posture, since if I wish to walk, I will quite unconsciously stand up from the ground to do so. Immersed in the ideas of this first chapter, I am rarely conscious even of where I am." (1976, p. 22) Jaynes likens the lack of consciousness in this case to the lack of consciousness in early visual processing and in blindness due to cortical damage—cases generally regarded as obviously and uncontroversially unconscious. He invites us to agree on the basis of our own sense of our experience; he does not defend these claims further.

A war of philosophical intuitions thus threatens. Never to my knowledge has such a war had a happy outcome.

iv

We might look for empirical arguments favoring one view over the other—arguments that go beyond mere appeal to our intuitive sense of our own experience. As far as I know, those who see consciousness as abundant offer either no positive arguments or only question-begging ones such as Searle's (1993) bald assertion that our capacity to shift attention to previously unattended stimuli proves that we had pre-existing conscious experience of those stimuli.[6] (What the capacity to shift attention shows, of course, is that we do some perceptual processing outside attention, not—at least, not without considerable further argument—that that pre-attentive perceptual processing is conscious.)

Advocates of the sparse view often offer empirical arguments for their position, but these arguments too are badly question-begging. A favorite argument is this: Without attention, we fail to parse, respond to, notice, or remember what one might think would be salient stimuli—for example, a stream of speech coming in one ear (Cherry 1953; Moray 1959) or a woman in a gorilla suit walking through a ball game (Simons and Chabris 1999). Therefore, it is said, we are "blind" (or "deaf" or "numb") to these stimuli; we don't experience them (e.g., Dennett 1991; Mack and Rock 1998; Wright 2005; Kouider et al. 2010). Here is the flaw in that argument: It is one thing (indeed a very interesting thing) to show that we don't do much processing of unattended stimuli; it's quite another to say that we have no experience whatsoever of those unattended objects. The conclusion simply doesn't follow, and many psychologists refrain from drawing it. We may not *parse* the speech semantically (very much) or *represent* the black blob in the middle of the ball game as an ersatz gorilla, but we may still experience that unattended speech and that gorilla in some more inchoate or unreportable way (Simons 2000; Most et al. 2005; Mole 2008; Ford 2008; Smithies, forthcoming). Furthermore, unless we really *are* blind, or deaf, or numb, we do process the unattended stimuli to some extent—as Searle points out, and as is acknowledged on all sides of the debate. One is drawn to an unexpectedly looming object, to an unanticipated call of one's name, to a familiar ringtone or doorbell that others can barely hear, or to a gentle tap on one's shoulder. To call our attention, such things must first register pre-attentively in some way. The question is whether whatever limited processing or responsiveness or preparedness to respond we have prior to attention is enough to underwrite actual sensory consciousness. The present argument doesn't address that question, nor do similar arguments involving "change blindness" (see, e.g., Rensink 2000, 2004).

Some of Mack and Rock's experiments (Rock et al. 1992 and Mack and Rock 1998) may give us pause. For example, subjects directed to judge the relative lengths of the arms of a cross presented for a fifth of a second, followed by a mask, often fail to report some other stimulus (such as a dot or a triangle) that is simultaneously and unexpectedly presented in a nearby visual region. When asked immediately after seeing the display, they may say that all they saw was the cross. Mack and Rock describe these subjects as "inattentionally blind"—as having had no experience whatsoever of the unexpected figure.

The conclusion is tempting, but on reflection the Mack and Rock experiments should no more trouble those who see experience as abundant than does the obvious fact that someone deeply absorbed may fail to notice a distant (or even not-so-distant) shout, and may say afterward that she heard nothing or heard only the uniform buzz of traffic. Several interpretations consonant with abundance suggest themselves. One might accept that the unexpected figure (or the shout) was not experienced at all, yet still hold that the uniform unattended background color (or traffic hum), including at least some of its unattended parts, *was* experienced: Perhaps the sensory systems failed to register anything of enough interest to merit more than "filling in" or representing the unattended field as uniform; it doesn't follow that there is no conscious experience of that uniformity. Or perhaps the figure contributed in an inchoate and unparsed way to an experience reported as uniform but actually an immemorable jumble—part of a stream of visual experience fluctuating not only with major changes in the display, measured in fractions of a second, but also with each eye movement, blink, afterimage, accommodation, and glitch, and perhaps even with every spike and trough of neural or informational noise. Or maybe the subject's sensory representations were activated enough to underwrite some sort of experience but not enough to trigger a behavioral response. The experiments by Mack and Rock don't address these possibilities. Though participants may deny having seen the unexpected figure, this in no way implies that experience is limited to the targets of attention.

What evidence do we have, then, on the crucial, foundational question about consciousness posed at the beginning of this chapter? Only conflicting folk-psychological intuitions and badly question-begging arguments. In other words, we have essentially *no* evidence. Such is the infancy of consciousness studies.

v

How should we approach the issue, then? I don't think further studies of the relationship between attention and successful report of stimuli will help much. We already have the relevant data: People have some, but only a very limited, sensitivity to unattended stimuli. The question remains: Is that sensitivity (whatever it is) enough to underwrite phenomenology? At this point, the interpretive questions loom larger than the flat empirical ones. People sometimes deny having seen, heard, or felt unattended things, but does that mean that those objects, or the fields containing those objects, or the entire unattended modality, was entirely unexperienced, rather than inchoately or immemorably or unactionably experienced? The typical attention-and-reportability study presupposes, rather than addresses, these larger interpretive issues, or else remains silent on them.

If we knew the neural basis of consciousness, perhaps we could use that knowledge to address the sparse-vs.-abundant question. But we don't know the neural basis of consciousness. In fact (a point I will return to later), we may never be able to know it until we determine whether experience is abundant, since (it seems) we need at least a rough understanding of what processes are conscious and what processes aren't conscious before we go looking for a common neural basis among the conscious ones; and until we settle the sparse-vs.-abundant question we don't have even a rough understanding of what neural processes are the conscious ones.

Are we left, then, with introspection—with simply *asking* ourselves, or experimental subjects, whether experience is sparse or abundant? Well, scholars *have* tried addressing the question introspectively—James, Jaynes, and Searle, for example—and have come to different conclusions. I assume that this is not because James and Searle really experienced every morsel and modality whereas Jaynes lived largely in blankness.

Advocates of the sparse view have often remarked on another problem, too, that plagues attempts to address this question introspectively: the "refrigerator-light" problem, so named after the mistaken impression a child might have that the refrigerator light is always on because it is on whenever he checks it (Thomas 1999; Block 2007). Jaynes puts the point nicely:

It is like asking a flashlight in a dark room to search around for something that doesn't have any light shining on it. The flashlight, since there is light in whatever direction it turns, would have to conclude that there is light everywhere. And so consciousness can seem to pervade all mentality when actually it does not. (1976, p. 23)

Does it seem to me that I have tactile experience of my feet in my shoes? Yes it does, now that I think of it. That I have auditory experience of the hum of the computer? Yes, I guess I seem to be experiencing that now too. But of course I can't conclude from such observations that I continually experience such things when I am *not* thinking about them. The mere fact of thinking about whether I experience my feet in my shoes may *create* that experience. What we want to know is whether I was experiencing my feet in my shoes before the matter came to mind. But that's now in the irretrievable past. I've been thinking too much about introspection, about my feet. I'm corrupted.

The question is, thus, rather difficult to study. The most obvious methods fail.

vi

But perhaps we haven't introspected carefully enough. Maybe we can dodge the problem through better introspective method. After all, the sparse view and the abundant view posit radically different phenomenal worlds. It seems that there should be *some* introspectively discoverable difference between them.

To avoid the refrigerator-light problem, we might try giving participants beepers to wear during their normal daily activities—beepers that sound only at long intervals, when the participants are likely to be immersed in other things—and instructing the participants to reflect, each time the beeper sounds, on what their experience was immediately before the beep, when (in most cases, presumably) they won't have been thinking about the sparseness or abundance of experience, or about their feet, or about the traffic in the background. Some participants might be asked to report everything in their experience, others only whether or not they had visual experience, and others only whether they had tactile experience in the left foot. A beeper is appealing because it has a sharp onset, targeting a specific moment of experience, while at the same time allowing subjects to become immersed in their normal, everyday activities. And because participants can be told in advance what to reflect on in the targeted experience, no seconds-consuming and potentially confusing verbal query is necessary. It thus combines the advantages of surprise and preparation. With a little practice, the participant ideally could reflect on her naturally occurring experience within a second of each sampled event (see Hurlburt and Heavey 2004 and Hurlburt and Schwitzgebel 2007).

I tried exactly this, and in the remainder of the chapter I will discuss the procedure, the results, and the questions that arise. I am not convinced that this approach can resolve the question of the sparseness or abundance of experience, but unless we plan to disregard subjective report completely, it seems that knowing what people say about their experience when prompted to reflect on it is an essential starting point. I offer this chapter in much the same spirit in which I offered chapter 5: If we want to be serious about consciousness, we must find some better methods for getting at it than casual observation by untrained introspectors. But the problems that ensue reveal the long and difficult path before us.

vii

I lent beepers to 21 people, about half of them philosophy graduate students and about half miscellaneous well-educated other folks. I divided participants into five conditions: the *full-experience* condition, the *full-tactile* experience condition, the *full-visual* experience condition, the *tactile-left-foot* condition, and the *far-right-visual-field* condition. (The experiment is described in more detail in Schwitzgebel 2007a.) I told participants in the full-experience condition only that our aim was to explore everyday conscious experience generally; they did not know the specific purpose of the research. Participants in the other four conditions were fully informed and asked for their initial opinion about the sparse-vs.-abundant debate, which I explained using intuitive examples like those mentioned at the beginning of this chapter.

Participants wore the beeper for 3–4 hours a day, at their convenience, for four days over the course of about two weeks. The beeper sounded at random intervals approximately 6–8 times during each 3–4 hour period, and each time it sounded the subject was to immediately write down what she had been experiencing in the last undisturbed moment before the beep. Participants in the four informed conditions (full-visual, full-tactile, far-right-visual field, and tactile-left-foot) were emphatically instructed to begin by simply noting whether they were having any conscious experience in the targeted modality, and only after that to record specific aspects of their experience, if any, in that modality and potentially relevant features of the environmental situation. I also emphasized that participants should skip any sample that seemed too private or to which they could not respond instantly. Skipped samples were uncommon, and no participant reported skipping more than two samples in a single interview day.

Within 24 hours of each 3–4 hour period, I interviewed each participant for an hour about her experiences. I asked the participants to report everything they could remember of the details of the experiences reported, and I had them describe their general environmental situation and what they were doing at the time (e.g., sitting in the passenger seat of a car, looking out the window at two women, thinking they looked young) as well as aspects of their situation that seemed directly pertinent to the targeted modality (e.g., in the tactile-left-foot condition, what if anything they were wearing on their feet and how their feet were positioned), always focusing as precisely as possible on the last instant before the beep. My idea in asking for such detail was to communicate a serious interest in conscientious accuracy, to convey in the context of specific reports what sort of phenomena participants should be noting the presence or absence of, and to give the participants ample opportunity to clarify ambiguities in their reports, to resolve or discover confusions, to express concerns about the methods of the study, and to develop their own sense of the phenomena. In general, I encouraged theoretical discussion. I clarified as much as possible what is meant by "consciousness" or "experience" in hopes of avoiding question-begging conceptions. I played devil's advocate, gently (I hope), raising potential doubts and concerns both about reports of experience and about reports of lack of experience, giving participants an opportunity to respond to those concerns.

Generally, the first time a participant in one of the visual conditions (the full-experience, full-visual, and far-right-visual-field conditions) denied visual experience in a sample, I introduced what I called the "phenomenal blindness" thought experiment. I explained phenomenal blindness as follows: There is a difference between blindness as pure blackness (like in the dark, though see chapter 8 for more on this) and blindness as genuine absence of visual experience, like the lack of visual experience you have of what is behind your head. (Or does it seem to you that there is a curtain of blackness behind your head?) A phenomenally blind person is one who is blind in the absence-of-experience sense. Once I felt that the participant understood this distinction, I asked the following question: At the sampled moment, could a phenomenally blind person, a twin of you in all respects except lacking visual experience, have had the same conscious experience as you at that moment? I mentioned that, of course, a real blind person might differ in several ways—in potential to respond to a looming object, in quality of auditory experience, in a lack of visual imagery, and so on. However, I asked participants to disregard such differences if they could. A few participants rejected the thought experiment as too much of an imaginative reach (I invited them to reject it if they didn't like it), but most said they found the comparison helpful. I emphasized that my aim was merely to ask as clearly as possible whether she completely lacked visual experience. I emphasized that either answer was acceptable, and that it was also acceptable to say "I don't know" or "I don't remember." I would occasionally return to this thought experiment if it seemed helpful. I offered the participants in the tactile conditions a corresponding "numbness" thought experiment, with a distinction between numbness positively felt and numbness as absence of tactile experience.

Of course my interview approach utterly violated the ordinary methodological advice (ordinary by contemporary standards, that is—see chapter 5) that participants be as naive as possible. Regarding the sparseness or abundance of experience, I think it is practically impossible to be naive, to have no initial inclinations or implicit assumptions. Given that, I thought it better to introduce my participants to competing alternatives and sources of skepticism than to leave them to the silent guidance of their own initial or emerging theories.

At the end of the last interview, I asked participants to guess whether I was more inclined toward a sparse view or toward an abundant view (or, in my labels of the time, a "thin" or a "rich" view). I also asked whether their opinion had changed over the course of sampling.

viii

From each participant I collected from 9 to 30 samples (with a mean of 17), excluding samples not discussed in the interviews. (For most participants, an hour was not enough time to carefully explore all the sampled experiences, especially on the first two interview days.) For analysis, I classified participants' answers into three categories, "yes or leaning yes," "undecided or don't know," and "no or leaning no," usually getting the participant's explicit assent to the label. (Most participants also used "yes" and "no" in their written notes.) I excluded from analysis undecided samples and samples in which the participant reported having been thinking about the experiment (usually a small minority of sampled experiences).

Table 6.1 outlines the main results. In sum, the majority of participants in the three visual conditions (which includes the full-experience condition)—8 out of 13—reported visual experience in every single one of their

Table 6.1

Type of experience	Conditions included	Number of people reporting the type of experience in 100 percent of their samples	Median reported percentage of the type of experience	Distribution of reported rates (one percentage rate for each participant)[a]
Any visual experience	Full experience, full visual, far right visual field	8 out of 13	100	56%, 73%, 74%, 85%, 89%, 100%, 100%, 100%, 100%, 100%, 100%, 100%, 100%
Far right visual experience	Far right visual field	0 out of 4	63	50%, 55%, 71%, 89%
Any tactile experience	Full experience, full tactile[b]	0 out of 8	76.5	50%, 56%, 69%, 75%, 78%, 79%, 86%, 89%
Tactile left foot experience	Tactile left foot	0 out of 4	49	16%, 18%, 80%, 92%

a. The percentages in the full-visual condition differ statistically from all other conditions (Mann-Whitney, one-tailed, $p < .05$).

b. So as not to interfere with their focus on the foot, participants in the tactile-left-foot condition were not asked to report their general tactile experience. In contrast, participants in the far-right-visual condition found it quite natural to discuss the general presence or absence of visual experience.

samples. However, a significant minority, the other 5, reported no visual experience whatsoever in some of their samples, by the very stringent standard implied in the "phenomenal blindness" thought experiment described in section vii above. Although no one reported far right visual experience or tactile experience in every single sample, every participant reported such experiences in at least half her samples. Two participants reported occasional tactile-left-foot experiences (one reported it in 3 of 19 samples, another in 4 of 22), and two others reported such experiences very frequently (12 of 15 and 11 of 12).

Taken at face value, these results appear to conflict with both the sparse view and the abundant view. Advocates of abundance typically assume that we have constant or very nearly constant visual and tactile experience—probably even constant tactile experience in the left foot. (Recall James's statement that every "morsel" is "sensibly alive.") The tactile data appear to contradict that claim. So too do some of the data from the visual conditions: Participants often denied peripheral visual experience, and some of them denied having any visual experience whatsoever in a substantial minority of samples.

Against the sparse view, every participant reported experience of unattended objects or in unattended modalities in some samples. I haven't attempted to quantify this, since the self-report of attention is fraught with perils and confusions I didn't even attempt to prevent or remedy; however, I explicitly asked participants about it from time to time. Every participant but one was unambivalently confident, at least once, of having had a conscious experience without attention—including those who began the experiment seemingly committed to a very sparse view of experience. Even if we disregard self-reports of attention, it seems unlikely that participants were attending to events in their far right visual field more than half the time or to tactile events in their left foot 16 percent or more of the time during the course of several hours of normal activities, unless wearing the beeper dramatically altered their run of experience.

Thus, one might read the data as supporting a moderate view—a view somewhere between the very sparse or very abundant views normally espoused by those who write on this topic. All my participants exited the experiment with a moderate view of some sort, thinking that experience extends well beyond the field of attention but does not include the entire field of every major modality anywhere near 100 percent of the time. Typically, they expressed some degree of what seemed to be genuine surprise at their results, with those initially inclined to think of consciousness as sparse (10 of the 21 participants, on the basis of the preliminary interview) surprised to seemingly find experience where they thought there would be none, and with those initially inclined toward abundance (11 of the 21) surprised at what they took to be the absence of experience in some cases. Most reported moderating their view by the end of the experiment.

I would love to be able to agree with the consensus of my participants. Unfortunately, I find myself overwhelmed with qualms. These qualms, I think, generalize beyond my own experiment and cast serious doubt on the scientific tractability of the sparse-vs.-abundant dispute—and consequently on any theories that turn on resolving it, such as (I will argue) all general theories of consciousness.

ix

Before I discuss the methodological worries, let me mention a concern about the theoretical viability of a moderate view. Theorists tend to split between seeing consciousness as very sparse and seeing it as very abundant. Here is why (I think): To make sense, theoretically, of the moderate view, one must introduce an extra moving part into one's theory of sensory consciousness. We already have good theoretical reasons, independent of any specific commitments about consciousness, to allow into our perceptual theories the phenomena of attention and supraliminal (that is, non-subliminal) perception. It is easy and natural to suppose that conscious experience co-occurs with one of these—the former on the sparse view, the latter on the abundant. There isn't as natural a theoretical space, however, for something that might explain why, if we accept a moderate view, some unattended sensory stimuli are consciously experienced and others aren't. If perceptual consciousness isn't causally inert (or even, on some theories, if it is), it ought to have some important, fundamental, cognitive-functional correlate. But what could that be, on the moderate view? The sparse view has attention, and the abundant view has supraliminal perception; however, for the moderate view nothing of broad currency in contemporary psychology seems to play quite the right role.

That is not to say there aren't candidates. Maybe there is a kind of *diffuse* attention, distinct from focal attention, that is capable of being spread broadly across multiple sensory modalities and objects, but not across all major modalities all the time. Or perhaps intense concentration or high-demand tasks pull enough resources away from non-focal sensory processing to prevent unattended stimuli from entering consciousness, whereas less intense concentration permits those stimuli to be (peripherally) experienced (Ward 1918; Lavie 2006; Hine forthcoming). Such views may be plausible, but we should be leery of embracing them without a broad range of corroborating support. Other advocates of moderate views, such as Lamme (2003, 2005) and Koch and Tsuchiya (2007), have suggested other candidate functional roles that decouple consciousness and attention but do not imply that conscious experience is abundant. Maybe such views can be sustained; maybe the functional roles will even map nicely onto introspective reports. But, as I will explain in the next section, I am inclined to think that introspective reports on this topic are problematic almost beyond hope.

x

I will divide my concerns into concerns about *overreporting* and concerns about *underreporting*—the first, of course, suggesting that experience is sparser than participants say, the second suggesting that it is more abundant.

Overreporting concern 1: The effects of wearing the beeper Many participants expressed concern that participating in the experiment would cause them to think more about the relevant modality or region and thus experience it more, distorting their results toward the abundant side. I grant the likelihood of some effect of this sort. However, since the experiment is not concerned with small differences, only a very large effect of this type would invalidate the general results—only a pervasive transformation of experience, moment to moment, for hours at a time. That doesn't seem especially plausible. Furthermore, it seems reasonable to suppose that if there were such a large effect we would see either rising rates of experience (as participants were trained to think about that modality or region) or declining rates (as participants grew more accustomed to the beeper and let it affect them less), depending on the mechanism guiding the supposed beeper-caused transformation of experience. But average rates of reported experience were stable between the first and last days. (Eight participants reported more experience on the last day, eight less, and 13 (mostly at ceiling) the same amount.[7]) And of course I excluded from analysis samples in which participants reported thinking about the experiment—only eight samples total, less than half a sample per participant. Most participants reported quickly becoming absorbed in their ordinary activities, largely forgetting about the beeper until it sounded.

Overreporting concern 2: Bias Experimenter-bias effects are, of course, pervasive in psychological research (as Robert Rosenthal in particular has emphasized, from Rosenthal and Fode 1963 through Rosnow and Rosenthal 1997; see also my brief discussion in chapter 3). Such effects seem especially likely to play a role in consciousness research and in research involving open-ended interviews. I came into the experiment not neutral between the theses but thinking that experience was probably abundant (though I found my conviction shaken as the experiment progressed). Thus, I sympathize with the advocate of the sparse view who suspects that it's mainly my bias driving the results and that the subjects of a more even-handed researcher would have reported sparser experience. One test of this, of course, would be for a sparse-minded researcher to replicate my methods. To assess my own bias, I did two things. First, at the end of the experiment I had subjects guess which view I favored. Only seven of the 21 subjects guessed than I favored the abundant view, whereas 13 guessed that I favored the sparse view (one declined to guess). Second, I asked Russ Hurlburt to review some of my interview tapes. I sought Hurlburt's opinion in particular because he is the world's leading practitioner of open interviews on randomly sampled experiences, because he repeatedly emphasizes the importance of being open-minded in interviewing style (e.g., in Hurlburt and Heavey 2006 and Hurlburt and Schwitzgebel 2007), and because he appears to favor a sparse view. He said he thought my interviews were even-handed. I conclude that at least my overt bias was not extreme. Of course, it is still possible that covert bias affected participants' responses.

At first, I also thought participant bias would be a major factor in the results. However, I was fortunate to have participants evenly balanced in their initial inclinations toward sparseness or abundance (10 vs. 11). Also, there was a surprisingly weak relationship between participants' initial inclinations and their final results. Participants inclined toward a sparse view were only slightly more likely to report relatively sparse results than participants with an abundant view. Counting the full-experience and far-right-visual-field groups twice—once for each type of recorded experience (for the full-experience subjects, any visual and any tactile; for the far-right-visual-field subjects, any visual and far right visual)—I found that in 17 cases participants' results tended in the direction of their initial inclinations, relative to the results of the group as a whole, and in 12 cases the results went against their bias—not a statistically significant tendency. For example, one subject who initially expressed a strong inclination toward the abundant view nonetheless reported visual experience in only five of her nine samples. I doubt that either of these facts—the equal distribution of initial bias or the weak relationship between initial bias and final results—should entirely dispel concerns about participant bias, but I do think it's reasonable to be optimistic that it isn't *mainly* participant bias driving the results.

Overreporting concern 3: Timing errors Participants might have reported more experience than they actually had either if they reached too far into the past, gathering up the last conscious experience, whenever it was, in the relevant modality or region, or if they inadvertently reported on their experience after the beep—experience that may have been created by the beep. I repeatedly emphasized the importance of trying to home in as accurately as possible on the last undisturbed moment before the beep. For what it's worth, the participants all felt they could do this, most of the time, with reasonable if not perfect accuracy; but still, people are certainly subject to illusions of timing.[8]

Another version of this third overreporting concern turns on the idea that the target experience may be affected by the beep even if the participant *accurately* reports the beep as being experienced only after the target experience. This needn't be as exotic a matter as backward causation. The beep is presumably experienced only some time after it stimulates the ear—only after, perhaps, some tens of milliseconds of neural processing. Maybe that preliminary processing, before the beep is experienced, affects the experience of the event that is experienced as having happened immediately before the beep. Maybe, even, experienced temporal order, when events are near enough together, is to some extent an after-the-fact reconstruction (see Dennett 1991). We could hardly expect participants to be able to assess such matters introspectively.

Overreporting concern 4: Stimulus error, reporting the plausible, or reporting the sensory store   Participants may have reported on states of the world rather than on their experience of the world, leading to overly abundant or otherwise erroneous reports; or they may have reported on what seemed plausibly to have been their experience rather than on the actual experience itself; or they may have reported the contents of their short-term sensory memory even if (on the sparse view) those memories are not of events sensorily experienced before the beep. For example, a participant asked to report on visual experience in the far right visual field may simply have reported on what objects she visually remembers having been to her right, regardless of whether those objects were in fact experienced before the beep. Wearing the beeper in piloting this experiment, I sometimes had the following reaction: The beep sounded, I closed my eyes (some participants did this, some didn't, I left it up to them), and I attempted to recall my immediately prior visual experience. There was a black street in front of me, green trees to my left. But was I simply now recalling the objects that I remembered to have been before me—or perhaps what was in my short-term "iconic memory" or "sensory store" (see Sperling 1960; Massaro and Loftus 1996)—or was I recalling my *experience* of those objects? The two judgments are different—on the sparse view, very different—but it is no trivial task to pull them apart introspectively.[9] Titchener and Boring call the mistake of reporting on outward objects rather than on one's experience of those objects "stimulus error" or "R-error." Their suggestions for how to avoid stimulus error, however, are sketchy and not especially helpful in this context. (See Titchener 1901–1905, 1910, 1912b; Boring 1921.)

On behalf of my experiment, I offer four facts as a partial response to this concern: (1) Every participant (except perhaps one) appears to have understood the distinction between reporting experience and reporting remembered objects, at least on a superficial level; and each at least once denied experience of something in her sensory environment that *could* have been experienced (e.g., an object in her field of view, the contact between flesh and shoe). (2) If participants generally reported on what was in their environment—that is, on what the abundant view would predict they would be experiencing—we would see near ceiling results in every condition, which we don't. (3) In the far-right-visual-field condition, participants quite readily reported blurriness or vagueness in their experience— properties, of course, of the experience itself, not of objects in the outside world. (4) Participants favoring a sparse view should, it seems, have been less prone than others to report in accord with an expectation that everything in their sensory fields would be experienced. Presumably they had no such expectation. They should have been quite ready to recognize a difference between knowing that an object is nearby (or having a lingering sensory representation of that object) and having had a sensory experience of that object, since their view demands that the two often come apart. And yet their results looked very much the same as those of the participants favoring the abundant view (see overreporting concern 2 above). Unfortunately, none of these four responses fully addresses the central problem, which has become increasingly lively to me: that it seems often to be practically impossible—except perhaps on the basis of questionable and circular assumptions about the sparseness or abundance of experience— to disentangle ordinary sensory memories (perhaps indistinct) of features of the outside world (e.g., that the trees were green and the pavement was black) from memories of one's sensory experience of that world (e.g., that I had a visual experience of green and black).

Underreporting concern 1: Preference for mixed reports　Experimental subjects often prefer moderate or mixed responses to extreme ones. I attempted to counter this preference by stating explicitly in the interviews (in the four informed conditions) that it would be acceptable to respond entirely with "yes" answers or entirely with "no" answers and that in fact that would be interesting as support for the theoretical views at stake—but I doubt I was entirely successful. Since participants gave nearly uniform "yes" answers to general visual-experience questions, pressure to mix it up can't explain the entire pattern of the results, of course; but a friend of abundance might suggest that only in the "obvious" case of central vision will participants have had the self-confidence to present an extreme pattern of data. (No parallel argument is available to the friend of sparseness, who will need something other than the middle-of-the-scale bias to explain the visual results that run counter to her position.)

If I had browbeat people into changing their report from sparse to abundant and vice versa, that could have generated an overall pattern of intermediate data. There was, indeed, some risk of this, since I tried to counteract participants' biases by occasionally raising concerns or pointing out the plausibility of the alternative view. Fortunately, an analysis of first-day vs. final-day results shows no consistent pattern of browbeaten conversions. Twenty subjects stayed either above or below the median report rates for the type of experience in question, and nine crossed the median (again counting full-experience and far-right-visual-field participants twice, once for each of their coded reports).

Underreporting concern 2: Subtle experience   In the tactile-left-foot condition, one participant—a philosophy graduate student who reported tactile-left-foot experience in 11 out of 12 samples—typically said he had a general sense of the position and disposition of his body, its posture, and its contact with things. He usually claimed not to have experienced his left foot separately and distinctly, but only as a small and subtle part of this holistic bodily sense. This pattern of reporting apparently surprised him: He initially expressed an inclination to the sparse view. Indeed, within the full-tactile and tactile-left-foot conditions, four of the participants (three initially sparse-biased, one initially abundant-biased) reported discovering a holistic bodily sense of this sort, and those four all had above-median results. Is this just a compelling theoretical idea that, once entertained, inclined these participants to invent experience to match it (see overreporting concern 4 above)? Or did this idea reflect a discovery of, and allow them to report, a subtle sort of background experience that others might easily miss?[10]

Underreporting concern 3: Memory error   I don't think we should be too concerned about long-term memory error. In the four informed conditions (that is, all but the full-experience condition), the basic data point was very simple, and I permitted participants to consult their notes during the interview. If a participant gets it right in the first few seconds after the beep, it seems unlikely she will misreport later. (Obviously there is much more room for long-term memory error in the full-experience condition, but fortunately those results fit with the results in the other conditions.) The bigger issue is this: What is the likelihood of failing to remember the targeted moment of experience, or non-experience, between the time of its occurrence immediately before the beep and the act of judgment shortly after the beep?

It is noteworthy how much we fail to remember over even very short intervals if our attention is not on it as it occurs. Perhaps the most striking recent experiments on this topic are the "change-blindness" experiments of Ronald Rensink (Rensink et al. 1997, 2000) and others (e.g., Simons and Levin 1998). You look at a picture. It flickers and is replaced by a very similar picture, with one major change. For example, a large railing changes position substantially, or a large jet engine near the middle of the picture disappears and then, after another flicker of the picture, reappears. It is often difficult to detect such a change, even when the stimuli are presented repeatedly. In another change-blindness experiment, the subject is having a conversation with a stranger. In the middle of the conversation, two people carrying a door briefly walk between the subject and the stranger, and the stranger is surreptitiously replaced by another person in different clothing, with a slightly different build but a similar social category (for example, male construction worker). Many people fail to notice the change. Experiments like this—along with older experiments on the unreliability of eyewitness testimony (Münsterberg 1927; Loftus 1979; Haber and Haber 2000) and on the forgetting of mundane everyday details such as the direction in which Abraham Lincoln faces on the penny (Sanford 1917/1982; Nickerson and Adams 1979)—suggest that we may fail to encode or remember surprisingly large aspects of our perceived external environment.

Whether we similarly fail to encode or remember large tracts of our stream of conscious experience, as distinguished from our outward environment, is an open question, but I see no reason to suppose it merits a different answer, especially if experience is abundant. If sensory experience is a complex and highly detailed flux, it may be at least as expensive and pointless to retain as are the unimportant or readily available environmental details we so easily forget. The beeper method brings to a practical minimum the delay between experience and reflection, but the experience and reflection still aren't simultaneous (they can't be, if we are to avoid the refrigerator-light error), and that non-simultaneity may be enough to guarantee the forgetting of substantial portions of experience that are never recorded even in short-term memory.

How should we assess these various concerns? Three strike me as fairly tractable, perhaps with further experiments: the effects of wearing the beeper, participant and experimenter bias, and the preference for mixed reports. The timing error issue seems a bit trickier. Perhaps it could be addressed by asking participants to focus on their experience not *immediately* before the beep but rather, say, a full second before the beep; but that seems likely to aggravate at least the memory issues, and perhaps also stimulus error and bias. The subtle experience error and the stimulus error seem to me trickier still. The subtle experience error raises some of the same tangled issues as the combination-tones case discussed in chapter 5: How do we know when someone is introspecting well enough that we can trust her assertion that she lacks some subtle experience? Though I was able to say a few things against the worry about stimulus error, it seems to me that such reassurances should leave an advocate of sparseness largely unmoved. The visual memory of a peripherally seen object and the memory of having visually experienced that object seem awfully hard to tease apart. And the concern about short-term memory seems to me absolutely intractable if we take its possibility seriously: How could anyone introspectively discern whether an experience, however recently past, never occurred, or whether, instead, it occurred but was never encoded into memory?

If all the concerns pointed the same direction, we could perhaps reach some rough conclusions nonetheless. For example, if the only really troubling concerns suggested underreporting, we might conclude that experience was *at least* as abundant as participants suggest. That would still leave us no basis for deciding between a moderate and a radically abundant view—no basis in a retrospective self-report experiment like this one, at least. (Whether there might be other bases for deciding will be addressed shortly.) Unfortunately, there are daunting concerns on both sides. Experience might still, for all we know given subjective reports like these, be anywhere from radically sparse to radically abundant.

xi

The phenomenological difference between sparseness and abundance is vast. If defenders of abundance are right, our stream of experience is aswarm with detail in many modalities at once, both inside and outside the field of attention; if defenders of sparseness are right, experience is limited to one or a few attention-occupying activities or objects at a time. On the first view, unconscious perception exists only in the margins if it exists at all; on the second, *most* of our perception is unconscious. On the first view, we always have a complex flow of visual experience; on the second, we may quite often have no visual experience at all. Shouldn't it be easy to decide between these two views? Shouldn't a moment's reflection settle the matter incontrovertibly?

The fact that it doesn't is striking, and methodologically very important. One might take the apparent evasiveness of what is seemingly an obvious issue to suggest some merely linguistic or communicative trouble, a problem of speaking past each other, of disagreement or inconsistency in the use of words—an issue I raised in section ii. I doubt that we can justifiably comfort ourselves with that thought. Forget about the interpretations of James and Jaynes and Searle, and just consider the issue in a single vocabulary. No matter how you think of "consciousness," exactly how far consciousness spreads is an open question. If the methodological difficulties are as serious as I have suggested they are, there should be a broad range of substantively distinct plausible views—perhaps even all the way from very sparse to very abundant. Such views remain live despite the phenomenological gulf between them because the refrigerator-light problem hobbles concurrent introspection and because stimulus error, memory error, and the potential subtlety of the target experiences make even carefully collected retrospective reports difficult to interpret.

Could this experiment, or another on the same topic, have been done appreciably better, so as to avoid these concerns? Can we construct, even if only in fantasy, a better experiment? Let's consider self-report methods first. Any concurrent self-report method—any method that asks the participant to report on his experience as it occurs—will be polluted by the introspective act itself. Any retrospective self-report method will invite concerns about short-term memory at least. Both approaches probably will accrue charges of participant bias, stimulus error, conceptual confusion, and potential insensitivity to subtle experiences. Different approaches will, perhaps, involve different trade-offs between these potential failings: Emphasizing the possibility of subtle experience may increase sensitivity to those experiences but also increase the risk of confabulation; selecting unsophisticated subjects may reduce certain sorts of theoretical bias but raise the risk of conceptual confusion; and so on. But no self-report method can, I think, effectively avoid the sorts of concerns raised here. My experiment, no matter how flawed, is not *contingently* flawed.

How about more objective or theoretical methods? Could we do away with subjective reports—at least, with subjective reports on this particular issue—and simply, say, look at the brain, or at patterns of behavior? Cognitive-behavioral approaches without the aid of self-report will not, I think, solve our problem. Either they operationalize "consciousness," equating it by definitional fiat with some behavioral or cognitive pattern, or they beg the question. Does mere behavioral responsiveness, for example, or above-chance responding on retrospective forced-choice questions about the presence of stimuli, demonstrate "consciousness" of those stimuli? Not in any way that should move an advocate of the sparse view. Does failure to report stimuli outside of attention show that they weren't consciously experienced? Not in any way that should satisfy an advocate of abundance. We simply don't know enough yet about the relationships between cognition and phenomenology to take any objective cognitive-behavioral measure of consciousness as valid without begging the question at hand.

The same holds for purely neural approaches. One might think we could resolve the issue by discovering what neural features are shared by indisputably nonconscious mental episodes and what neural features are shared by indisputably conscious mental episodes and then see whether our brain's response to unattended stimuli looks more like the former or the latter. Unfortunately, the gap between the indisputably conscious and the indisputably nonconscious is too wide to be bridged in this way. Early visual processing and early lexical processing are indisputably nonconscious (at least in mainstream opinion); focal visual attention and deliberate episodes of inner speech are indisputably conscious. There will be many neural and functional features the latter share that the former lack, and some of those features will be shared with tactile processing of an unattended foot. But which of those features are essential for consciousness? We don't know.

Furthermore, we may *never* know until we resolve the sparse-vs.-abundant dispute. As I mentioned in section v, the search for neural correlates of consciousness makes no sense unless we have in advance at least a *rough* idea of the sorts of mental states that are conscious, and we don't have even a rough idea of the sorts of mental states that are conscious until we settle the sparse-vs.-abundant question. Suppose we find a neural state that occurs when and only when a sensory process involves focal attention. Is that a neural correlate of consciousness? Not if experience is abundant; it might just be a correlate of attention. Suppose we find a neural state that occurs whenever there is sensory responsiveness. Is that a neural correlate of consciousness? Not if experience is sparse; it might just be a correlate of sensory sensitivity. Suppose we find a neural state that correlates with something like *diffuse* attention (as postulated in section ix). To declare that to be the neural correlate of consciousness, thus adopting a moderate view, begs the question against both sparse and abundant views, unless further arguments can be marshaled; but those further arguments must turn on self-report (which, as we saw, appears to be highly problematic in this domain) or else must turn on further behavioral, cognitive, or neural measures, which will be equally question begging.

xii

If there were a theory of consciousness so elegant and so nicely articulated with available scientific data that it compelled acceptance independent of the sparse-vs.-abundant question, perhaps we could turn to it to resolve the dispute. But there is no such theory. An obstacle to constructing such a theory is that the sparseness or abundance of experience appears to be a part of the basic data *in light of which* a theory of consciousness must be constructed. Arguably, we must know whether experience is sparse or abundant *before* we can justifiably embrace a general theory of consciousness.

Consider some actual theories. Bernard Baars (1988, 1997) advances a "global workspace" theory of consciousness according to which sensory content is conscious just in case it is in the narrow theater of working memory, where only a small amount of attended content can be manipulated at a time and broadcast across the cognitive system. Francis Crick (1994) argues that the neural correlate of consciousness is synchronized 40-hertz neural oscillations in the subset of neurons corresponding to an attended object. Rafael Malach (2006) suggests that consciousness may emerge from the tightly integrated activity of anatomically local neural groups, whether or not they interact with other cognitive processes. David Chalmers (1996) suggests that consciousness may be present wherever there is information processing (and thus virtually everywhere). Built into these views, virtually from the start, is a commitment to a view of consciousness as sparse (Baars, Crick) or abundant (Malach, Chalmers). Such theories will not and should not seem convincing to researchers with different antecedent opinions on the sparse-vs.-abundant question. Those of differing inclinations may quite reasonably regard such theories as, at best, theories of something *else*, not consciousness per se—perhaps focal attention, perhaps availability as a potential target of attention, perhaps information processing.

The distribution of consciousness across the range of animals and machines raises similar issues, at least for those theories of consciousness that purport to treat consciousness in general and not just human consciousness. From the beginning, such theories will include commitments on the distribution of consciousness—commitments that probably can't be grounded independently of the theory, in view of the difficulty in evaluating non-human behavior and biological processes for signs of phenomenology. Problems of this sort may be insurmountable. Consequently, a methodologically well justified scientific consensus on a theory of consciousness may be beyond our reach.

In the long run, the ingenuity of scientists nearly always embarrasses naysayers about science, so maybe I shouldn't be so pessimistic. Maybe I should say only that the obstacles are formidable.

7 The Unreliability of Naive Introspection

Is it not one and the same "I" who is now doubting almost everything, who none-theless understands some things, who affirms that this one thing is true, denies everything else, desires to know more, is unwilling to be deceived, imagines many things even involuntarily, and is aware of many things which apparently come from the senses? Are not all these things just as true as the fact that I exist, even if I am asleep all the time, and even if he who created me is doing all he can to deceive me? . . . Lastly, it is also the same "I" who has sensory perceptions, or is aware of bodily things as it were through the senses. For example, I am now seeing light, hearing a noise, feeling heat. But I am asleep, so all this is false. Yet I certainly *seem* to see, to hear, and to be warmed. This cannot be false. . . .

—Descartes, *Meditations on First Philosophy* (1641/1984), p. 19

i

Current conscious experience is generally the last refuge of the skeptic against uncertainty. Though we might doubt the existence of other minds, that the sun will rise tomorrow, that the earth existed five minutes ago, or that there is any external world at all, still, it is said, we can know the basic features of our ongoing stream of experience. Descartes espouses this view in his first two *Meditations*. So does Hume, in the first book of the *Treatise*, and so does the ancient skeptic Sextus Empiricus (as I read him).[1] Other radical skeptics, including Zhuangzi and Montaigne, though they appear to aim at very general skeptical goals, don't grapple specifically and directly with the possibility of radical mistakes about current conscious experience. Is this an unmentioned exception to their skepticism? Is it an uninten-tional oversight? Do they dodge the issue for fear that it is too poor a field on which to fight their battles?[2] Where is the skeptic who says we have no reliable means of learning about our own ongoing conscious experience, our current imagery, our inward sensations—we are as in the dark about that as about anything else, perhaps even more so?

Is introspection (if that's what is going on here) simply that good? If so, that would be great news for the blossoming (or should I say recently resurrected?) field of consciousness studies. Or does contemporary discord about consciousness—not just about the physical bases of consciousness but seemingly about the basic features of experience itself—point to some deeper, maybe fundamental, elusiveness that somehow escaped the notice of the skeptics and that perhaps partly explains the first death of consciousness studies a century ago?

ii

One must go surprisingly far afield to find major thinkers who unambiguously hold, as I do, that the introspection of current conscious experience is both (i) possible, important, and central to the development of a full scientific understanding of the mind and (ii) highly untrustworthy, at least as commonly practiced. In some Eastern meditative traditions, I think, this conjunction is common. And the fiercest advocates of introspective training in the first era of scientific psychology (circa 1900) endorsed both claims— especially Edward Titchener. (On Titchener, see chapter 5; for a brief discussion of the early "phenomenologists," see note 3 to the present chapter.) Both the meditators and Titchener, though, express optimism about introspection "properly" conducted; thus, they hardly qualify as general skeptics or pessimists. It is as though their advocacy of a regimen sets them free to criticize introspection as ordinarily practiced. But might they be right more in their doubts than in their hopes? Might understanding the human mind require introspection, even though the prospects are bleak?

I won't say much to defend (i), which I take to be both common sense and the majority view in philosophy. Of course we have *some* sort of attunement to our ongoing conscious experience, and we impoverish ourselves if we try to do without it. Defending (ii) is my project. In less abbreviated form: Most people are poor introspectors of their own ongoing conscious experience. We fail not only in assessing the *causes* of our mental states or the processes underwriting them; and not only in our judgments about nonphenomenal mental states like traits, motives, and skills; and not only in determining the proper labels for or essences of states otherwise perfectly well known; and not only when we are distracted, or passionate, or inattentive, or self-deceived, or pathologically deluded, or when we are reflecting about minor matters, or about the past, or only for a moment, or when fine discrimination is required. We are both ignorant and prone to error. There are major lacunae in our self-knowledge that are not easily filled in, and we make gross, enduring mistakes about even the most basic features of our currently ongoing conscious experience, even in favorable circumstances of careful reflection, with remarkable regularity. We either err or stand perplexed, depending—rather superficially, I suspect—on our mood and our caution.

Present-day philosophers and psychologists often doubt the layperson's talent for assessing such nonconscious mental states as personality traits, motivations, skills, implicit beliefs and desires, and the bases of decisions, and they sometimes describe such doubts as doubts about "introspection." But it's one thing not to know why you chose a particular pair of socks (Nisbett and Wilson 1977) and quite another to be unable accurately to determine your currently ongoing visual experience as you look at those socks, your auditory experience as an interviewer poses a question, or the experience of pain in your back that is making you want to sit down. Few philosophers or psychologists express plain and general pessimism about the latter sorts of judgment. Or, rather, I should say that I have heard such pessimism mainly from behaviorists, and their near cousins, who nest their arguments in a theoretical perspective that rejects the psychological value, sometimes even the coherence, of attempting to introspect conscious experience at all—and who thus reject (i) above—though indeed even radical behaviorists often pull their punches when it comes to ascribing bald error. (See, for example, Watson 1913; Skinner 1945, 1953; Ryle 1949; Bem 1972.[4])

Accordingly, although infallibilism—the view that we cannot err in our judgments about current conscious experience—is now mostly out of favor, mainstream philosophical criticism of it is meek. Postulated mistakes are largely only momentary, or about matters of fine detail, or under conditions of stress or pathology, or at the hands of malevolent neurosurgeons.[5] Fallibilists generally continue to assume that, in favorable circumstances, careful introspection can reliably reveal at least the broad outlines of one's currently ongoing experience. Even philosophers seen by most of the community as pessimistic about introspection are, by my lights, remarkably tame and generous. Paul Churchland, famous for his disdain of ordinary people's theories about the mind, nevertheless puts the accuracy of introspection on a par with the accuracy of sense perception (1984/1988, 1985). Daniel Dennett, who seems in some places to offer arguments for introspective error, in other places says that we can come close to infallibility when charitably interpreted.[6] Where are the firebrands?

A word about "introspection": I happen to regard it as a pluralistic confluence of processes involving attention to current conscious experience, but I do not defend that view in this book. (For that, see Schwitzgebel forthcoming a.) My project here, I hope, does not depend on my particular account of introspection. The reflections of this chapter and book should play a prior, constraining role on a theory of introspection. That is, we can and should consider the kinds of mistakes that people make about their stream of experience before we construct a detailed theory of introspection; it is only in light of conclusions about reliability that theories of the mechanisms can properly be developed. Think of introspection as you will, then, as long as introspection is the primary method by which we normally reach judgments about our experience in cases of the sort I will describe.[7] That method, whatever it is, is unreliable as typically executed. Or so I'll argue.

iii

I don't know what emotion is, exactly. Neither do you, I would guess. Is surprise an emotion? Comfort? Irritability? Is it more of a gut thing or a cognitive thing? If cognition isn't entirely irrelevant, how is it involved? Does cognition relate to emotion merely as cause and effect, or is it partly constitutive? I'm not sure there is a single right answer to these questions. The empirical facts seem ambiguous and tangled. (For a review, see Prinz 2004.) Probably we need to conjecture and stipulate, simplify, idealize, to have anything workable. So also, probably, for most interesting psychological concepts. But it is clear that, whatever emotion is, some emotions—joy, anger, fear—can involve or accompany conscious experience.

Now, you are interested, presumably, in philosophy and psychology, in introspection, consciousness, and the like—otherwise, you wouldn't be reading this book. You have had emotional experiences, and you have thought about how they feel either concurrently or retrospectively as they fade. If such experiences are introspectible, and if introspection is the diamond clockwork it is often supposed to be, then you have some insight. So tell me: Are joy, anger, fear, and other emotional states always felt phenomenally—that is, as parts of one's stream of conscious experience—or only sometimes? Is their phenomenology, their experiential character, always approximately the same, or does it differ widely from case to case? For example, is joy sometimes in the head, sometimes more visceral, sometimes a thrill, and sometimes an expansiveness, or, instead, does joy have a single, consistent core—a distinctive, identifiable, unique experiential character? Is emotional consciousness simply the experience of one's bodily arousal and other bodily states, as William James (1890/1981) and Jesse Prinz (2004) suggest? Or, as most people think, can it include, or even be exhausted by, something less literally visceral? Is emotional experience consistently located in space—for example, in particular places in the interior of one's head and body? Can it have color? For instance, do we sometimes literally "see red" as part of being angry? Does it typically come and pass in a few moments (as Buddhist meditators sometimes suggest), or does it tend to endure (as my English-speaking friends more commonly say)?

If you are like me, you won't find all such questions trivially easy. You will agree that someone—maybe even you—could be mistaken about some of them, despite sincerely attempting to answer them, despite a history of introspection, despite maybe years of psychotherapy or meditation or self-reflection. You can't answer these questions with the same easy confidence that accompanies your answers to similarly basic structural questions about cars—How many wheels? Hitched to horses? Travel on water? If you can—well, I won't try to prove you wrong. But if my past inquiries are indicative, you are in a distinct minority.

It's not just language that fails us—most of us?—when we confront such questions (and if it were, we would have to ask, anyway, why this particular linguistic deficiency?). Introspection itself fails us. The questions challenge us not simply because we struggle for the words to describe a patently obvious phenomenology. It isn't like knowing perfectly well what particular shade of tangerine your Volvo is, and being stumped only about how to describe it. Rather, in the case of emotion, the very phenomenology—the qualitative character of our consciousness—is not entirely evident, or so it seems to me. But how could this be so if we know the "inner world" of our own experience so much better than we know the world outside? Even the grossest features of our emotional experience largely elude us. Reflection doesn't remove our ignorance, or it delivers haphazard results.

Relatedly, most of us have a rather poor sense, I suspect, of what brings us pleasure and suffering. Do you really enjoy Christmas? Do you really feel bad while doing the dishes? Are you happier weeding, or going to a restaurant with your family? Few people make a serious study of this aspect of their lives, despite the lip service we generally pay to the importance of happiness. Most people feel bad a substantial proportion of the time, it seems to me. We are remarkably poor stewards of our emotional experience. We may *say* we're happy—overwhelmingly we do—but we have little idea what we're talking about.[8]

iv

Still, you might suggest, when we attend to *particular instances* of ongoing emotional experience we can't go wrong, or don't, or not by far. We may concede the past to the skeptic, but not the present. It is impossible—or nearly impossible—to imagine my being wrong about my ongoing conscious experience right now, as I diligently reflect.

Well, philosophers sometimes say this, or things that sound a lot like it—Descartes, for example, in the epigraph, as standardly interpreted[9]—but I confess to wondering whether they have really thought it through, contemplated a variety of examples, challenged themselves. You would hope they would have, so maybe I am misunderstanding or going wrong in some way here. But to me at least, on reflection, the claim that I could be infallible, or nearly so, in all or most of what I am inclined to say about my ongoing emotional phenomenology—even barring purely linguistic errors, and even assuming I'm being diligent and cautious and restricting myself to purely phenomenological claims about present experience, arrived at (as far as I can tell) "introspectively"—well, unfortunately, that seems just blatantly unrealistic.

Let's try an experiment. You are the subject. Reflect on, introspect, your own ongoing emotional experience right now. Do you even have any? If you're in doubt, vividly recall some event that still riles you until you are sure enough that you're suffering some renewed emotion. Or maybe your boredom, anxiety, irritation, or whatever in reading this chapter is enough. Is it completely obvious to you what the character of that experience is? Does introspection reveal it to you as clearly as visual observation reveals the presence of the text before your eyes? Can you, through introspection, discern the gross and fine features of your emotional phenomenology as easily and confidently as you can, through vision, discern the gross and fine features of nearby external objects? Can you trace its spatiality (or nonspatiality), its phenomenological viscerality or cognitiveness, its involvement with conscious imagery, thought, proprioception, or whatever, as sharply and infallibly as you can discern the shape, texture, and color of your desk? (Or the difference between 3 and 27?) I cannot, of course, force a particular answer to these questions. I can only invite you to share my intuitive sense of uncertainty.

Or consider this: My wife mentions that I seem to be angry about being stuck with washing the dishes again (although maybe washing dishes makes me happy?). I deny it. I reflect; I sincerely attempt to discover whether I'm angry—I don't just reflexively defend myself; I try to be the good self-psychologist my wife would like me to be—and I still don't think I'm angry. But I'm wrong, of course, as I usually am in such situations: My wife reads my face better than I introspect. Maybe I'm not quite boiling inside, but there is plenty of angry phenomenology to be discovered if I knew better how to look. Or do you think that every time we are wrong about our emotions, those emotions must be nonconscious, merely dispositional, not genuinely felt? Or felt and perfectly apprehended phenomenologically but somehow nonetheless mislabeled? Can't I also err more directly?

Surely my denial of anger is colored by my wanting to maintain a particular self-conception and by the same involvement in the situation that produces the anger itself. To that extent, this example is less than ideal as a test of my claim that, even in the most favorable circumstances of quiet reflection, we are prone to err about our experience. However, as long as we focus on judgments about ongoing emotional phenomenology, we can't insist that the reflection always be cool. If emotionality is enough consistently to undermine the reliability of our judgments about emotional experience, that rather better supports my thesis than defeats it, I think.

Excellent, nearly infallible, judges of our emotional phenomenology? I'm baffled. How could anyone believe that? Do *you* believe that?

V

Now, maybe emotional experience is an unusually difficult case. Maybe, though we err there, we are generally quite accurate in our judgments about other aspects of our phenomenology. Maybe my argument even plays on some conceptual confusion about the relation between emotion and its phenomenology or relies illegitimately on introspection's undercutting the emotion introspected. I don't think so, but I confess I have no tidy account to eradicate such worries.

So let's try vision. Suppose I am looking directly at a nearby bright-red object in good light, and I judge that I'm having the visual phenomenology, the subjective experience, of redness. Here, perhaps, even if not in the case of emotion, it seems rather hard to imagine that I could be wrong (though I could be wrong in using the term "red" to *label* an experience I otherwise know perfectly well). I grant that. Some aspects of visual experience are so obvious that it would be difficult to go wrong about them. So also would it be difficult to go wrong in some of our judgments about the external world—the presence of the text before your eyes, or the existence of the chair in which you are sitting and now (let's suppose) minutely examining. Introspection may admit obvious cases, but that in no way proves that it is more secure than external perception, or even as secure.

Of course, many philosophers have argued plausibly that one *could* be wrong even in "obvious" judgments about external objects, if one allows that one may be dreaming or that one's brain may have been removed at night and teleported to Alpha Centauri to be stimulated by genius neuroscientists with inputs mimicking normal interaction with the world. Generally, philosophers have supposed, with Descartes, that such thought experiments don't undermine judgments about visual phenomenology. Brain-in-a-vat skepticism suggests that I may be wrong about seeing a red tomato, but most philosophers would say it doesn't undermine my introspective knowledge that I am having *an experience as of* seeing a red tomato. So perhaps obvious introspective judgments (about "inner" experience) *are* more secure than obvious perceptual judgments (about how objects stand in the world outside), since they don't admit even this particular smidgen (usually it seems like only a smidgen) of doubt?

But in dreams we make baldly incoherent judgments, or at least very stupid ones. I think I can protrude my tongue without its coming out; I think I see red carpet that isn't red; I see a seal as my sister without noticing any difficulty about that. In dream delirium, these judgments may seem quite ordinary or even insightful. If you admit the possibility that you are dreaming, I think you should admit the possibility that your judgment that you are having red phenomenology is a piece of delirium not accompanied by any actual reddish phenomenology. Indeed, it seems to me not entirely preposterous to suppose that we have no color experiences at all in our sleep, or have them only rarely, and that our judgments about the colors of dream objects are on a par with the seal-sister judgment— purely creative fiction unsupported by any distinctive phenomenology. (See chapter 1 for more skepticism about color in dreams.) If so, the corresponding judgments about the coloration of our *experiences* of those dream objects will be equally unsupported.

Likewise, if malevolent neurosurgeons from Alpha Centauri might massage and stoke our brains, I see no reason to deny them the power to produce directly the judgment that one is having reddish phenomenology, while suppressing the reddish phenomenology itself. Is such a power so patently impossible?[10]

Thus, absolute security and immunity to skeptical doubt elude obvious introspective judgments as well as obvious perceptual ones. If we exclude radically skeptical worries, then we are left with judgments as obvious and secure as one could reasonably wish ("red phenomenology now," "book in my hands"). Whether the introspection of current visual experience warrants greater trust than the perception of nearby objects must be decided on different grounds.

vi

Look around a bit. Consider your visual experience as you do so. Does it seem to have a center and a periphery, differing somehow in clarity, precision of shape and color, richness of detail? Yes? It seems that way to me too. Now, how *broad* is that field of clarity? Thirty degrees? More? Maybe you are looking at your desk, as I am. Does it seem that a fairly wide swath of the desk (a square foot?) presents itself clearly in experience at any one moment, with the shapes, colors, textures all sharply defined? Most people, when I ask them, endorse something like that.[11] They are, I think, mistaken.

Consider, first, our visual capacities. It is firmly established that the precision with which we detect shape and color declines precipitously outside a central, foveal area of about one to two degrees of arc (about the size of your thumbnail held at arm's length). Dennett (1991) has suggested a way of demonstrating this to yourself: Draw a card from a standard deck without looking at it. Keeping your eyes fixed on some point in front of you, hold the card to one side, at arm's length, just beyond your field of view. Without moving your eyes, slowly rotate the card toward the center of your visual field. How close to the center must you bring it before you can determine the card's color, its suit, and its value? Most people are quite surprised at the result of this little experiment. They substantially overestimate their visual acuity outside the central, foveal region. When they can't make out whether it is a jack, a queen, or a king even though the card is nearly (but only nearly) dead center, they laugh, they are astounded, dismayed. (See also Dennett 2001.)

By itself, this says nothing about our visual experience. Surprise and dismay may reveal error in our normal (implicit) assumptions about our visual capacities, but it is one thing to mistake one's abilities and quite another to misconstrue phenomenology (a point Mike Gordon and I emphasized in our discussion of echolocation in chapter 4). Our visual experience depends on the recent past, on general knowledge, and on what we hear, think, and infer, as well as on immediate visual input—or so it is plausible to suppose. Background knowledge could thus fill in and sharpen our experience beyond the narrow foveal center. Holding our eyes still and inducing ignorance might artificially crimp the region of clarity.

Still, I doubt visual experience is nearly as sharp and detailed as most untutored introspectors seem to think it is. Here is the root of the mistake, I suspect: When the thought occurs to you to reflect on some part of your visual phenomenology, you normally move your eyes (or "foveate") in that direction. Consequently, wherever you think to attend, within a certain range of natural foveal movement, you find the clarity and precision of foveal vision. It is as though you look at your desk and ask yourself: Is the stapler clear? Yes. The pen? Yes. The artificial wood grain between them and the mouse pad? Yes—each time looking directly at the object in question—and then you conclude that they all are clear simultaneously. (This, then, would be a version of the "refrigerator-light problem," discussed in chapter 6; see also Dennett 1969, pp. 139–141. Another contributing factor may be an implicit analogy between visual experience and painting or photography; see chapter 2 and Noë 2004.)

But you needn't reflect in this way. We can pry foveation apart from introspective attention. Fixate on some point in the distance, holding your eyes steady while you reflect on your visual experience outside the narrow fovea. Better, direct your introspective energies away from the fovea while your eyes continue to move around (or "saccade") normally. This may require some practice. You could begin by keeping one part of your visual field steadily in mind while you allow your eyes to foveate anywhere but there. Take a book in your hands and let your eyes saccade around its cover while you think about your visual experience in the regions away from the precise points of foveation.

Most of the people I have spoken to who attempt these exercises eventually conclude to their surprise that their experience of clarity decreases substantially even a few degrees from the center. Through more careful and thoughtful introspection, they seem to discover—I think they really do discover—that visual experience does not consist of a broad, stable field, flush with precise detail, hazy only at the borders. They discover that, instead, the center of clarity is tiny, shifting rapidly around a rather indistinct background. Most of my interlocutors confess to error in having originally thought otherwise.[12] If I am right about this, then most naive introspectors are badly mistaken about their visual phenomenology when they first reflect on it. Even though they may be patiently considering their experience as it occurs, they will tend to go wrong unless they are warned and coached against a certain sort of error. And the error they make is not a subtle one; the two conceptions of visual experience differ vastly. If naive introspectors are as wrong as many later confess themselves to be, they are wrong about an absolutely fundamental and pervasive aspect of their sensory consciousness.

I am perfectly willing to doubt myself, though. Maybe I'm wrong and visual experience is broadly crisp and stable. But if so, I'm not the only person who is wrong about this. So also are most of my interlocutors (whom I hope I haven't browbeaten too badly) and probably a good number of philosophers and psychologists.[13] We—I, my friends, and co-believers—have erred through some theory or preconception, perhaps, some blindness, stupidity, oversight, or suggestibility. Okay, let's assume that. I need only, now, turn my argument on its head. We *tried* to get it right. We reflected, sincerely, conscientiously, in good faith, at a leisurely pace, in calm circumstances, without external compulsion, and we got it wrong. Introspection failed us. Since what I am trying to show is the aptitude of introspection to lead to just such errors, that result would only further my overall thesis. Like other skeptical arguments that turn on our capacity for disagreement, it can triumph in partial defeat.

My pessimistic argument does require this, though: People's judgments about their visual experience differ substantially. My interlocutors' opinions about their ongoing visual experience change significantly as a result of their reflections. The mistake in question, whichever side it is on, though perhaps understandable, is large—no minuscule, evanescent detail, no mere subtlety of language. Furthermore, opinions on both sides arise from normal introspective processes—the same types of process, whatever they are, that underwrite most of our introspective claims about consciousness. And finally, the argument requires that those who disagree don't differ in the basic structure of their visual experience in such a way as to mirror precisely their disagreements. Maybe you can successfully attack one of these premises?

vii

In 2002, David Chalmers and David Hoy ran a summer seminar in Santa Cruz, California, for professional philosophers of mind. They dedicated an entire week of the seminar to the "phenomenology of intentionality," including most centrally the question of whether thought has a distinctive experiential character.

There can be little doubt that sometimes, when we think, reflect, ruminate, dwell, or ponder, we simultaneously, or nearly so, experience imagery of some sort: maybe visual imagery, such as of keys on the kitchen table; maybe auditory imagery, such as hearing silently, in one's head, "That's where they are." Now, does the phenomenology of thinking *consist entirely* of imagery experiences of this sort, perhaps accompanied by feelings such as discomfort, familiarity, or confidence? Or does it go beyond such images and feelings? Is there some distinctive phenomenology of thought, additional to or conjoined with the images, perhaps even capable of occurring without them?

Scholars disagree. Research and reflection generate dissent, not convergence, on this point. This is true historically,[14] and it was true at the Santa Cruz seminar. Polled at week's end, seventeen participants endorsed the existence of a distinctive phenomenology of thought, while eight disagreed, either disavowing the phenomenology of thought altogether or saying that imagery exhausts it.[15]

If the issue were highly abstract and theoretical, like most philosophy, or if it hung on recondite empirical facts, we might expect such disagreement. But the introspection of current conscious experience is supposed to be easy, right? Thoughts occupied us throughout the week, presumably available to be discerned at any moment, as central to our lives as the seminar table. If introspection can guide us in such matters—if it can guide us, say, at least as reliably as vision—shouldn't we reach agreement about the existence or absence of a phenomenology of thought as easily and straightforwardly as we reach agreement about the presence of the table?

Unless people diverge so enormously that some have a phenomenology of thought and others do not, then someone is quite profoundly mistaken about his own stream of experience. If there is such a thing as a conscious thought, then presumably we have them all the time. How could you go looking for them and simply not find them? Conversely, if there is no distinctive phenomenology of thought, how could you introspect and come to believe that there is one—that is, how could you invent a whole category of conscious experiences that simply don't exist? Such fundamental mistakes almost beggar the imagination; they plead for reinterpretation as disagreements only in language or theory, not real disagreements about the phenomenology itself.

I don't think that's how the participants in these disputes see it, though; and, for me at least, the temptation to recast things this way dissipates when I attempt the introspection myself. Think about what you plan to do after you have finished reading. Now consider: Was there something it was like to have that thought? Set aside any visual or auditory imagery you may have had. The question is, was there something further in your experience, something besides the imagery, something that might qualify as a distinctive phenomenology of thinking? Try it again if you like. Is the answer so obvious that you can't imagine someone going wrong about it? Is it as obvious as that your desk has drawers, your shirt is yellow, your shutters cracked? *Must* disagreements about such matters be merely linguistic or about philosophical abstracta? Or, as I think, might people genuinely misjudge even this very basic, absolutely fundamental and pervasive aspect of their conscious experience, even after putting their best introspective resources to work?

viii

In my view, then, we are prone to gross error, even in favorable circumstances of extended reflection, about our ongoing emotional, visual, and cognitive phenomenology. In other chapters of this book I have argued that we are similarly inept in our ordinary judgments about the experience of visual perspective (chapter 2), of visual imagery (chapter 3), and of the echoic environment (chapter 4); and I have raised concerns about our judgments about the doubleness or singleness of visual experience (chapter 2), about difference tones, afterimages, and subtle illusions (chapter 5), and about the extent to which sensory experience is sparse or abundant (chapter 6). The treatment of dreams in chapter 1 doesn't concern concurrently introspected experience (except in those rare cases where one introspects one's dream experience while dreaming), but fits into the same general pattern. The final chapter, chapter 8, is a descent into confusion about normal, waking visual experience with one's eyes closed. Maybe I have erred in my interpretation of some of these cases. Still, taken together they are, I think, evidence enough for a generalization: The introspection of current conscious experience, far from being secure, nearly infallible, is faulty, untrustworthy, and misleading, not just sometimes a little mistaken, but frequently and massively mistaken, about a great variety of issues. If you stop and introspect now, there probably is very little you should confidently say you know about your own current phenomenology. Perhaps the right kind of learning, practice, or care could largely shield us from error (an interesting possibility that merits exploration), but as yet I see no robust scientific support for such hopes.[16]

What about pain, a favorite example for optimists about introspection? Could we be infallible, or at least largely dependable, in reporting ongoing pain experiences? Well, there is a reason optimists like the example of pain—pain and foveal visual experience of a single bright color. It *is* hard, seemingly, to go too badly wrong in introspecting really vivid, canonical pains and foveal colors. But to use these cases alone as one's inference base is to rig the game. And the case of pain is not always as clear as is sometimes supposed. There is confusion between mild pains and itches or tingles. There is the football player who sincerely denies he's hurt. There is the difficulty we sometimes feel in locating pains precisely (for a dentist, say) or in describing their character. I see no reason to dismiss out of hand the possibility of genuine introspective error in such cases. Psychosomatic pain, too. Normally we think of psychosomatic pains as genuine *pains*, but is it possible that some of them, instead, involve sincere belief in pain that doesn't exist?

Inner speech—"auditory imagery" as I called it above—can also seem hard to doubt—for example, that I am silently saying to myself "time for lunch." But on closer inspection, I find it too slipping from my grasp. I lean toward thinking that there is cognitive phenomenology of the sort described in the previous section, which can occur without imagery, but as a result I'm not always sure that some cogitation that seems to be in inner speech is not, instead, imageless. Also, does inner speech typically involve not only auditory images but also motor activity or motor imagery of the vocal apparatus? Is there an experiential distinction between (more active) inner speaking and (more passive) inner hearing? I almost despair.

Why, then, do people tend to be so confident in their introspective judgments, especially when queried in a casual and trusting way? Here is my guess: Because no one ever scolds us for getting it wrong about our experience and we never see decisive evidence of error, we become cavalier. This lack of corrective feedback encourages of hypertrophy of confidence. Who doesn't enjoy being the sole expert in the room—the person whose word has unchallengeable weight? In such situations, we tend to take up the mantle of authority, to exude a blustery confidence, and to genuinely feel that confidence (what professor doesn't know this feeling?) until we imagine the possibility of being proved wrong later by another authority or by unfolding events. About our own stream of experience, however, there appears to be no such humbling danger.

ix

An objection: Suppose I say, "I'm thinking of a pink elephant"—or even, simply, "I'm thinking." And suppose that I'm sincere and there is no linguistic mistake. Aren't claims of this sort necessarily self-verifying? Doesn't merely thinking such thoughts or reaching such judgments, aloud or silently, guarantee their truth? Aren't their truth conditions just a subset of their existence conditions—and if they are, might this not be useful in making a case for the trustworthiness of introspection?

I will grant that certain things plausibly follow from the very having of a thought: that I am thinking, that I exist, that something exists, and that my thought has the content it in fact has. Thus, certain thoughts and judgments will be infallibly true whenever they occur: whatever thoughts and judgments assert the actuality or possibility of the conditions or consequences of having them. But the general accuracy of introspective judgments doesn't follow.

Infallibility is, in fact, cheap. Anything that is evaluable as true or false, if it asserts the conditions or consequences of its own existence or has the right self-referential structure, can be infallibly true. The spoken assertion "I'm speaking" or "I'm saying 'blu-bob'" is infallibly true whenever it occurs. The sentence "This sentence has five words" is infallibly true whenever uttered. So is the semaphore assertion "I am holding two flags." So, sure, certain thoughts are infallibly true—true whenever they occur. This shouldn't surprise us; it is merely an instance of the more general phenomenon of self-fulfillment. It has nothing whatsoever to do with introspection; it implies no perfection in the art of ascertaining what is going on in one's mind. If introspection happens to be the process by which thoughts of this sort sometimes arise, that is merely incidental: Infallibly self-fulfilling thoughts are automatically true whether they arise from introspection, from fallacious reasoning, from evil neurosurgery, quantum accident, stroke, indigestion, divine intervention, or sheer frolicsome confabulation.

And how many introspective judgments, really, are infallibly self-fulfilling? "I'm thinking"—okay. "I'm thinking of a pink elephant"—well, maybe, if we are liberal about what qualifies as "thinking of" something. (See Hintikka 1962; Burge 1988, 1996.) But "I'm not angry," "my emotional phenomenology right now is entirely bodily," "I have a detailed image of the Taj Majal, in which every arch and spire is simultaneously well defined," "my visual experience is all clear and stable one hundred degrees into the periphery," "I'm having an imageless thought of a pink elephant"—those are entirely different. And, anyway, I'm not sure the objection doesn't change the topic. Does the thought "I'm thinking" or "I'm thinking of a pink elephant" really express a judgment about one's *conscious experience*? Philosophers might reasonably take different stands here, but it isn't clear to me that I am committed to believing anything, or anything particular, about my conscious experience in accepting such a judgment. I am certainly not committed to thinking that I have a visual image of a pink elephant, or an "imageless thought" of one, or that the words "pink elephant" are drifting through my mind in inner speech. I can hold "I'm thinking of a pink elephant" to be true while I suspect any or all of the latter to be false. Am I committed at least to the view that I am *conscious?* Maybe. Maybe this is one fact about our conscious experience that we infallibly know. (Could I reach the judgment that I am conscious nonconsciously?[17]) If that satisfies you, however, your ambitions for introspection must be modest indeed.

x

I sometimes hear the following objection: When we make claims about our phenomenology, we are making claims about how things *appear* to us, not about how anything really *is*. The claims, thus divorced from reality, can't be false; and if they are true, they are true in a peculiar way that permits no error. In looking at an illusion, for example, I may well be wrong if I say that the top line is longer; but if I say only that it appears or seems longer, I can't be wrong in the same way. The sincerity of the latter claim guarantees its truth. It's tempting, perhaps, to say this: If something *appears* to appear a certain way, necessarily it appears that way. Therefore, we can't misjudge appearances, which is to say phenomenology.

This reasoning rests on an equivocation between what we might call an *epistemic* sense and a *phenomenal* sense of "appears" (or "seems"). Sometimes we use the phrase "it appears to me that ____" simply to express a judgment—a hedged judgment, of a sort—with no phenomenological implications whatsoever. If I say "It appears to me that the Democrats are headed for defeat," ordinarily I am merely expressing my opinion about the Democrats' prospects. I am not attributing to myself any particular phenomenology. I am not claiming to have an image, say, of defeated Democrats, or to hear the word "defeat" ringing in my head. In contrast, if I am looking at an illusion in a textbook on vision science and I say that the top line "appears" longer, I am not expressing any sort of judgment about the objective length of the line. I know perfectly well that it isn't longer. I am making instead, it seems, a claim about my phenomenology, about my visual experience.[18]

Epistemic uses of "appears" *might*, under certain circumstances, be infallible in the sense I described in the previous section. Maybe, if we assume that they are sincere and normally caused, their truth conditions will be a subset of their existence conditions—I take no stand on that. (See Moran 2001 and Bar-On 2004.) But *phenomenal* uses of "appears" are by no means similarly infallible. This is evident from the case of weak, nonobvious, or merely purported illusions (as discussed in section v of chapter 5). Confronted with a perfect cross and told that there may be a "horizontal-vertical illusion" in the lengths of the lines, you may feel uncertainty, change your mind, and make what at least plausibly seem to be errors about whether one line "looks" or "appears" or "seems" in one's visual phenomenology to be longer than another. You may, for example, fail to notice—or worry that you might be failing to notice—a real illusion in your experience of the relative lengths of the lines, or you may (perhaps under the influence of a theory) erroneously report a minor illusion that really isn't part of your visual experience at all.

Philosophers who speak of "appearances" or "seemings" in discussing consciousness invite conflation of the epistemic and phenomenal senses of these terms. They thus risk breathing an illegitimate air of indefeasibility into our reflections about phenomenology. "It appears that it appears that such-and-such" may have the look of redundancy, but with disambiguation the redundancy vanishes: "It epistemically seems to me that my phenomenology is such-and-such." No easy argument renders this statement self-verifying.

xi

Suppose I am right about one thing—something that appears to be hard to deny: that people reach vastly different introspective judgments about their emotional experience, their imagery, their visual experience, their thought. If these judgments are all largely correct, people must differ immensely in the structure of their conscious experience.

You might be happy to accept such vast differences if the price of denying them is skepticism about the accuracy of introspective judgments. Yet I think there is good reason to pause. Human variability, though impressive, usually keeps to certain limits. For example, some people's feet are lean and bony, some fat and square, yet all show a common design: skin on the outside, stout bones at the heel, long bones running through the middle into the toes, appropriately arranged nerves and tendons. Only in cases of severe injury or birth defect is it otherwise. Human livers may be larger or smaller, but none is made of rubber or attached to the elbow. Human behavior is wonderfully various, yet we wager our lives daily on the predictability of drivers, and no one shows up at a department meeting naked. Is phenomenology the exception, varying radically from person to person—some of us experiencing one hundred degrees of visual clarity, some only two degrees, some possessed of a distinctive cognitive phenomenology that accompanies every conscious thought, some not, and so forth—with as little commonality as these diverse self-attributions seem to suggest? Of course, if ocular physiology differed in ways corresponding to the differences in report, or if we found vastly different performances on tests of visual acuity or visual memory, or if some of us possessed high-level cognition or sympathetic emotional arousal and others did not, that would be a different matter. But as things are, the variability-endorsing optimist must suppose that when two people walk into a room, their behavioral differences will normally be subtle, their physiologies essentially the same, and yet phenomenologically they will quite possibly be so alien as to be like different species. Hmm!

Here is another possibility: Maybe people are largely the same *except* when they introspect. For example, maybe we all have basically the same visual phenomenology most of the time, until we reflect directly on that phenomenology—and then some of us experience a hundred degrees of stable clarity while others experience only two degrees. Maybe we all have a phenomenology of thought, but introspection amplifies it in some people, dissipates it in others; analogously for imagery, emotions, and so forth.

That view has its attractions. However, one must surrender many things to work it so as to render our introspective judgments basically trustworthy. The view concedes to the skeptic that we know little about ordinary, unintrospected experience, since the view hobbles the inference from introspected experience to experience in the normal, unreflective mode. The view also threatens to make a hash of change in introspective opinion: If someone thinks that one of her previous introspective views was mistaken (a fairly common experience among people I interview—see, for example, section vi of this chapter and chapter 4)—she must, it seems, generally be wrong that her previous view was mistaken. She must, generally, be correct, now, that her experience is one way, and also correct, a few minutes ago, that it was quite another way, without having noticed the intervening change. This seems an awkward coupling of current introspective acumen with profound ignorance of change over time. The view renders foolish whatever uncertainty we may sometimes feel when confronted with what might have seemed to be introspectively difficult tasks (as in sections iv and vii of the present chapter, as well as elsewhere in this book). Why feel uncertainty if the judgment one reaches is bound to be right? It also suggests a number of particular—and, I am inclined to think, rather doubtful—empirical commitments (unless consciousness is causally irrelevant): major differences in actual visual acuity while introspecting between those reporting broad clarity and those reporting otherwise, major differences in cognition while introspecting between those reporting a phenomenology of thought and those denying it, and so on. The view also requires an entirely different explanation of why theorists purporting to use "immediate retrospection," including James (1890/1981, p. 189), Titchener (1912b, p. 491), and Hurlburt (1990, chapter 2), also find vastly divergent results, since immediate retrospection, if successful, postpones the act of introspection until after the conscious experience to be reported, when presumably it will not have been polluted by the introspective act.

Is there some compelling reason to adopt all these troubles?

xii

There are two kinds of unreliability. Something may be unreliable because it often goes wrong or yields the wrong result, or it may be unreliable because it fails to do anything or to yield any result. An employee is unreliable in one way if she botches the job, unreliable in another if she neglects it entirely. A program for delivering stock prices is unreliable in one way if it misquotes, unreliable in another if it crashes. Either way, they can't be depended on to do what they ought.[19] Introspection is unreliable in both ways. Reflection on basic features of ongoing experience leads sometimes to error and sometimes to perplexity or indecision. Which predominates in the examples in this chapter, and in the examples in this book generally, is not, I think, a deep matter, but rather a matter of context or temperament. Some introspectors will produce glib guesswork, while others will doubt. Some contexts—for example, a pessimistic essay on introspection—will encourage restraint. But whether the result is error or indecision, introspection will have failed—*if* we suppose that introspection ought to yield trustworthy judgments on the matters at hand.

You might reject that last idea. Maybe we shouldn't expect introspection to reveal (for example) the bodily or nonbodily aspects of emotion, or the presence or absence of a distinctive cognitive phenomenology. It wouldn't, then, tell against the reliability of introspection if such cases baffle us. It doesn't tell against the reliability of a stock quote program if it doesn't describe the weather. A passenger car that overheats while going 120 miles per hour isn't thereby unreliable. Maybe I have pushed introspection beyond its proper limits, illegitimately forcing it into failure.

What would be the proper limits of introspection, then? Perhaps we can restrain it, rendering it reliable, by restricting ourselves to the very easiest of judgments—self-fulfilling thought ascriptions, judgments about foveal colors and severe canonical pains, maybe one or few other cases where we really do seem dependably to get it right. (But what cases are those? Sometimes when I think I have found one, further inquiry proves me wrong. See the brief reflections on inner speech in section ix; I had also thought the experience of foveal shape quite straightforward until considering the issues about perspective discussed in chapter 2.) Such restraint hardly seems natural: The scientific or philosophical introspector wants to reach judgments about peripherally experienced color, not just foveally experienced color, about the location and character of pain, not just its presence or absence; and the processes in these various cases are not palpably different. Worse, the restraining move deprives introspection of most of its philosophical and psychological value. We wanted to know (didn't we?) general facts about the stream of experience—for example, about the structure of visual experience and inner speech, and about the range and types of phenomenology we possess. If introspection is to yield knowledge of such matters, it must be permitted to traverse them; and if it doesn't dependably yield accurate judgments about them, then for the purposes at hand it is not reliable. Alternatively, if one's aim is to advance the traditional philosophical foundationalist project of grounding knowledge of the outside world in knowledge of the sensory experience that the outside world produces in us, a narrowly caged introspection will not suffice: The foundationalist's introspection had better yield detailed knowledge of our sensory experience, and not just a few coarse judgments about foveal color and the like, to underwrite our detailed knowledge of the outside world. If we care about the reliability of introspection, we should care about its reliability in a broad range of cases, not just in a sliver. It helps none to lop its limbs, hoping thereby to prevent its sin.

xiii

Descartes, I think, had it quite backward when he said the mind—including especially current conscious experience—was better known than the outside world. The teetering stacks of paper around me I'm quite sure about. My visual experience as I look at those stacks, my emotional experience as I contemplate the mess, and my cognitive phenomenology as I drift in thought, staring at them—of such things I'm much less certain. My experiences flee and scatter as I reflect. I feel unpracticed, poorly equipped with the tools, categories, and skills that might help me dissect them. They are gelatinous, disjointed, swift, shy, changeable. They are at once familiar and alien.

The tomato in my hand is stable. My visual experience as I look at the tomato shifts with each saccade, with each blink, with each observation of a blemish, with each alteration of attention, and with the adaptation of my eyes to lighting and color. My thoughts, my images, my itches, and my pains all leap away as I think about them, or remain only as interrupted, theatrical versions of themselves. Nor can I hold them still, even as artificial specimens—as I reflect on one aspect of the experience, it alters and grows, or it crumbles. The unattended aspects undergo their own changes too. If outward things were so evasive, they also would mystify and mislead.

I know better what is in the burrito I am eating than I know my gustatory experience as I eat it. I know it has cheese. In describing my experience, I resort to saying, vaguely, that the burrito tastes "cheesy," without any very clear idea of what that involves. Maybe, in fact, I am merely—or partly—inferring: The thing has cheese, so I must be having a taste experience of "cheesiness." Maybe also, if I know that the object I am seeing is evenly red, I will infer a visual experience of uniform "redness" as I look at it. Or if I know that weeding is unpleasant work, I'll infer a negative emotion as I do it. Indeed, it can make great sense as a general strategy to begin with judgments about plain, easily knowable facts of the outside world, then infer to what is stranger and more elusive: our conscious experience of that world.[20] I doubt we can fully disentangle such inferences from more "genuinely introspective" processes.

Descartes thought, or is often portrayed as thinking, that we know our own experience first and most directly and then infer from it to the external world.[21] If that is right—if our judgments about the outside world, to be trustworthy, must be grounded in sound judgments about our experiences—then our epistemic situation is dire indeed. However, I see no reason to accept any such introspective foundationalism. Indeed, I suspect that the opposite is nearer the truth: Our judgments about the world tend to drive our judgments about our experience. Properly so, since the former are the more secure.

8   When Your Eyes Are Closed, What Do You See?

What they were asked to do was briefly this: to close the eyes, allow the after-images completely to die away, and then persistently and attentively *to will* that the color-mass caused by the *Eigenlicht* should take some particular form,—a cross being the most experimented with.

—George Ladd, "Direct Control of the Retinal Field" (1894, p. 351)

i

I would rather end this book with a tangle of questions than with the pessimism of the previous chapter. I am not an utter skeptic, nor do I think we should abandon efforts to understand the stream of experience. Let's plunge once more into the thicket, with a fresh topic. My aim is not as much to establish pessimism as to see how things look through a pessimistic lens.

The first scholar I am aware of who seriously considered what we see when our eyes are closed was the eminent early-nineteenth-century Czech physiologist—the first great introspective physiologist—Johann Purkinje (a.k.a. Jan Purkyne, 1787–1868), in his doctoral dissertation *Contributions to the Knowledge of Vision in Its Subjective Aspect* (1819/2001), a work ground-breaking in its attention to phenomenological detail.[1]

Purkinje begins his dissertation with a phenomenon he discovered in a childhood game:

I stand in bright sunlight with closed eyes and face the sun. Then I move my out-stretched, somewhat separated, fingers up and down in front of the eyes, so that they are alternately illuminated and shaded. In addition to the uniform yellow-red that one expects with closed eyes, there appear beautiful regular figures that are initially difficult to define but slowly become clearer. When we continue to move the fingers, the figure becomes more complex and fills the whole visual field (figs. 1–4 [figure 8.1 in this book]).

  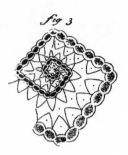 

Figure 8.1
"Light and shade figures," from p. 69 of Purkinje 1819/2001.

This is what happens in general. Now to the single instances and to closer definition of the conditions. I will first consider the observations of the figures in my right eye, and will mention those for the left eye later.

In general, I differentiate primary and secondary forms in the whole figure. The primary patterns define the background while the secondary are superimposed on it. The primary forms are larger and smaller squares (fig. 2) alternately light and dark, which cover most of the field, resembling a chess board.

At the borders of the squares longer and shorter zigzag lines develop that appear here and there and then vanish. Outward from the center, which is marked by a dark point surrounded by a light area, I see a field of larger hexagons, with gray sides and white centers. To the lower left of the central spot I see overlapping half circles, the direction of which continuously changes. They resemble tree rings or roses with many petals. . . . [Purkinje's descriptions continue for another page and a half.]

Further I must stress that the patterns I have described, especially the squares, have been seen by the majority of people with whom I have carried out the experiment, in so far as they can be communicated by verbal reports not accompanied by drawings. . . .

The patterns in my left eye, which is weak sighted, can only be seen incompletely. The primary patterns appear as curvilinear networks rather than as regular squares. The secondary patterns, however, are the same, only they are placed at opposite sides. (1819/2001, pp. 69–71)

Several other authors attest to such phenomena: Helmholtz says that such figures emerge in conditions of a "rapid change of light and shadow" (1866/1909/1962, volume 2, p. 257). John Smythies (1957) and Steven Stwertka (1993) call them "stroboscopic patterns" and find that they can be induced by a strobe light flashing about 10 times per second. G. Bard Ermentrout and Jack Cowan (1979) provide a mathematical explanation of why such geometrical figures may appear in hallucinations. So far, I have not been able to find such geometric organization in my own case—neither using Purkinje's splayed fingers technique, nor with a stroboscope. In both cases, I seem to experience an unsteady, quickly flashing, light and dark, noisy background and small colored figures that come and go.

In the passage reproduced above, Purkinje comments only briefly on *non*-stroboscopic experience while facing the sun with one's eyes closed—that "one expects" a "uniform yellow red." Elsewhere in his dissertation, and in an 1823 follow-up volume, Purkinje discusses various striking subjective visual phenomena, some occurring with eyes closed, others with eyes open. Among the eyes-closed experiences he discusses are the "cross-spiderweb" figures he sees when he suddenly wakes up with the sun shining on his closed eyes (1823/1919, §VIII), the "wandering cloudy stripes" he sees with eyes closed in darkness (see section iii below), the various "pressure figures" induced by pressing on his eyes (1819/2001, §II-III), the "galvanic light figures" produced by running electric current through his face (1819/2001, §IV), the squares he sees when he restricts the flow of blood to his head (1819/2001, §III), and the ellipse he sees when, after closing his eyes and attending to things non-visual for a while, with a sudden jerk of the eyes he attends to his darkened visual field (1823/1919, §V). But experience in ordinary daylight with his eyes closed seems never to have attracted Purkinje's attention. Perhaps the casual remark in the passage above reflects his final opinion: It's a simple yellow-red, hardly worth further discussion.

ii

Like Purkinje, later authors almost entirely ignore the question of what we normally experience with our eyes closed in well-lit environments. I can find no serious treatments.[2] (More commonly discussed is visual experience with eyes closed in the dark; I will get to that soon.) But can't we, if we want, just go out, lie in the sun, and see what it's like with our eyes closed? Will we then be doing cutting-edge science?

Here is what I am inclined to report: a bright, relatively uniform field that fluctuates in color from warm hues (including red, orange, brilliant scarlet) to white or dull gray, sometimes with a faint bluish tinge. The changes of hue are sometimes seemingly spontaneous, at other times precipitated by moving my eyes or tightening my lids. The field seems to churn throughout with a darker color, and I see flashes of brightness at the extreme periphery. The field seems broader than it is high, and either

flat and a few inches before me or—alternatively and quite differently—
entirely lacking any features of distance or depth or flatness.

I coaxed three acquaintances into reporting their visual experience
while facing the sun for seven minutes with their eyes closed. All independently described experiences similar to mine: bright fields fluctuating in
color from red to orange or yellow or white. All described the field as fairly
uniform, though with some perturbations (one reported diagonal lines that
came and went, another reported squiggles and lightning-like branching
figures, the third drifting dark spots and patches and crisscrossing lighter
strands or threads). When I asked about the periphery, all three described
it as similar to the center, though perhaps a bit darker. This similarity of
report is, perhaps, encouraging. Incidentally, the pupils of all three observers were fairly contracted by the end of the experiment, suggesting that
appreciably more light penetrates the closed eyelid when facing the sun
than enters the open eye in normal indoor environments.

I also lent random beepers (of the sort used in chapter 6) to five experimental subjects, asking them to report on their visual experience with their
eyes closed in a variety of circumstances. More on that later.

Who cares what we visually experience when the sun shines through
our eyelids? Well, here are two possibilities: (i) Everyone reports pretty
much the same thing, in which case there is probably no reason to doubt
the reports, and simply by lying on our backs in the sun we have discovered something new, despite having almost two centuries of consciousness
studies behind us. (ii) People disagree, and we have the same wonderful,
horrid mess on our hands that erupts in every other chapter of this book.

iii

More theoretically valuable, perhaps, or more intrinsically interesting, and
in any case much more discussed, is what we experience when our eyes
are virtually or entirely darkened, as when one sits with eyes closed in an
unlit room at night. Purkinje calls this the "dark field" and discusses it in
a section titled "Wandering Cloudy Stripes":

When I fixate the darkness of an eye, well protected from all external light, sooner
or later weakly emerging fine, hazy patterns begin to move. At first they are unsteady
and shapeless, later they assume more definite shapes. The common feature is that
they generate broad, more or less curved bands, with interpolated black intervals.
These either move as concentric circles toward the center of the visual field, and
disappear there, or break down and fracture as variable curvatures, or as curved radii
circle around it (figs. 17–19 [figure 8.2 here]). Their movement is slow, so that I

Figure 8.2
"Wandering cloudy stripes," from p. 80 of Purkinje 1819/2001.

usually need 8 seconds until such a band completes the journey and disappears completely. Even at the beginning of the observation the darkness is never complete. There is always some weak, chaotic light. It is strange that in this darkness the sense of proportions fails completely. The darkness is finite, extended in width. It is possible to measure it from the center, but one cannot determine precisely the peripheral limit. The closer we come to the periphery, the more difficult and finally impossible it gets to establish a visible peripheral limit. . . .

The figures described were seen with my right eye, because the left eye, which is somewhat weak, would not notice these delicate phenomena. In individuals in whom the two eyes are identical, probably the figures would unite just as the two fields of vision fuse into one. (1819/2001, pp. 79–80)

In his 1823 volume Purkinje adds:

In most cases after some minutes the . . . wandering cloudy stripes begin their game, often developing such vivacity that they appear colored themselves. Later a profusion of straight and crooked lines of different lengths appear, the straight frequently standing parallel and vertical, the crooked irregular and fragmentary. Sometimes a checkerboard appears or fragments of an eight-ray star. . . . With sensitivity becoming increasingly tender, the slightest involuntary movements bring forth a variety of light phenomena, even more toward the outer part of the visual field than in the middle. (1823/1919, pp. 105–106, my translation)

Johann Wolfgang von Goethe (whom Purkinje credits in his 1823 book but not in his 1819 dissertation) somewhat anticipated Purkinje's wandering cloudy stripes:

If the eye is pressed only in a slight degree from the inner corner, darker or lighter circles appear. At night, even without pressure, we can sometimes perceive a succession of such circles emerging from, or spreading over, each other. (1810/1840/1967, §96)

Let's follow these wandering cloudy stripes down through the nineteenth century, as they change and disappear.

iv

The next discussion I can find of the dark field is by the nineteenth century's next great introspective physiologist, Johannes Müller, some fourteen years after Purkinje's second volume:

If we direct our attention to what takes place in the eyes when closed, not merely do we see sometimes a certain degree of illumination of the field of vision, but also occasionally an appearance of light developed in greater intensity; sometimes, indeed, this luminous appearance spreads from the centre to the circumference, in the form of circular waves, disappearing at the periphery. At other times the appearance has more the form of luminous clouds, nebulae or spots; and, on rare occasions, it has been repeated in me with a regular rhythm. (1837–1840, p. 742)

Though in some ways strikingly similar to Purkinje's description (and Müller mentions Purkinje four times on this page, but oddly not on this topic), Müller's description of the stripes is more limited, characterizing them only as circular and not in the other forms Purkinje reports. Müller also describes them as moving in the opposite direction: not toward the center but outward toward the periphery.

Nineteen years after Müller's discussion, Helmholtz at first characterizes the dark field quite differently:

When the eyes are closed, and the dark field is attentively examined, often at first after-images of external objects that were previously visible will still be perceived. . . . This effect is soon superseded by an irregular feebly illuminated field with numerous fluctuating spots of light, often similar in appearance to the small branches of the blood-vessels or to scattered stems of moss and leaves, which may be transformed into fantastic figures, as is reported by many observers. (1856/1909/1962, volume 2, p. 12)

But then he adds that many people, including Goethe and Purkinje, report wandering cloudy stripes. Helmholtz continues:

The author's experience is that [wandering cloudy stripes] generally look like two sets of circular waves gradually blending together towards their centre from both sides of the point of fixation. The position of this centre for each eye seems to correspond to the place of entrance of the optic nerve; and the movement is synchronous with the respiratory movements. One of Purkinje's eyes being weaker than the other, he could not see those floating clouds except in his right eye. The background of the visual field on which these phenomena are projected is never entirely black; and alternate fluctuations of bright and dark are visible there, frequently occurring in rhythm with the movements of respiration. . . . (pp. 12–13)

In describing *two* sets of circular waves, Helmholtz departs from both Purkinje and Müller (though with a nod to Purkinje's weak eye). Helmholtz calls such visual experiences without outside light the *Eigenlicht* (intrinsic light) of the eye.

Nine years later, Hermann Aubert, adopting a phrase from Purkinje, calls our visual experience in darkness "light chaos" ("Lichtchaos," 1865, p. 333). Although no previous author claims that cloudy stripes are the only stable inhabitants of the dark field, in Aubert's account they jostle against multiple competitors. Aubert describes the light chaos as "a swarm of spots, lines, and splotches of light, difficult to describe, spread over the entire visual field" and specifies five forms: (1) black, but not deepest black, with yellow spots and lines of light like "hovering threads of fiber," (2) colorless wandering cloudy stripes in Purkinje's sense, moving in all directions, (3) fogballs in the middle of the visual field, expanding and contracting without much other movement, brighter in the center and fading toward the edges without a distinct boundary, (4) very bright lights at the far periphery, usually disappearing quickly, and (5) zigzag lines, like bright lightning, blue or violet in color, moving slowly and disappearing within a few seconds (ibid., pp. 333–334, my translations). Aubert estimates the brightness of the black background as similar to that of a sheet of white paper illuminated by a single candle 130 meters away (p. 64).

Despite their impressive pedigree in Goethe, Purkinje, Müller, and Helmholtz (and who could ask for more expert witness in the early nineteenth century?), the wandering cloudy stripes seem to dissipate after Aubert. The next serious discussion of them is in an 1897 journal article by Edward Scripture. Scripture rejects Helmholtz's claim that people see one figure for each eye, and describes the stripe as a "spreading violet circle." After Scripture, I can find no psychologist who treats wandering foggy stripes as the characteristic inhabitants of the dark field.

V

Meanwhile, another tradition—really a set of conflicting traditions—was arising that did not venture to predict any *particular* pattern of shapes in the visual field of the light-deprived eye.

Gustav Fechner offers the first substantial treatment of eyes closed visual experience with no reference to Purkinje's cloudy stripes. His term for the experience, *Augenschwarz* (literally "eye-black"), emphasizes its darkness. He writes:

The blackness that is present when the eyes are closed is rather just the same impression of light as we get when viewing a black surface, one which can change through all gradations to the most intense visual sensation. Indeed, this intrinsic blackness of the eye changes occasionally through purely internal causes into bright light and contains, so to speak, a sprinkling of light phenomena.

By paying strict attention, one discovers in the blackness that is seen when the eyes are closed a kind of fine dust composed of light, which is present in different people and under different conditions of the eye in various states of abundance, and in certain diseases may increase to a lively phenomenon of light. In my own eyes there exists, since the time when I had a lengthy disease of the eye, a strong continuing flickering of light, which increases according to the stimulation of my eyes and is subject to great fluctuations. (1860/1966, p. 138)

Fechner doesn't cite Purkinje, Müller, or Helmholtz here. Although his brief discussion on pages 136–138 doesn't preclude the possibility that wandering cloudy stripes may be among the "sprinkling of light phenomena," they remain unmentioned. Throughout his *Elements of Psychophysics*, especially in the second volume, Fechner treats the Augenschwarz as near the lowest bound of blackness, and he discusses the self-reports of several correspondents who describe their visual field with their eyes closed as either purely black or very nearly so (1864/1889, pp. 478–483).

Whereas Fechner evidently regards the regular experience of bright light in the Augenschwarz as pathological (see also Rüte 1845/1855; Maury 1861/1878), the American psychologist George Ladd suggests that it is only amateurish introspection that leads to reports of the field as mostly dark:

I have found by inquiry that a large proportion of persons unaccustomed to observe themselves for purposes of scientific discovery are entirely unacquainted with the phenomena of the retinal *eigenlicht*. Ask them what they customarily see when their eyes are closed in a dark room and they will reply that they see nothing. Ask them to observe more carefully and describe what they see, and they will probably speak of a black mass or wall before their eyes, with a great multitude of yellow spots dancing about on its surface. Some few will finally come to a recognition of the experience with which I have long been familiar in my own case. By far the purest, most brilliant, and most beautiful colours I have ever seen, and the most astonishing artistic combinations of such colours, have appeared with closed eyes in a dark room. I have never been subject to waking visual hallucinations, but I verily believe there is no shape known to me by perception or by fancy, whether of things on the earth or above the earth or in the waters, that has not been schematically represented by the changing retinal images under the influence of intra-organic stimulation. (1892, p. 300)

Galton writes:

[B]efore I thought of carefully trying, I should have emphatically declared that my field of view in the dark was essentially a uniform black, subject to an occasional light-purple cloudiness and other small variations. Now, however, after habituating myself to examine it with the same sort of strain that one tries to decipher a signpost in the dark, I have found out that this is by no means the case, but that a kaleidoscopic change of patterns and forms is continually going on, but they are too fugitive and elaborate for me to draw with any approach to truth. I am astonished at their variety, and cannot guess in the remotest degree the cause of them. They disappear out of sight and memory the instant I begin to think about anything, and it is curious to me that they should often be so certainly present and yet be habitually overlooked. (1883/1907, pp. 114–115)

Note that although Galton says that the patterns and forms disappear when he thinks about anything (else), it isn't clear whether he thinks that there is no visual experience whatsoever or that instead the field persists without attention, only darker or blander. (This is pertinent to the "sparseness" issue I will raise in section ix.) I have found no other author who goes even as far as Galton in asserting the relationship between attention and experience of the Eigenlicht. For what it's worth, I share Galton's impression that attention to the Eigenlicht tends to make its forms livelier.

Still differently, Ewald Hering calls the phenomenon *Eigengrau*, meaning "intrinsic gray" (1905, 1920/1964; in 1878 he was still using Helmholtz's term, Eigenlicht). His choice of gray over Fechner's black is deliberate: In the absence of contrast, especially after a long time, Hering suggests, we experience not so much darkness as neutral gray:

If we awake at night when it is still completely dark, at first we distinguish no objects at all, but see the whole visual field filled merely by those weak, more or less unsteady, cloudy or spotty colors which one can call the *intrinsic gray* (intrinsic brightness or darkness). (1920/1964, pp. 74–75)

That the field should be gray and not black fits nicely with Hering's emphasis on opponent processes in vision, according to which visual sensation involves competition between light and dark, between red and green, and between blue and yellow, all arising in contrast to a neutral resting state toward which one gravitates with adaptation. On such a view, it is natural to suppose that with persistent non-stimulation one would revert to a neutral sensation, not a dark one (see also G. E. Müller 1896, pp. 30–33; 1897, pp. 40–46). Why, then, might people misreport the experience? Hering suggests that the gray and the weak colors we experience when the eye is not stimulated have less "weight" (*Gewicht*)—that is, "the impressiveness or expressiveness that a visual quality or color possesses," which causes us to notice and remember it (1920/1964, pp. 115–116). (Afterimages and peripherally seen objects also lack weight, in Hering's view.) This is not at all the same as their being dark, but perhaps the casual introspector would confuse the two. Or—though I recall no hints of this thought in Hering—perhaps it is an instance of "stimulus error" (see chapter 6 above and Boring 1921)—the mistake of confusing the features of the outside world (that it is dark, or that no appreciable light is entering the eyes) with the features of the sensory experience the outside world produces in us.

Other psychologists offer passing comments on visual experience of the dark field. Alfred Volkmann describes the field as absolute blackness but with a "light dust" that varies between people (1846, p. 311). Louis-Ferdinand Alfred Maury says that when people have maladies or congestion and close their eyes or look into darkness they sometimes see hallucinatory figures (1861/1878, p. 84). Adolf Fick describes the field as "consisting of all kinds of moving splotches, in places colored, in places colorless, with shape and color steadily changing" (1879, p. 230, my translation). William James calls it "a curdling play of obscurest luminosity" (1890/1981, p. 583). Edmund Sanford invites students to consider the "shifting clouds of [idio-retinal] light" in the darkened eye (1892, p. 485, brackets in original). George Frederick Stout describes "the retina's own light" as "medium gray" with "specks and clouds of color" (1899/1977, p. 151). Edward Titchener describes "hazy or cloud-like patches of dull grey" (1901, volume 1, p. 510) and says "we see a grey, . . . an 'intrinsic' brightness sensation" (1896/1906, p. 79). An observer quoted at length by George T. Ladd (1903), referred to only as a "Mr. H.D." with an 1896 Yale Ph.D., says that his Eigenlicht ordinarily has "the appearance of a dancing mass of vari-colored dust, red predominating" and that it is normally circular, centered at the bridge of the nose, while "the radius extends to the corner of the eye and sweeps over the forehead to the other eye" (p. 145). Wilhelm Wundt describes "weak subjective light sensations" in the form of "light nebulas and light sparks" (1908a, p. 660, my translation). William Peddie describes the "self-light" as an "irregularly flecked shimmer" of yellowish-white (1922, pp. 44, 84). Leonard Troland says that the visual field is "relatively homogeneous and lacking in stereoscopic character" and that "faint patterns of colors . . . idio-retinal whirlings and the like, may be present" (1922/2008, p. 16). Frank Allen says we experience a "misty dark gray light" (1924, p. 275). Burch writes that with "prolonged resting of the eye in an absolutely dark room, the self light slowly diminishes and finally disappears" (quoted in Allen 1924), while Boring remarks in contrast that "the black of complete darkness gets subjectively lighter as it continues" (1942, p. 163). Karol Koninski says "the visual field appears as regular bluish-(ink-)black grains (the grains millet- to lentil-sized) on a yellow background" (1934, p. 362, my translation). Donald Purdy describes the "self light" as "a uniform dim expanse of gray" (1939, p. 531). Phenomenological reporting went out of style in psychology, and thoughtful descriptions of the Eigenlicht become harder to find after the 1930s. (See note 3 for some later quotes and note 4 for a few words on sensory deprivation and *Ganzfeld* experiments.)

Is it possible that all the men mentioned in the preceding paragraph just had different experiences, and that each of them was reporting his own experiences accurately? Maybe Hering genuinely experienced gray, Fechner black, Ladd fantastic colors, Purkinje a parade of cloudy stripes converging inward, and Scripture a crimson band spreading outwards. Deprived of stimuli and free to play, our brains could fall into different habits. And yet Ladd is convinced that people who manage to introspect carefully will come to agree with him. Presumably, this was his experience in conversation, at least with his students. Most researchers represent their experiences not as idiosyncratic but as typical. One would hope that they would base such claims partly on reports gathered from others, and Fechner, at least, does so explicitly. It would be strange if all of Fechner's acquaintances happened to see black and all of Hering's acquaintances gray. The historical arc of the reports of wandering cloudy stripes reminds me of the arcs of opinion about black-and-white dreams (chapter 1) and the elliptical appearance of tilted coins (chapter 2), possibly further grounds for suspicion of the accuracy of the reports.

Could people experience more or less what they *expect* to experience? That might explain the historical arcs and the similarity among researchers' students and acquaintances. Against this, though, at least some people say they are surprised at what they discover. Galton said so, as have some of the acquaintances and subjects I have interviewed.

vi

We might turn to neuroscience. Neurons are always active, even in the absence of stimulation. Tal Kenet and colleagues (2003), for example, looking at cats, found that "spontaneous activity" (in the dark or looking at a gray screen) in area 18—an area associated with selectivity for the orientation of visual stimuli—often closely resembled, with somewhat less organization, ordinary area-18 activity in response to visually presented gratings. Kun Wang and colleagues (2008) also found spontaneous activity in human primary visual cortex, especially in areas associated with imagery and memory, when subjects rested with their eyes closed inside an fMRI scanner. But there is no straightforward inference from neural firing patterns to phenomenology, and phenomenological studies are lacking: Despite the fact that subjects often lie in the dark in MRI machines, neuroscientists interested in vision understandably tend to focus on what occurs not in the darkness but rather when visual stimuli are presented.

One exception is a paper by Yuval Nir and colleagues (2006). Their subjects spent two minutes with eyes closed inside a dark MRI machine, and were asked to "pay close attention to any visual-like percepts that might occur during darkness (e.g., visual-like dots) and to report it following the scan" (p. 1314). Five of the seven subjects reported no visual-like percepts whatsoever; one reported afterimages in the first few seconds, and nothing otherwise; and one reported "visual-like" dots (thus adopting the terminology of Nir et al.). Although there is something to be said for brevity and neutrality in instructions on introspection, Nir et al. posed the introspective question too casually. What does it mean for a subject to report "nothing"? Does that mean blackness, or no visual experience at all (like the lack of visual experience of things behind your head; see the discussion of the "phenomenal blindness" thought experiment in chapter 6 and section viii of this chapter), or nothing that seems important, or nothing that the subject would confuse with a sensation caused by an ordinary outward object? The experimenter who has theoretical conversations with her subjects invites the charge of imposing her own views and thus biasing the reports. But sometimes, as here, without such conversations, the reports are uninterpretable, creating a methodological dilemma. Anyhow, Nir et al. found considerable fluctuation in visual cortical activity among their subjects, despite the subjects' minimal reports.

I see no reason neuroscientific studies couldn't cast some light. (Thus, I am more hopeful of progress here than I am about progress on the sparse/abundant issue discussed in chapter 6.) However, I have found no studies that are even close to methodologically adequate.

vii

I close my eyes right now, in my fluorescent-lit office, and consider my visual experience. I feel little room for doubt. The field is mainly black, with hints or tintings of color. After contemplating it for ten seconds, I place my palms gently over my eyes. Ah, I think, *now* it's black! I remove my palms and the field now seems like an intermediate gray—and that seems to me now to be the color it was before, originally, when I thought it was black. Was that first assessment, which seemed so easy, mistaken?

Or have I failed to track the changes in my experience over even these brief periods of time? Does my concept of blackness or darkness apply well only to the outside world, or to my experiences of the outside world, so that it's always something of a distortion to apply it to my experience with my eyes closed? Why does even so apparently easy an introspection confound me?

Helmholtz writes:

Another general characteristic property of our sense-perceptions is, that *we are not in the habit of observing our sensations accurately, except as they are useful in enabling us to recognize external objects. On the contrary, we are wont to disregard all those parts of the sensations that are of no importance so far as external objects are concerned.* Thus in most cases some special assistance and training are needed in order to observe these latter subjective sensations. It might seem that nothing could be easier than to be conscious of one's own sensations; and yet experience shows that for the discovery of subjective sensations some special talent is needed, such as Purkinje manifested in the highest degree; or else it is the result of accident or of theoretical speculation. For instance, the phenomena of the blind spot [where the optic nerve exits the eye] were discovered by Mariotte from theoretical considerations. Similarly, in the domain of hearing, I discovered the existence of those combination tones which I have called summation tones [see chapter 5, section iv]. . . . It is only when subjective phenomena are so prominent as to interfere with the perception of things, that they attract everybody's attention. . . . Even the after-images of bright objects are not perceived by most persons at first except under particularly favorable external conditions. . . . No doubt, also, there are cases where one eye has gradually become blind, and yet the patient has continued to go about for an indefinite time without noticing it, until he happened one day to close the good eye without closing the other, and so noticed the blindness of that eye. (1856/1909/1962, volume 3, pp. 6–7)

Immediately after this passage comes Helmholtz's assertion, quoted in section vii of chapter 2 above, that people typically are astonished to discover that most of the objects in their visual field, most of the time, are seen double. Later on the same page, Helmholtz lists "the 'luminous dust' of the dark field" among the subjective phenomena that are difficult to heed.

Here, as in my discussion of the subjective "flight of colors" after exposure to bright light (chapter 5, section v), I find myself torn. On the one side, I feel intuitively confident. I have a sense that I couldn't really go *too* far wrong—that I can doubt only inauthentically, as dogmatic skeptics are prone to do. On the other side, I am concerned that my, or our, subjective confidence may be poorly tuned in this domain—as suggested by Helmholtz and Ladd, who studied the phenomena with (presumably) more subjects than I and who insist that it is remarkably easy for untutored introspection to go astray.

viii

One thing that everyone in this literature appears to agree on (except perhaps Galton) is that we normally have *some* visual experience when our eyes are closed—at least, they all seem naturally to invite that reading, and they don't guard against it. Recall, however, the sparse view of consciousness from chapter 6. On the sparse view, we don't normally experience, even peripherally, the unattended hum of traffic in the background, the pressure of the shoes on our feet, or even the road before our eyes when we are driving inattentively. If it seems to us that we constantly experience all sensory inputs simultaneously, that is only because the act of attending *creates* the experience whose presence or absence we aim to assess. And if visual consciousness does indeed sometimes slip away, it might do so least conspicuously when our eyes are closed—unless, of course, for some reason we happen to be thinking specifically about our eyes-closed visual experience. Maybe we don't so much discover the Eigenlicht when we think about it, as bring it into being.

Adapting the beeper methodology described in chapter 6, I lent randomly sounding beepers to five volunteers, who wore them for two hours at a stretch, keeping their eyes closed the entire time. I left it up to them what their activities and lighting environments should be, though I did ask them to collect no more than half of their samples in any single type of situation. When the beep sounded, they were to consider whether they had any sort of visual experience—blackness, colors, fantastic figures, whatever—in the last undisturbed moment before the beep, or whether they had no visual experience whatsoever, not even of blackness or grayness. If they did believe they had some experience, I asked them to describe it in as much detail as possible. I interviewed them closely about their sampled experiences (or non-experiences); I encouraged open questioning of the methodology; I attempted to clarify as much as possible what was being asked, while minimizing or hiding my own inclinations; and I aimed to elicit the participant's best judgment about the matter at hand under the pressure of frank but gentle expression of concerns.

I made as clear as I could the difference between no visual experience and the experience of black or gray. My standard technique was as follows: First I asked participants if it seemed to them that they experienced blackness or grayness or anything else visual in the region behind their heads and beyond the farthest boundary of their peripheral vision, or whether it seemed, instead, empty or blank—not black, but rather entirely devoid of visual experience. All expressed the view that beyond the periphery it was visually blank, not black. I then asked them to imagine the blankness encroaching, the periphery narrowing, until no visual experience whatsoever remained but only blankness. My question then was: Is *that* what it's like when your eyes are closed and you're caught up in thinking about something else, or is it more like seeing black, or gray, or colors, or figures?

I also distinguished *sensory* visual experience from visual *imagery* experience. Visually imagine a setting sun in a cloudy sky. If you did that successfully, presumably you experienced visual imagery that was somewhat different in kind—or at least in vividness (Hume 1740/1978; Perky 1910)—from your sensory visual experience when you look at a real setting sun. People usually don't seem to have difficulty distinguishing imagery experience from sensory experience when their eyes are open, but when their eyes are closed the distinction sometimes loses it grip. I invited participants to consider whether that distinction made sense to them, and if so to report whether any visual experience they had seemed more sensory or more imagistic. All participants accepted the distinction and confidently classified each of their visual experiences in one or the other category. In some cases, they reported both sensory and imagery experience. Always, in such cases, the two were experienced as distinct—for example, a sensory experience of a uniform, bright orange field and simultaneously a visual image of two men dressed in black.

Table 8.1 displays the results, by subject, collected over three (or, for subject 1, four) separate beep-and-interview days. My sense of the subject's bias was based on what the subject said in the preliminary interview. Only S2 ever reported thinking about the experiment or about his ongoing visual experience in the moment immediately before the beep. Unfortunately, he reported this in six of his ten samples. All other participants were quickly swept up in radio programs, telephone conversations, and the like. As is evident from the table, their reports varied enormously. S2 reported sensory visual experience in every single sample; S4 never reported visual experience of any sort. Overall, the five subjects reported no visual experience of any sort—whether sensory or imagistic—in 25 percent of the samples, and they reported sensory visual experience (with or without a simultaneous experience of visual imagery) in 58 percent of the samples.

Four of my beeper subjects had their eyes closed in near darkness in at least one sample. Considering, then, only those samples, the ones collected

Table 8.1

Reported visual sensory and visual imagery experience in randomly sampled moments, with eyes closed.

Subject	Initial bias	Total number of samples	Number of samples with only sensory experience reported	Number of samples with only imagery experience reported	Number of samples reporting both sensory and imagery experience	Number of samples reporting neither type of experience
S1	sparse	14	1 (7%)	8 (57%)	3 (21%)	2 (14%)
S2	abundant	10	9 (90%)	0 (0%)	1 (10%)	0 (0%)
S3	sparse	12	9 (75%)	0 (0%)	0 (0%)	3 (25%)
S4	sparse	9	0 (0%)	0 (0%)	0 (0%)	9 (100%)
S5	abundant?	10	8 (80%)	1 (10%)	1 (10%)	0 (0%)
Total		55	27 (49%)	9 (16%)	5 (9%)	14 (25%)

in darkness: S1 reported no sensory visual experience at all, not even of blackness, in six such samples (though plenty of visual *imagery*). S2 reported, in two dark samples, a sensory visual experience of "undulating blackness" with small flashes of color. S3 reported a sensory visual experience of turbulent blackness on one occasion, like water before a boil, but no visual experience at all on a second occasion. S5 reported a sensory visual experience of grayish, angular wisps of foggy light against a black background in one sample and no sensory visual experience (but vivid visual imagery) in another.

S2 collected four samples outside, facing the sun. In each sample, he described complex latticeworks similar to a "squashed Bucky-ball"; in two samples he also reported a glowing light in the center (though not quite in the direction of the sun, and too large to be a direct perception or ordinary afterimage of the sun). When I showed him Purkinje's "light and dark figures" (figure 8.1), he said that his experience was similar but less geometrically regular. S5 collected two samples facing the sun. He reported neither S2's latticework nor my own relatively uniform field fluctuating from red or yellow to white or gray. In one sample, S5 described the field as a dark orange oval becoming bright white near the center, with a horizontal orange band dividing it across the middle, and bright, iridescent spots throughout, fading in and out. In the other sample he reported a bright yellowish-white field riddled with whitish-blue vertical stripes and spots, accented with flecks of orange.

We might take the reports at face value, as indicating substantial variability in people's experiences with their eyes closed. Or we might doubt the truth of the reports. The same issues arise that I noted in section x of chapter 6. Also, the experimental situation—demanding closed eyes through extended wakeful activity—differs, perhaps importantly, from ordinary eyes-closed situations, such as sinking into sleep or shutting them wakefully but only briefly. In the beeper experiment I described in chapter 6, two subjects did, by chance, have their eyes closed at the moment of the beep. One was closing her eyes in frustration; the other had fallen asleep. Neither reported any visual experience.

ix

So what do people typically experience when their eyes are closed? Either there are specific characteristic figures, such as wandering cloudy stripes (Purkinje, J. Müller, Helmholtz, Aubert) or there aren't (Ladd, Hering); the field is either very nearly black (Fechner) or middling gray (Hering, G. E. Müller) or highly variable with fantastic figures (Ladd, Galton); or maybe there is usually no visual experience of any sort at all (Nir et al., and presumably most of the advocates of sparse views as described in chapter 6). Maybe eyes-closed visual experience (or the lack of it) varies radically from person to person, and the diverse reports are mostly accurate; or maybe we all experience about the same range of phenomena but many of us misdescribe it. Nothing at all is settled.

I will conclude by mentioning some related issues almost untouched by existing research—issues so little studied that researchers have not yet occupied the full range of initially plausible positions.

What is it like to see through your eyelids? If I am in an illuminated room and I wave my hand before my face, I seem to experience motion of some sort—fluctuations of the visual field synchronous with the motions of my hand; so also, though less reliably, if a friend waves her hand.[5] Acquaintances and loitering undergraduates, I have found, differ substantially in their reports and in their apparent skill at detecting position and motion through their lids. I have also noticed that if I hold an occluding object like a book over half my visual field, the motion I see still spreads over the whole field, especially when the angle of occlusion matches the angle of motion (as when the occluding object is covering the lower half of the visual field and my hand is moving from right to left).

Is the eyes-closed field cyclopean? Purkinje thought not, in his own case—he distinguishes what he sees through his right eye from what he sees through his left. However, as quoted above, he also thought that the two fields would unite for "individuals in whom the two eyes are identical." My eyes are presumably not identical in the relevant sense: My left eye is much more nearsighted than my right (though also dominant and more effectively corrected by a lens). When I close my eyes, however, it seems to me that, although I can distinguish between the right and left halves of the darkness (yes it still seems like darkness to me), I don't feel any impulse to ascribe different fields to my two eyes. However, I can undermine my confidence in this as follows: First, with eyes open I press on the outside corner of my left eye and note the figure, called a phosphene, that appears in the opposite corner. (For me, this phosphene is usually a dark ring with a bright aura; see also Purkinje 1819/2001 and Helmholtz 1856/1909/1962.) Then I close my eyes and repeat the procedure, ignoring the colored smudge that now seems to appear at the point of pressure. I find myself torn between locating this phosphene about two thirds of the way toward the right border of a cyclopean dark field and locating it near the far edge of a field specifically associated with the disturbed left eye. Furthermore, it helps in seeing the phosphene if I do something that feels a bit like shifting my energies or attention toward that eye.

Does a single closed eye have a visual field?   Begin with both eyes closed, then open one; or begin with both eyes open and close one. Does the one closed eye see darkness or figures in the Eigenlicht? Some people I have interviewed have said so. I have the contrary impression myself. With one eye open, it seems to me that I have only one visual field, centered on the open eye. There is a margin of darkness at the inside edge of that field, in the direction of the closed eye, but that darkness is as though seen from the perspective of the open eye, not the closed eye. It appears to be located behind the nose. When I create a phosphene in that darkness behind the nose, the apparent spatial location of the phosphene is on the open-eye side of the nasal mid-line.

How broad and how tall is the eyes-closed visual field?   Recall that Purkinje says that, although the peripheral limit is finite, it is impossible to establish. With my eyes open I am inclined to say that there is a fairly straightforward (though indistinct) border to my visual field, but with my eyes closed things seem less straightforward. The darkness feels somehow more enveloping—though at the same time it feels to be more in my forward perspective than in my rear perspective. Does it really extend over a greater degree of arc? Well, I'm not sure I'm quite ready to say that. Others I have asked give diverse reports. With the eyes open, the visual field seems wider than it is tall. Is that also true of the eyes-closed field? Most of my interviewees seem willing to say that it is. However, as you may recall, Ladd's subject H.D. states that it is circular. (See the quote from Ladd 1903 in section v above).

Is the eyes-closed visual field flat? I find this thought much more tempting than the parallel thought about my eyes-open visual field (chapter 2). Purkinje's descriptions of his field seem always, implicitly, to treat it as flat. His checkerboard shapes, for example (figure 8.1) are drawn as though on a plane perpendicular to the line of sight rather than as within a three-dimensional space (where they might recede into the distance at an angle). Likewise, Purkinje does not portray his cloudy stripes as moving forward or back or twisting in three dimensions. Although a number of authors (and most of my subjects mentioned in section viii above) describe a "background" (often black or gray, or more brightly colored if the observer is in the sun) against which other figures sometimes move, this doesn't necessarily imply that the field has any real depth. None of my subjects ever reported that one object in the eyes-closed field seemed to be farther away than another, though I was careful to explicitly ask each subject (except S4, who reported no experience) several times, with several different samples, whether the field had depth or distance. C. E. Ferree, on the other hand, talks about "look[ing] deep into the field vision . . . beyond the background as usually observed" (1908, pp. 114–115). E. R. Jaensch says that although most subjects describe the Eigengrau as a "surface" [*Fläche*], others describe it as a "space" [*Raum*] (1923, p. 52).

Does the eyes-closed field appear to be any particular distance away? Most of the people I have interviewed deny that the field appears to be any particular distance from them—an inch or a foot or a mile. But I confess that I am tempted to describe my afterimages and my Eigenlicht as about two inches in front of my subjective center, or right about at the backs of my eyes. This temptation seems to me oddly specific. I would not before have said that my subjective center is two inches behind my eyes. In your own case, do figures in the closed-eye field appear to be any particular *size*? If so, then perhaps from their visual angle a distance is implied.

Do figures in the Eigenlicht stand in any spatial relation to one's imagery? Jaensch says they do, since his subjects reported their images as being drawn in the Eigengrau, or ringed around by it (1923, p. 52). Jean-Paul Sartre, however, argues that perceptual experience and imagery cannot co-occur (1940/1972, p. 138). Stephen Kosslyn's view that the same cortical areas subserve both perception and imagery (see e.g. Kosslyn et al. 2001) suggests that there will be competition between them, and presumably a

common spatial framework. Russell Hurlburt's beeper subjects have sometimes reported experiencing, simultaneously and without interference,
both visual imagery and sensory visual experience (1990, esp. pp. 48–51).
Three of my five beeper subjects reported at least one sample containing
both visual sensory experience and visual imagery simultaneously. (See
table 8.1.) S1 (with three instances) and S2 (with one instance) said that
the imagistic and the sensory experience did not appear to interact or to
be (in S2's words) "in the same co-ordinate space." S5, in contrast, in his
one report of this type, said that the imagery and sensory experience were
"in the same field of space" though "not of a piece."

Can we control the Eigenlicht?   Most people don't believe they can control
their sensory experience directly through acts of will (though of course we
can control it indirectly, for example by averting our eyes). One can't form
a sensory visual experience of a cross shape, for example, simply by willing
that a cross appear. Some scholars even make passivity the mark by which
sensory experience can be distinguished from imagery (Berkeley 1710/1965;
Sartre 1940/1972; Wittgenstein 1967; McGinn 2004; though see Thomas
2010). This lack of responsiveness to the will may be one reason to regard
the Eigenlicht as sensory rather than imagistic. In 1894, however, Ladd
asserted that he and his students could form Eigenlicht experiences by
direct willing:

What they were asked to do was briefly this: to close the eyes, allow the after-images
completely to die away, and then persistently and attentively *to will* that the color-
mass caused by the *Eigenlicht* should take some particular form,—a cross being the
most experimented with. . . . Of the sixteen persons experimenting with themselves,
four only reported no success; nine had a partial success which seemed to increase
with practice and which they considered undoubtedly dependent directly upon
volition; and with the remaining three the success was marked and really phenomenal. It should be said, however, that of the four who reported "no success," only
one appears to have tried the experiment at all persistently. (pp. 351–352; see also
Tatibana 1938, p. 129)

I can find no recorded attempts to replicate Ladd's experiment.

The uncharted wilderness is behind your eyelids.

x

Why did the scientific study of the mind begin with the study of conscious
experience? And why, despite that early start, have we made so little
progress? The two questions can be answered together if we are victims of
an epistemic illusion—if, though the stream of experience seems readily

available, though it seems like low-hanging fruit for first science, in fact we are much better equipped to learn about the outside world. We are tempted to approach consciousness incautiously, and it rebels. It leaps away or presents different faces when we approach it, and it won't comfortably wear our conceptions; we may never entirely master it. Should we leave it be, then, and study something less frustrating? Should we pursue only what yields easily to our methods?

Despite the pessimism of chapters 6 and 7, my view is not uncompromisingly bleak. Though some crucial, foundational issues about consciousness may be intractable, or nearly so, at least in the medium term, other issues are, I think, merely difficult. Eyes-closed visual experience illustrates the situation—the historically patterned variety of opinion, the weird bloom of ensuing questions, the limited existing research, the dependence on probably unstable introspective judgments. Exactly how much progress we will make isn't clear, in part because we haven't yet, really, given the scientific study of consciousness a proper try in full appreciation of its hazards.

Notes

Chapter 1

1. Simon's shift from reality's being black-and-white in 1973 to imagination's being black-and-white in 1981 is, I'm afraid, the reverse of what I would conjecture on the basis of the ideas of this chapter. However, Simon has said that he isn't sure which way he originally wrote the lyrics, and that he alternates between singing it the two ways. I am attracted to the view that Simon's original thought was "better" and that in revising he changed it to "worse" to cohere better with the song's celebration of color.

2. Oddly, Middleton found almost identical percentages to report *hearing* in color, 11 percent saying they did so frequently or very frequently, 21 percent saying occasionally, and 68 percent saying rarely or never. Middleton makes clear to his readers (and he claims he made it clear to the respondents too) that by "hearing in color" he means the synaesthetic experience of having sensations in one sensory modality when stimulated in another—for example, literally seeing streaks of green when hearing C-sharp or seeing swirling yellow when hearing the long "a" vowel sound. Recent estimates of the percentage of people who experience *any* form of synaesthesia (sound-color synaesthesia being only one subtype) run from virtually zero to about 4 percent (see, e.g., Simner et al. 2006; Hochel and Milán 2008). I can imagine a researcher in Middleton's time doubting the very existence of color dreaming on the basis of these data. If "color hearing" is very rare and thus presumably virtually or entirely non-existent in Middleton's respondents and so being grossly overreported by them, then perhaps "color dreaming" should be interpreted similarly. Tapia's finding that psychiatric patients reported color dreaming more frequently than others might seem to bolster such skepticism. One needn't believe all one's respondents. For some reason, though, skepticism about color dreaming didn't seem to tempt researchers of the era. I can find no evidence that anyone doubted the veracity of reports of color in dreams.

Incidentally, my respondents (Schwitzgebel 2003; Schwitzgebel, Huang, and Zhou 2006) reported color hearing at about the same high rates as Middleton's respondents, which suggests that many of my respondents either answered wrongly or misunderstood the question—or perhaps that occasional bouts of synaesthetic phenomena are fairly widespread. Recent research on synaesthesia generally attempts to verify subjective reports with some sort of objective measure, which seems very desirable but which will verify the existence of synaesthesia only in people who experience it dependably.

3. Among the twentieth-century claims based on personal experience or psycho-therapy are the following: Beaunis's (French, 1903) report that colors in his own dreams tend to be limited and grays common; Savage's (1908) claim that color is rarely or never present in his dreams; Ellis's (1911) statement that "in the dreams of most people color is rare" (though he also remarks that in his own experience "it is difficult to decide whether the absence of color is due to its actual absence from the dream imagery, or merely its failure to make any impression on memory"); Paul Köhler's (German, 1912) discussion of the phenomenology of dreaming, which appears to take the coloration of dreams for granted; Titchener's (1912a) report of dinner companions divided about whether they experienced only gray in their dreams; Bellamy's (1915) remark that "every one has noticed the rarity with which colors and sunshine appear in dreams; I have found, however, that colors and sun-shine always appear if there is any necessity for their doing so"; Rapport's (1949) report that in his own dreams color is usually present but easily forgotten; Kubie's (1950) view that "for most people the visual images of dreams consist largely of black, white, and grey"; Calef's (1954) view that color is not predominant but may be more frequent than is typically assumed; Huxley's (1956) view that most dreams lack color; Garma's (Argentine, 1961) view that "dreams are like old silent films without sound or technicolor"; Tauber and colleagues' (1962) view that color is very common and underreported; Blum's (1964) view that color may often be present but quickly forgotten; Miller's (1964) view that color is generally present but unat-tended; and Yazmajian's (1964, 1968) view that when color is present it is for highly affective dreams and elements, especially those involving viscera and genitalia. Thus, we see the same shift in the personal reports as in the systematic studies.

Two studies have been repeatedly mishandled in the literature and are not included in table 1.1. Knapp (1956) is sometimes cited as claiming that about 15 percent of most people's dream reports involve color—he is cited this way, for example, by Kahn et al. in their influential 1962 article—but Knapp is including reports of black, white, and gray as "color" reports, and he offers no estimate of the ratio of reports of chromatic colors as opposed to black, white, and gray. Monroe (1898), who has also sometimes been cited in connection with the view that dreams are often black-and-white (including again by Kahn and colleagues), said that color was a "pronounced feature" in 21 percent of dreams reported in the morning after experimental subjects studied colored patches at night, but he neither asserted nor denied the presence of colors in the other 79 percent of dreams in which it was not a "pronounced feature" (nor did he, unfortunately, use a control group). Furthermore, like Knapp, Monroe treats black, white, and gray as "colors" for his purposes, so discovering the ratio of black-and-white experiences to color experiences appears not to have been his interest. Since Monroe, unlike Knapp, breaks down his results by color, we can see by reanalyzing the data that the ratio of chromatic colors to black, white, and gray is about 3.5:1, in contrast with Bentley's (1915) finding (briefly discussed in the body of the chapter) of about four times as many grays as chromatic colors.

4. A potential exception to this trend is the *philosophical* literature on dreams circa 1950. Although Manser (1956) mentions the possibility that dreams are black-and-white, this doesn't appear to be a very common remark among philosophers of the time, and there are several cases of philosophers mentioning colored objects in dreams without further remark: Yost and Kalish's "this is green" (1955), Thomas's "pink rats" (1956), Wolgast's "great blue grasshopper" (1958), and Malcolm's blue walls (p. 64) and red cloak (p. 86) in his notorious book *Dreaming* (1959). However, I cannot find any philosophers of that period who explicitly resist the opinion that dreams are mostly black-and-white, and of course reporting a single colored object is consistent with the view that dreams are *mostly* black-and-white. I would guess that, if philosophers tended to resist the dominant view, that resistance may have had something to do with the huge influence of Descartes on philosophers' thoughts about dreaming. (Malcolm's book, by the way, was notorious for arguing that dreams do not occur when one is asleep and that they contain no feelings, imagery, sensations, or the like. Instead, Malcolm says, when we wake, we are inclined to confabulate stories of a certain sort. Telling such a story is what we call "relating a dream," but there is no sense in which the dream exists independent of or prior to the story we tell about it, and there is no sense in which such a story can be evaluated as an accurate or an inaccurate description of occurrences during sleep.).

5. We also replicated (with different respondents) version 2 of my 2003 questionnaire, briefly described above, and found the same tendency for results to align with socioeconomic status. Let me also take this occasion to correct some data erroneously reported in the 2006 article. Contrary to table 3 on page 40 of that article, among the intermediate group 26 percent reported dreaming in color, 20 percent reported dreaming in black-and-white, 26 percent reported dreaming in both, none reported dreaming in neither, and 29 percent said they didn't know. These data fit better with the overall trends and with our hypotheses than do the misreported numbers in the original article. (Thanks to Michael Schredl for noticing this error in our reporting.)

6. Other cross-cultural data are a bit thin. I have found three studies from Japan: Tatibana 1938, Yamanaka et al. 1982, and Okada et al. 2005. Tatibana says that 25 percent of his observers reported colors in their dreams. Yamanaka's 1982 estimates are intermediate between the 1950s and 1960s U.S. estimates and differ greatly by gender, with 30 percent of men and 64 percent of women reporting color dreaming. By 2005, Okada found 85 percent of respondents reporting dreaming in color at least occasionally, comparable to my own 2003 U.S. finding of 81 percent. Japan was an early adopter of color television but slower than the U.S. to adopt color

movies, so these results fit with my overall finding that the coloration of movies synchronizes better with opinion about dreams than does television. In Mexico, López et al. (1986) found high levels of reported color dreaming (89 percent of subjects). Color movies were commonplace in Mexico by 1986, but I can't say with confidence that they were more commonplace than in Japan in 1982. In Austria, Stepansky et al. (1998) found a surprisingly low rate of reported color dreaming (37 percent reported dreaming in color, 47 percent said they did not dream in color, and 16 percent said they didn't know). In Germany, Schredl et al. (2008) found respondents to estimate that, among dreams whose coloration or lack thereof they could recall, about 85 percent were in color. Bolton (1978), reporting on the Quechua Indians in Peru, who presumably had little media access at the time, found black, white, and gray to be mentioned in dream reports more frequently than color (32 vs. 19 occurrences in 498 reports); however, without knowing the overall rates of color-term use in the language, Bolton's results are difficult to interpret. (Note 4 above also includes a few personal observations by non-Anglophone researchers, indicated as such.)

7. My four sources were Cynthia Richmond's columns on dream interpretation in the *Los Angeles Times* in 1999; a website featuring monthly dream reports from a variety of subjects (http://www.lifetreks.com) from January 1997 to January 2000 (accessed February 2000); a sample of 81 dreams collected from women at University of California at Santa Cruz in 1996, made available by Adam Schneider and G. William Domhoff at http://psych.ucsc.edu/dreams (accessed October 2001); and a sample of dreams from 4th–9th grade San Francisco Bay Area girls in 1996–1997, also from Schneider and Domhoff's site. In 72,886 words from these four sources, colors other than black, white, and gray are mentioned approximately 153 times (depending on what counts as a color term—e.g., "golden" can be a color or a material, and it isn't always clear which it is), i.e., as 0.20 percent of all words. In the Hall–Van de Castle dream reports on Schneider and Domhoff's site, I found approximately 228 color words out of 122,280 (0.19 percent). "Black," "white," and "gray" appeared 92 times (0.13 percent) in the late-twentieth-century reports and 109 times (0.09 percent) in the Hall–Van de Castle reports. Schredl (2008) reports similar results: 0.21 percent for color terms excluding black and white and 0.08 for black and white.

8. I estimated rates of color-term use in ordinary English using word-frequency charts from a variety of sources: Carroll, Davies, and Richman 1967, Kučera and Francis 1967, Dahl 1979, Johansson and Hofland 1989, and a search, at my request, of the HAL database of Internet usegroup text by Curt Burgess. (On HAL, see Burgess and Lund 2000.) Of course, such a comparison is only suggestive, since it could reasonably be argued that these samples of English are not the appropriate comparison class. None of them, for example, is confined to narratives about experienced events. Schredl (2008) reports German-language color term use of 0.41 percent in 444 people's descriptions of the same 5-minute sequence from a film presented without sound.

9. This claim is based on taking each of four individual media-exposure variables separately as a predictor, along with status group, in two-predictor logistic regressions of binary-coded response on the target question, for each version of the questionnaire. I further confirmed the results by looking at various Spearman rank correlations and chi-square tests. Murzyn, in her 2008 British study, does find a relationship between individuals' history of media exposure and their reports of black-and-white versus color dreaming within a group of respondents over age 55. However, as she acknowledges, age differences within that broad group may be confounding her results; a finer discrimination by age might have washed out the effects of the individual history variable. In any case, the thesis of this chapter does not require that I deny the possibility of differences in dream reports driven by individual exposure. If capture by media metaphor explains differences in dream reports, it would not be surprising if people sometimes differed in their attraction to the metaphor owing to different histories of media exposure. My view is consistent with either result. What is relevant to the present argument is the potential difficulty, for the defender of the view that the dreams themselves have changed, of explaining the weak relationship in China between personal history of media exposure and reporting of color in dreams.

10. In the study published as Schwitzgebel, Huang, and Zhou 2006, we presented the Braun and Wehrle studies as tentatively suggestive of color experience during sleep because they showed activity in V4 and other extrastriate visual cortical areas. However, V4 is not exclusively associated with color, and Braun and Wehrle did not focus specifically on that area; furthermore, they found deactivation of V1, which is also involved in color vision (though *perhaps* too early in the visual stream to be necessary for consciousness), so I now think that suggestion was premature. Accordingly, Nir and Tononi (2010) overstate the neuroscientific case for dreaming in full color.

Chapter 2

1. Malebranche seems to be to be fairly clear on this point at I.7.iii–iv (p. 34). However, Michael Jacovides has suggested to me that it may be possible to interpret him as holding that the perspectivally distorted "impressions" and "errors" are not experienced sensorily but are somehow pre-experiential, while experience is limited to the veridical "compound sensations" and "judgments of sense."

2. Somewhat confusingly, Locke follows up the quote in the epigraph as follows: "But we having by use been accustomed to perceive, what kind of appearance convex Bodies are wont to make in us; what alterations are made in the reflections of Light, by the difference of the sensible Figures of Bodies, the Judgment presently, by an habitual custom, alters the Appearances into their Causes: So that from that, which is truly a variety of shadow or colour, collecting the Figure, it makes it pass for a mark of Figure, and frames to it self the perception of a convex Figure, and a uniform Colour; when the *Idea* we receive from thence, is only a Plain variously

color'd, as is evident in Painting." (1690/1975, p. 145) Here Locke is not distinguishing between "ideas" and "appearances" (one looks in vain through the text for a
systematic distinction between these two); rather, as is evident from the remainder
of the section, he is saying that the sensory "idea" of a flat circle variously shadowed
is normally *followed* by a second idea, framed by the judgment, of a globe. That
second idea is not itself sensory, but rather follows swiftly and automatically from
the sensory idea much as the ideas of the objects referred to in speech follow from
the sensations of speech sounds. Normally, then, we no more notice the idea of a
flat circle when looking at a globe than we notice the auditory sensations of speech
when listening to someone attentively and with understanding.

3. In a previous article on this topic (Schwitzgebel 2006), I described Ayer as having
a dual-aspect view. I now think that was mistaken. See his decisive rejection on pp.
118–122 of his earlier (e.g., p. 16) characterization of the tilted coin as looking
elliptical. Hatfield (2009, chapter 5) offers an intermediate view, on which there is
a projective transformation of experience that would appear to make the coin only
slightly elliptical. (See also Thouless 1930–1931; Mundle 1971.)

4. However, on p. 207 of the same book, Price seems to accept that the obliquely
viewed penny *does* look elliptical. I don't see how all his remarks can be made fully
consistent.

5. On Reid's "geometry of visibles," see van Cleve 2002; Yaffe 2002, Belot 2003;
Meadows forthcoming.

6. Aristotle does claim that the sun seems to be one foot wide (*De Anima* 428b; *On
Dreams*, 4th c. BCE/2001, 458b), a claim repeated often in antiquity. However,
perception of the sun was acknowledged in the period to be an unusual case, perhaps
sui generis, perhaps not involving the ordinary rules of perception, and perhaps
involving illusion or misperception—not, in other words, ordinary projective distortion. For more on the size of the sun, see Cleomedes II.1 (ca. 2nd c. CE/2004) and
references therein.

7. The term "impression," which appears to have derived from the signet metaphor,
continued to have prominence in philosophy into the seventeenth and eighteenth
centuries. However, I suspect that the metaphorical liveliness, the power of the suggestion of impressed wax, declines in these later uses. Furthermore, Locke at least
seems to shift the significance of the impression metaphor away from the wax signet
toward the printing press (e.g., 1690/1975 II.i.25, II.x.5), and, as quoted in the epigraph, he thinks of the sensory "Ideas" impressed on our minds as flat.

8. Consider the oar's looking bent in water. Should we say that the oar's bent
appearance is an illusion? That seems natural. But if so, then presumably the look
of things through a glass of water, which will be similarly distorted, is also an illusion. But then will the look of things through a magnifying glass held (improperly)
at arm's length also be illusory? And if that, then also the look of things through a

magnifying glass held appropriately close? Through a telescope? Through ordinary corrective lenses? Presumably we don't want to go that far. On the other hand, if we say that the oar's "bent appearance" is not an illusion—that it is just part of an oar's looking straight (to an experienced oarsman or someone facile with the laws of the refraction of light) that it present a certain sort of bent appearance when submerged in water, then will we also say that the double vision I get when I press my eye is not an illusion (because I know that's how things should look when I press my eye)? Should we also then say that the "moon illusion" is no illusion to the knowledgeable observer aware of the effect? And Poggendorff's illusion (figure 5.1 in chapter 5)—is it just what it is for the segments to look aligned, that they look like that? If so, then it seems no one sufficiently familiar with an illusion could experience it as illusory. The resolution of these difficulties would seem to turn on where exactly in the cognitive chain the visual experiences and the compensating judgments arise (if indeed there is an exact "where"). It might be helpful to ask people how things "look" vs. how things "are"—indeed, some researchers have done that for perception of tilted figures of various sorts, with results intermediate between the flat and the three-dimensional view (Thouless 1930-1931; Epstein et al. 1962)— but my reflections in this chapter and book make me nervous about putting too much weight on people's answers to such questions. Dispute about the distinction between perceptual illusion and perceptual accuracy coupled with erroneous judgment has a long history in philosophy, going back at least to the Indian philosophers Dignāga (6th c./1968) and Dharmakīrti (7th c./1958). (For reviews of the Indian material, see Matilal 1986; Dreyfus 1997; Rao 1998.)

9. I object to the use of the term "foreshortened" in Annas and Barnes's 1994 translation of the colonnade example, with its implications of painterly projection. Bury (2nd c. CE/1933) uses "curtailed," Mates (2nd c. CE/1996) "tapering," and Bett, in a related passage (*AL* I.244, 2nd c. CE/2005), "narrowing."

10. From a very different cultural perspective, the ancient Chinese philosopher Xunzi makes some remarks that seem to suggest substantial size distortion in visual appearance:

Looking down at oxen from the top of a mount will make them appear the size of a sheep, but someone looking for sheep will not go down to lead them away. The distance has obscured their true size. If from the foot of a mountain you look up at the trees, trees ten cubits high look like chopsticks, but someone looking for chopsticks would not climb up to break them off. (3rd c. BCE/1999, chapter 21.13, p. 697)

I am not aware of any comparisons of vision and painting in the literature of the period, but Xunzi does, in the same chapter and elsewhere, liken the mind to a pan of water (21.12, 25.16), with the attendant suggestion, perhaps, that perceptions are like images reflected in the water. (Whether mirror images are flat is an open question, but some people seem to think so.) In the same era, Zhuangzi famously likens the mind to a mirror (3rd c. BCE/1968, chapter 7, p. 97); in medieval Chinese philosophy, the mind-mirror analogy was commonplace, as Wang Yangming notes (early 16th c./1963, p. 45). However, ancient Chinese discussions of visual appearance are too brief and scattered to provide much of a test of the hypothesis.

11. In his 2006 article Sacks bases his claims about this on the reports of others, especially "Stereo Sue." However, the following year—as chance (I assume) would have it—he himself went blind in one eye. He now says that he experiences the world as flat (as reported in Cohen 2008).

12. Some other stereoscope enthusiasts who describe visual experience as pervasively doubled are Hering (1868/1977) (if I read him right), Schön (1876, 1878a,b), Le Conte (1881/1897), Külpe (1893/1895), Wundt (1896/1897), Stout (1899/1977), and Sanford (1901). Despite having invented the stereoscope, Wheatstone rejects the pervasive doubling of the visual field (1838/1983, pp. 86–90; his discussion also mentions a number of other early advocates of pervasive doubling).

Chapter 3

1. On such "non-imagers" see Faw 1997, Faw 2009, and N. Thomas, "Are There People Who Do Not Experience Imagery?" (http://www.imagery-imagination.com/non-im.htm). Thomas is more skeptical than Faw about purported non-imagers, though he doesn't dismiss the possibility (personal communication, 2009). I recommend his 1989 account of the behaviorist John Watson's apparently theory-driven shift from claiming that he had vivid visual imagery to claiming that he had none. Russ Hurlburt (personal communication, 2002) says that several self-described non-imagers have reported visual imagery when given beepers and interviewed about randomly sampled moments of ordinary experience (and conversely that sometimes people who expect to find lots of imagery find none).

2. If you aren't familiar with phosphenes, press gently on the corner of one eye. A little spot should appear in the opposite corner (perhaps a gray spot with a bright ring). Wiggling your finger a little to make the spot move can help bring it out.

3. The view that there is often no determinate fact about the extent to which imagery is indeterminate has not been widely discussed, though some readers of this chapter have urged it upon me. A theoretical attraction to higher-level indeterminacy may arise from a view on which talk about visual imagery is a useful fiction and there is no fact of the matter whether a fiction that posits a determinate number of stripes is more useful than a fiction that does not; or it may arise from a view on which visual images are insufficiently stable to support predications about the determinacy or indeterminacy of their features over even the smallest duration of attention; or it may grow from an account of the nature of vagueness or from some other motivation. If one accepts some such species of higher-level indeterminism about visual imagery, one may deploy it to explain why people are often baffled by the kinds of questions posed in the second paragraph of this section—but this explanation must be handled delicately if it is meant to preserve the view that introspective judgments about visual imagery are largely accurate, since many

people are confident in their diverse (and on this view not determinately true) assessments of their imagery experiences.

4. However, Reisberg, Peason, and Kosslyn (2003) argue, partly on the basis of a retrospective survey, that, at least in the early period of the debate around 1980, differences in researchers' own imagery experiences partly predicted their theoretical stances, theoreticians who had more vivid imagery (as measured by the VVIQ: see below) being more attracted to the pictorial view.

5. For contemporary reviews, see Angell 1911 and Ogden 1911; for a recent review, see Kusch 1999. Monson and Hurlburt (1993) argue that the actual experiential reports of the subjects on both sides of the debate were very similar but were interpreted differently by the disputing parties. If that is so, it tangles the issue at hand; and yet I think it remains the case that—regardless of what their subjects may have said—Titchener and Külpe genuinely disagreed about the phenomenology of thinking. In chapter 7 I will discuss the recent revival of a similar controversy.

6. Since Locke says "idea," not "image," it is possible to interpret him as thinking of the idea of the triangle as non-imagistic. However, the standard interpretation of Locke seems to be that ideas, in his view, are always imagistic (though not always visually imagistic). In any case, James (1890/1981), Huxley (1895), and others clearly acknowledge the possibility of images with vague or indeterminate features, so they could substitute for Locke as opponents to Berkeley.

7. McKelvie finds three studies (all reported in one article: Shaw and DeMers 1986) suggesting a relationship between VVIQ scores and visual creativity for high-IQ subjects. Interestingly, he finds a parallel result for *verbal* creativity: no relationship to the VVIQ unless participants are specially selected for high IQ. What to make of these results is not clear. In light of the vast number of studies McKelvie considers and the various sources of spurious correlation (discussed below), I wouldn't put too much weight on these results.

8. McKelvie does find less variability in imagery reports than one might expect from reading Galton: McKelvie's meta-analysis yielded a mean VVIQ score of 2.307 and a standard deviation of 0.692 on the five-point scale. Demand characteristics of the survey may explain some of this trend toward the low (vivid) end of the scale. As Ahsen (1990) notes, the survey begins by asking the subject to "think of some relative or friend" and then to "consider carefully the picture that comes before your mind's eye." The latter phrase implies that a picture-like image will be experienced. However, Galton's survey employs similar language. It is possible that the narrative format of Galton's questionnaire was more encouraging of extreme responses than the five-point scale of the VVIQ. Or maybe cultural or subject-pool differences explain the apparent decline in the variability of self-reports of imagery. Heavey and Hurlburt (2008), having lent beepers to thirty people and asking them to report on ten randomly sampled moments of experience, found very high variability in the rate

at which imagery was reported, ranging from 0 percent to 90 percent of the sampled experiences.

9. For reports of correlations between the VVIQ and visual or imagery-related tasks, see Wallace, Allen, and Propper 1996; Campos and Fernández 1997; Campos and Fernández 1998; Keogh and Markham 1998; Riske, Wallace, and Allen 2000; Lanca and Bryant 2001; Petrova and Cialdini 2005; Keng and Lin 2006; Hills, Elward, and Lewis 2008; Lobmaier and Mast 2008. For reports of no statistically detectable relationship, see Antonietti, Bologna, and Lupi 1997; Campos and Pérez 1997; Campos, Pérez, and González 1997; Eton et al. 1998; Antonietti 1999; Heaps and Nash 1999; Kunzendorf et al. 2000; Lewis and Ellis 2000; Tomes and Katz 2000; Kilgour and Lederman 2002; Laeng and Teodorescu 2002; Pérez-Mata, Read, and Diges 2002; Burton and Fogarty 2003; Dean and Morris 2003; Sebastiani et al. 2003; Kozhevnikov et al. 2005; Gemignani et al. 2006; Wyra, Lawson, and Hungi 2007; Gyselinck et al. 2009; Blazhenkova and Kozhevnikov 2009; Mohr et al. 2009. For studies with mixed results, see Crawford and Allen 1996; Campos and Fernández 1997; Tomes and Katz 1997; Winograd, Peluso, and Glover 1998; Walczyk and Taylor 2000; Eberman and McKelvie 2002; Blajenkova, Kozhevnikov, and Motes 2006; Mast, Merfeld, and Kosslyn 2006; Carretti, Borella, and De Beni 2007. I exclude from these lists studies looking only at the relationship of the VVIQ to other self-report measures (e.g., personality measures or other imagery measures). The above listings should include most of the works published since 1995 in ISI-indexed journals.

A related issue is whether there is a relationship between VVIQ score and brain activity while engaging in visual imagery. Amedi et al. (2005) and Cui et al. (2007) instructed participants to form visual images while in an fMRI machine. They found that participants scoring toward the vivid end of the VVIQ exhibited greater differences between activity in visual and non-visual areas of the brain during the imagery than those reporting less vivid imagery on the VVIQ. (See also Belardinelli et al. 2009 on the QMI.) Although these results are encouraging, Ganis et al. (2004, clarified by a personal communication) and Schienle et al. (2008) fail to find such a relationship, and Kosslyn et al. (1996) report mixed results. Given all the potential sources of spurious correlations, I think we have to regard the issue as open.

10. This section concerns what has come to be called "typographic eidetic imagery" as opposed to "structural eidetic imagery" of the sort posited (but not in my view very clearly characterized) by Ahsen (1977), Marks and McKellar (1982), and Hochman (2002).

11. A few studies continued to be done. Kaylor and Davidson (1979), Paine (1980), and Miller and Peacock (1982) report somewhat better memory performance among self-described eidetikers, Wasinger, Zelhart, and Markley (1982) report no difference, and Richardson and DiFrancesco (1985) report a non-significant trend. Kunzendorf (1984) reports electroretinogram differences and differences in physiological control between eidetikers and non-eidetikers; Matsuoka (1989) finds eidetikers to report

more absorption in sensory and imaginative experiences; and Glicksohn, Steinbach, and Elimalach-Malmilyan (1999) suggest a connection between eidetic imagery and synaesthesia. Brang and Ramachandran report a self-described eidetic with good visual memory. For retrospective personal reports of frustration in searching for relationships between self-reported eidetic imagery and performance on objective tasks, see Furst 1979 and Sommer 1980. Also, as mentioned at the end of section iv, work is occasionally done on established prodigies, who sometimes claim high imagery capacities.

12. For some recent philosophical discussions of epiphenomenalism, see Flanagan 1992; Chalmers 1996; Nichols and Grantham 2001. Note that the purest kind of metaphysical epiphenomenalism is not what is at issue here. Consciousness could be metaphysically epiphenomenal in the sense that it itself has no causal power while still being nomologically connected to some causally efficacious process such that we could always scientifically discern, by appeal to the causally efficacious process, whether the accompanying conscious process was present. Such purely metaphysical epiphenomenality would not explain the lack of correlation between imagery self-reports and performance in cognitive tasks.

13. I exclude from discussion here the literature on the "bizarreness" of imagery and its memorability (e.g. Einstein and McDaniel 1987), since bizarreness seems be more closely related to the strangeness of the situation depicted than to the phenomenological features of the image itself.

Chapter 4

1. Nagel, by the way, is a philosopher of mind with no particular background in perceptual psychology. He offers this claim simply as an obvious, commonsensical point. Nagel acknowledges in a footnote on a later page that blind people can use something like bat sonar when tapping with a cane. He appears to have trouble imagining even what that is like, writing in the subjunctive: "Perhaps if one knew what that [i.e., the sonar of the blind] was like, one could by extension imagine roughly what it was like to possess the much more refined sonar of a bat." (1974, p. 442)

2. I, Eric, am the one who emphasizes the specifically *auditory* character of echolocation. Mike writes: "I am more doubtful than Eric seems to be about whether echolocation, or really any form of perception, can be phenomenologically or even biologically separated from the other modalities (barring organisms—paramecia?—with only a single sensory system). Humans, bats, and dolphins all echolocate, *and* will use visual, tactile, vestibular, olfactory, and any number of other signals as they become available. Consider that the bat does not detect its echolocatory capacities; rather echolocation is a means by which it can detect an insect flying past. To suggest that the phenomenology of the bat is different in kind from any other species is to suggest that the principal determinant of phenomenology is the

medium by which sensory information is detected—and not the content of that information. Furthermore, while in this chapter we have outlined some of the literature to suggest that echolocation is a valid sensory channel for both blind and sighted humans, in a larger sense one could argue that all of our perception is part of a unified multisensory experience (including various forms of hearing) that informs us about the world and the objects therein. Did perception evolve to inform us about how we detect the world, or to inform us about the things in the world that will support successful actions? While most perceptual psychologists still embrace the classic Aristotelian division of the sensory systems, this perspective has caused me to favor a more continuous amodal/modality-neutral approach that distinguishes sensory experiences by their organization in the environment (i.e., the object and events occurring in the world), and not by the sensory channels by which they are detected." The case for error about experience becomes somewhat more complicated on the modality-neutral approach, since people are more often right, in my view, about the fact that certain environmental objects are sensorily present than they are about the specific sensory character of their experience of those objects. However, even from the modality-neutral approach, people are still mistaken when they deny having *any* sensory experience of the wall, the book, etc., with their eyes closed.

3. Traditionally, echolocation was defined only "monostatically," as the detection of the reflections of self-generated sounds, as in Griffin 1958 and Simmons 1989. However, some researchers (e.g., Lee 1990; Xitco and Roitblat 1996; Rosenblum et al. 2000) have also emphasized the importance of sounds generated from other sources. Since the cognitive and functional demands seem to be similar in the two cases, we opt for the broader definition.

4. Prior (1999) describes training a dolphin to use eye covers (a dolphin blindfold) for a marine show intended to exhibit the dolphin's excellent echolocation abilities. Although the eye covers were designed not to be physically irritating, the dolphin resisted wearing them. Through a series of ingenious training methods, Prior managed to convince the dolphin to accept the eye covers, but the dolphin's resistance is interesting. How much do dolphins know about their sensory abilities? Experiments by Gopnik and Graf (1988) and O'Neill and Gopnik (1992) suggest that three-year-old children often don't know very well the sensory bases of their knowledge or what information comes through what sensory modality. Could dolphins have the same difficulty? (Alternatively, this particular dolphin may simply not have wanted to sacrifice its visual input, despite the safe environment and the ease of the task.)

5. Rosenblum and Robart (2007) found that sound intensity (measured in decibels) was virtually identical for the triangle, the circle, and the square when measured at listeners' average head position, and listeners were still able to detect the shape differences at rates above chance. Gordon and Rosenblum (2004) tested the effects of intensity by randomly varying, along with the aperture size, the sound intensity of

the crowd noise from the speakers. The sound at the listener's average head position was always substantially quieter in the lowest-sound-intensity condition, regardless of aperture size, than it was in the highest-sound-intensity condition, so that if participants were judging strictly by intensity they would judge all the apertures more passable in the high-sound-intensity condition than in the low-sound-intensity condition. Gordon and Rosenblum found, on the contrary, that although sound intensity did have an effect on judgments of passability (with apertures less likely to be judged passable at lower sound intensities), the larger apertures were much more likely to be judged passable than the smaller apertures, regardless of sound intensity. For example, the largest aperture was judged passable 69 percent of the time at the lowest sound intensity, whereas the smallest aperture was judged passable only 47 percent of the time at the highest sound intensity.

6. Sometimes we experience vibration both tactilely and auditorily (for example, when we feel a loud, thumping bass line), but that is not so much auditory input being experienced tactilely as a single event experienced simultaneously through two different senses. It's like both seeing and feeling a square. On synaesthesia, see Simner et al. 2006 and Hochel and Milán 2008.

7. Still another view is that of Kells (2001), who extensively interviewed eight blind people about the phenomenological character of their ability to detect silent objects. She characterizes the experience neither as auditory nor as involving facial pressure but rather as a sensation of its own unique kind—a hard-to-convey sense of the presence of something in space or of openness or closedness. However, not all blind echolocators seem to talk this way—not, for example, Kish (2009), nor the participants in the study by Worchel and Dallenbach (1947) who denied having the ability to detect objects at all in the echolocatory tasks despite pretty good performance.

Chapter 5

1. The first psychology journal, founded by Alexander Bain in 1876, was the British journal *Mind*. Wundt's journal was second. *Mind* is now one of the "big three" leading *philosophy* journals, with rarely more than a whiff of empirical psychology. Notably, *The Journal of Philosophy*, another one of the current big three philosophy journals, underwent a similar transition. Founded in 1904 as *The Journal of Philosophy, Psychology, and Scientific Methods* by philosopher Frederick Woodbridge and psychologist James McKeen Cattell, it featured in its inaugural issues work by Titchener, George Trumbull Ladd, and other leading psychologists. The words *"Psychology, and Scientific Methods"* disappeared from its title with volume 18 in 1921.

2. The consequent amnesia for early introspective procedures was compounded by the simultaneous rise of Gestalt psychology (see, e.g., Köhler 1929/1947) as the chief competitor to behaviorism in academic research psychology. Gestalt psychology, though it gave an important role to introspection, regarded classical introspective techniques as objectionably reductionist in their analysis of experience into discrete

sensory elements. Gestalt theorists held the holistic sensory Gestalt (literally figure or form or shape) to be primary in ordinary experience. (Freud, his competitors, and his followers played a large role, of course, in *clinical* psychology—a field that during the twentieth century overlapped surprisingly little, scientifically or sociologically, with laboratory research psychology.)

3. My references to Titchener's laboratory manual will list the volume in capital Roman numerals, the part in Arabic, and (following Titchener) the page in Arabic (if it is from the main text) or lower-case Roman (if it is from an introduction). The second part of each volume was intended only for use by the laboratory instructor. In the 1971 reprint of *Experimental Psychology*, the second part of the first volume is omitted, though this may be easy to miss because each part of the first volume is itself misleadingly divided into two further "parts."

4. For more specific discussions and examples of the benefits of practice in focusing on stimuli, steadying one's sense organs, and controlling one's attention, see I.2.30–31, I.2.121, II.2.cliv–clvi, and II.2.307. On the benefit of practice in attaining a consistent standard of judgment, see I.2.87, II.1.xxxiii, II.1.1–2, II.1.25–26, and II.2.307. On knowing what to abstract, attend to, or look for in a complex sensation, see I.1.41–42, I.2.48, I.2.52, I.2.75, I.2.87, I.2.217, and I.2.300. On reporting lapses of attention and interfering influences, see I.2.167, I.2.220–222, I.2.341–345, and II.2.402; and when considered in conjunction with each other II.1.104–106, II.2.2–3, and II.2.260. See also Nahmias 2002.

5. However, E. G. Boring claims that later in his career Titchener put "considerable faith" in the method of naive phenomenological report that he criticizes here, though he never published on the subject (Boring 1929/1950, p. 416; see also Boring 1927, p. 502; Evans 1972).

6. Frequency is a physical measurement of rate of vibration, in this case of a sound wave, in hertz (that is, cycles per second). Pitch is a subjective phenomenon pertaining to how high or low a tone sounds on the musical scale. Generally speaking, higher-frequency tones sound higher in pitch (doubling the frequency increases the pitch by one octave), though as with most psychophysical phenomena the relationship between stimulus and experience is complex when examined in detail.

7. I am not entirely convinced that there isn't a sense in which difference tones exist in the environment (see Hall 1981), but the philosophical and acoustic issues are complex, turning in part on what counts as a proper component of a sound wave. Ultimately, I think, no major points in this chapter hang on the issue, as should become evident later in this section.

8. A possible objection would go as follows: I know about the outside world—about things such as tones in my environment—by knowing, in the first instance, about the *stream of conscious experience* that that world produces in me, then inferring from there to what the world itself must be like (views of this sort have been associated

with Descartes (1641/1984), Locke (1690/1975), and Russell (1912)), and it is by introspection that I know the stream of experience. Therefore, *all* perceptual knowledge, including the detection of combination tones, is grounded in introspection. My opinion on this issue is rather complicated: I think we do have a sort of attunement to our experience that serves as part of the epistemic ground for our judgments about the outside world, but I don't think that such attunement rises to the level of classificational judgment, and I don't think it is properly called introspective. (See Schwitzgebel forthcoming a.) As I will suggest in chapter 7, our introspective judgments are so unreliable that they could not plausibly serve as a basis for our knowledge of objects and events in our environment.

"Transparency" theorists in philosophy argue that introspective attention to experience is impossible—attention always "passes through" experience to the outside world (Harman 1990; Shoemaker 1994/1996; Dretske 1995; Tye 1995, 2000, 2003; for critical discussions, see Kind 2003 and Siewert 2004). Harman writes: "When Eloise sees a tree before her, the colors she experiences are all experienced as features of the tree and its surroundings. None of them are experienced as intrinsic features of her experience. Nor does she experience any features of anything as intrinsic features of her experiences. And that is true of you too. There is nothing special about Eloise's visual experience. When you see a tree, you do not experience any features as intrinsic features of your experience. Look at a tree and try to turn your attention to intrinsic features of your visual experience. I predict you will find that the only features there to turn your attention to will be features of the presented tree." (1990, p. 667) If this is correct, it would certainly explain the apparent similarity between the introspective and the perceptual tasks in discerning combination tones. However, on a plausible psychological notion of attention as involving the dedication of central cognitive resources or working memory, it seems clear, contra Harman and others, that we *can* attentively consider the visual experience of a tree. At a minimum, we can *reflect on* or *think about* what our visual experience is, in an attention-hogging way. Harman might say that he meant only that we don't *visually* attend to the experience of the tree; but if that is the correct interpretation of his claim, it doesn't seem to do the work he wants it to do in support of functionalism. Also, it is hard to see how anyone would be tempted in the first place to think that we visually attend to our visual experience: We don't *see* our visual experience, after all; no light reflects from it into our eyes. Siewert advances a more moderate claim that seems more sustainable: We don't *withdraw* attention from the tree in attending to our experience of the tree.

My own position is that introspective attention and perceptual attention differ mainly in the *goal* that is implicit or explicit in the attentive process. In introspection, the goal is to discern features of your own conscious experience or phenomenology; in perception, the goal is to discern features of the outside world. These goals need not compete; often they nest. Discerning features of your perceptual phenomenology generally involves, as an integral part, reaching perceptual conclusions about the outside world. Introspection differs from ordinary perception principally in what further things you do with those perceptual conclusions, in what other processes are integrated with the perceptual process, and in what the standards of success are (for example, reporting a tone generated by tinnitus would be a mistake if your purposes were perceptual but not if your purposes were introspective). We attend to the features of our experience in part *by* attending to the features of the outside world. The two kinds of knowledge intermix. Consider looking at a tree through a slightly warped window: You may want simply to learn about the tree, or you may want to learn about the window. If the latter, you do so in part by noting how the tree looks through the window. Analogously for introspection: We learn about properties of our sensory experience in part by noting the apparent properties of the perceived world. I develop this view of introspection further in Schwitzgebel forthcoming a. The entanglement of perceptual knowledge with introspective knowledge of perceptual experience, combined with the fact (mentioned in the present chapter) that introspective training need not always involve introspective activity, explains, I think, the subtlety of the difference between musical training, conceived non-introspectively, and Titchener's training here.

9. One might try to avoid the puzzle by adopting the position that all mathematically simple combination tones contribute to any auditory experience of a musical interval. However, this position faces two obstacles: First, where to draw the lines isn't clear. Could we experience 7L – 4U? 10U – 14L? 16L – 11U of the third harmonic? Second, even the best-trained experts (e.g. Plomp) don't report dozens of combination tones in every experience of an interval, so the position seems to imply a wealth of combination tones that no one can discern.

10. Blue and yellow are generally treated as opposing colors in visual perception, as are red and green.

11. Wallace (1979) takes individual variability in the flight of colors for granted; Young (1948) and Feldman et al. (1974) assume the contrary. Brown (1965), in his influential general review of the literature on afterimages, seems at one point (p. 480) to agree roughly with Titchener's description of the flight of colors but at another point (p. 490), apparently inconsistently, to endorse Berry's claim that the flight of colors varies greatly between people. A related issue is whether afterimages produced by exposure to colored light are consistent between people. The evidence on this question is also divided. See Homuth 1913, Weve 1925, Judd 1927, Brown 1965, Stamper et al. 2000, and Taya and Ohinata 2002. Other papers of interest include Fröhlich 1921 and Shuey 1924.

12. Many researchers have discussed ambiguous figures that appear to reverse perspective, the best-known example being the Necker cube (the famous drawing that looks like a transparent cube consisting of two partially overlapping squares with lines connecting the corresponding corners). The idea that attention to a particular vertex tends to bring it forward goes back to Necker himself (1832). More recent research suggests that this tendency is not perfect and a number of other factors

may be involved (Köhler and Wallach 1944; Hochberg 1950; Pritchard 1958; Gregory 1970; Girgus et al. 1977; Peterson and Hochberg 1983; Long and Olszweski 1999).

13. Earlier sources for the horizontal-vertical illusion include Oppel (1854–1855) and Künnapas (1955). Titchener claims that every object in figure 5.3 shows this illusion except the last, which he says shows no illusions. (Do you think you would have written that in your lab book if you had been his student?)

14. Titchener attributes to Kundt (1863) the view that in monocular vision the outer limb appears longer than the inner, an illusion also supposedly present in figure 5.3E. I informally tested this claim by having acquaintances monocularly bisect, with a pen stroke, horizontal lines of varying length, but I found no consistent trends. Titchener attributes the view that the upper limb looks longer than the lower to Delboeuf (1865; see also Nicolas 1995) and claims the illusion is also present in figure 5.3B. Contemporary research appears to run contrary to Delboeuf, with subjects bisecting vertical lines too high (Post et al. 2006).

Chapter 6

1. In earlier work (Hurlburt and Schwitzgebel 2007; Schwitzgebel 2007a), I used the terms "rich" and "thin" instead of "abundant" and "sparse." But people complained to me that "rich" and "thin" don't sound like opposites (consider Steve Jobs), and the terms have been used widely by philosophers to mark other distinctions (even by me in chapter 5, where I described auditory experience as "rich" if it has many aspects). Hence the new terminology.

2. For critiques of this literature, see Holender 1986; O'Brien and Opie 1999; Holender and Duscherer 2004.

3. Usually Dennett seems to espouse the sparse view, and he has confirmed this in conversation. However, on p. 137 of his 1991 book he seems to tilt the other way on the absent-minded driving case, and on page 138 he seems to express the view that, at least in some cases, there may be no fact of the matter. In general, I don't see how all of Dennett's statements about consciousness can be reconciled, an issue I explore in Schwitzgebel 2007b. Dennett responds to these concerns in the same journal issue.

4. Although clearly there is a usage of "conscious" on which people are not conscious when they are dreaming, that is not the usage employed in this book or in most contemporary philosophy of mind. Unless you have a very unusual view of dreaming (perhaps one like Norman Malcolm's (1959)—see note 4 to chapter 1), you will probably grant that dreams are experienced; there is "something it's like" to dream, perhaps involving imagery or perception-like phenomenology as well as felt emotions or quasi-emotions. To grant that is just to grant that dreams are conscious, in the relevant sense of "conscious."

5. However, on page 430 of the same work James writes: "The pressure of our clothes and shoes, the beating of our hearts and arteries, our breathing, certain steadfast bodily pains, habitual odors, tastes in the mouth, etc., are examples from other senses, of the same lapse into unconsciousness of any too unchanging content." This may either qualify or contradict the passage on pages 1066–1067, though it still fits nicely with a relatively abundant view, since it posits excessive constancy rather than inattention as the cause of lapse into unconsciousness. See also pages 402–403, where James discusses the differences between sense experiences with and without attention.

6. Block (2007) and Koch and Tsuchiya (2007; see also Srinivasan 2008; Tye 2009), while not defending broadly abundant views, argue empirically against at least very sparse views. Block argues, in part introspectively and in part empirically, that the conscious experience of a briefly presented visual display (for example on a computer) extends considerably beyond the focally attended features that can be reported. Koch and Tsuchiya mention that people can report the gist of a briefly presented visual scene (saying, for example, whether the scene contains an animal) even when their attention is largely consumed in a demanding task presented elsewhere in the display. But such discussions don't in fact touch the issue at hand. As Koch and Tsuchiya emphasize, experimental results (or phenomenological observations) in such paradigms at best show consciousness in the *near*-absence of attention: There may be some attention spread across the entire visual display, even if attention is mostly concentrated on the central task. More directly pertinent to the question of this chapter is whether subjects experience the frame of the computer monitor, or the picture on the wall behind the computer, or the pressure of their flesh against the chair, when they are concentrating intensely on a computer display. On such matters, Block is silent and Koch (2004, p. 165) falls back on intuition rather than empirical argument. Mole (2008) presents an intuitive defense of a moderate view.

7. The total of 29 reflects the fact that I counted the full-experience and the far-right-visual-field participants twice each—the full-experience participants for both their visual and tactile reports and the far-right-visual-field participants for both their full-visual and their far-right-visual-field reports. See also note b to table 6.1.

8. See James 1890/1981; Geldard and Sherrick 1972; Libet 1985; Dennett 1991; Nijhawan 1994; Spence et al. 2001; Danquah et al. 2008. Boring (1929/1950) describes nineteenth-century astronomers' appreciation of illusions of timing as the increasing accuracy of astronomical observation began to expose individual astronomers' different impressions of when, to a tenth of a second according to the heard beats of a clock, a star passed a telescopic cross-wire. Boring portrays this discovery in astronomy as playing an important role in the emergence of reaction time studies in psychology. Although it is sometimes argued (for example, in Danquah et al. 2008) that visual processing is slower and more subject to temporal illusion than auditory or tactile processing, the findings on this topic appear to me to be fairly inconsistent.

9. The discussion in chapter 5 above (especially in note 9 to that chapter) of whether we introspect combination tones relates to the present issue.

10. One might suggest that, as experiences become more subtle and less intense, it becomes a vague, indeterminate matter whether conscious experience is present or not, and this vagueness in the target phenomena may be responsible for some of the variability in the reporting. I myself have difficulty making sense of the idea that consciousness is a vague phenomenon: Though I am willing to grant that most concepts are vague enough to admit of borderline cases, I can't seem to conceive of vague cases of consciousness—cases in which I would be tempted to say that whether a state is conscious or not is indeterminate. Even a little bit of conscious-ness, it seems—a tiny gray patch, a barely felt twinge—is determinately a case of consciousness (Searle 1992; Antony 2008). (Note that the *content* of a conscious state may be indeterminate, as perhaps in the case of a sketchy image, while it is none-theless determinately the case that the state itself has a phenomenal character.) On the other hand, I am inclined to think that consciousness must be a vague phenom-enon, at least ontogenetically and phylogenetically, even though I have difficulty conceiving of vague cases: Why should consciousness suddenly pop into existence at some particular point in the course of evolutionary change or at some particular point in the course of fetal or infant development, given that the physical and behavioral changes that seem most pertinent to consciousness are gradual (Dennett 1991; Papineau 1993)? Perhaps this apparent inconsistency reveals a flaw in my conceptualization of consciousness, or, to the extent that I am typical, in the con-temporary everyday or mainstream philosophical conceptualization. In any case, even if we allow that it may be a vague matter whether unattended peripheral stimuli are consciously experienced, that does not resolve the difficulties at hand in this chapter; in fact it seems likely to worsen them, for now we have three possibili-ties (or a spectrum of possibilities) with respect to the consciousness or noncon-sciousness of some stimulus: determinately conscious, determinately nonconscious, or somewhere in the gray area between. The problems of memory, stimulus error, etc. discussed in this section by no means ensure that all contentious cases would straightforwardly belong in the gray area.

Chapter 7

1. See Descartes 1641/1984, especially page 19, as quoted in the epigraph at the beginning of this chapter; Hume 1740/1978, especially pp. 190 and 192 of I.4.2, and p. 232 of I.4.5, (though Hume may change his mind in his *Enquiries* of 1748/1975; see p. 13 of I.1 and p. 60 of I.7); Sextus 2nd c. CE/1994, especially chapters 7 and 10. Pierre Bayle takes a similar position in the entry on Pyrrho in his *Dictionary* (1702/1734–1738, volume 4; see especially remark B on p. 654).

2. See Zhuangzi, 3rd c. BCE/1964, chapter 2; Montaigne 1580/1948, "Apology for Raymond Sebond." Sanches's brief treatment of the understanding of the mind

(1581/1988, especially pp. 243–245 [57–59]) is at most only a partial exception to this tendency. Unger (1975, III.9) seems to envision only the possibility of linguistic error about current experience, and his skepticism in this instance seems to turn principally on an extremely demanding criterion for knowledge. Huet (1694/2003) is nicely explicit in extending skepticism to internal matters of ongoing thought, though his examples and arguments differ considerably from mine here.

3. It is possible that some phenomenologists in the tradition of Brentano, Husserl, Heidegger, and Merleau-Ponty held that introspection was both important and highly untrustworthy, at least in the untrained, as some philosophers have suggested to me in conversation. I find these authors difficult to interpret. Brentano seems the clearest, however, and he does not appear to hold this view. In *Psychology from an Empirical Standpoint* (1874/1973) he argues that introspection [*innere Beobachtung*] is impossible or scientifically useless because the act of attentive introspective observation necessarily interferes with the mental state under investigation (a charge that goes back to Comte 1830). In its place Brentano recommends "inner perception" [*innere Wahrnehmung*], which does not require attention; and this inner perception, he says, is "infallible and does not admit of doubt" (p. 35). Thus, to judge by these remarks, in Brentano's view what is difficult or impossible (introspection) is not scientifically important, and what is important (inner perception) is infallible.

4. B. F. Skinner, for example, writes:

In summary, a verbal response to a private stimulus may be maintained in strength through appropriate reinforcement based upon public accompaniments or consequences. . . . [Thus] we may understand why terms referring to private events have never formed a stable and acceptable vocabulary of reasonably uniform usage. . . . The answer lies in the process by which "terms are assigned to private events," a process which we have just analyzed in a rough way in terms of the reinforcement of verbal responses.

None of the conditions that we have examined permits the sharpening of reference which is achieved, in the case of public stimuli, by a precise contingency of reinforcement. . . . It is, therefore, impossible to establish a rigorous scientific vocabulary for public use, nor can the speaker clearly "know himself" in the sense in which knowing is identified with behaving discriminatively. (1945, pp. 274–275)

The principal flaw of introspective report, according to Skinner (and Bem following him), is vagueness or instability of vocabulary due to the impossibility of precise differential reinforcement.

5. A representative passage:

I report "I am in pain now." Now if we take the view that the latter is a piece of indubitable knowledge, to what period of time does the word "now" refer? Not to the time before I started speaking, for there I am depending on memory, which can be challenged. Not the time after I finish speaking, for then I depend on knowledge of the future, which can be challenged too. The time in question must therefore be the time during which the report is being made. But then it must be remembered that anything we say takes time to say. Suppose, then, that I am at the beginning of my report. My indubitable knowledge that I am in pain can surely embrace only the current instant: it cannot be logically indubitable that I will still be in pain by the time the sentence is finished. Suppose, again, that I am just finishing my sentence. Can I do better than remember what my state was when I began my sentence? (Armstrong 1963, pp. 420–421)

Thus, according to Armstrong, self-knowledge must involve memory or projection, with the consequence that error is possible, in principle at least, if only momentarily. Another representative passage, from Churchland:

[T]he taste-sensation of lime sherbet is only very slightly different from the taste-sensation of orange sherbet, and in blindfold tests people do surprisingly poorly at telling which sensation is which. An orange-expectant subject fed lime sherbet may confidently identify her taste-sensation as being of the kind normally produced by orange sherbet, only to retract the identification immediately upon being given a (blind) taste of the genuinely orange article. (1984/1988, p. 77)

The introspective error is small and easily repaired. See also Lycan 1996; Shoemaker 1996; Kornblith 1998 (reading with a careful eye to distinguish error about current conscious experience from other sorts of error); Dretske 2000; Jack and Shallice 2001; Nichols and Stich 2003; Goldman 2004, 2006; Horgan, Tienson, and Graham 2005; and most of the essays collected in Gertler 2003. Gertler (2001), Chalmers (2003), and Horgan and Kriegel (2007) have recently attempted to revive restricted versions of (something like) infallibilism. Chalmers's infallibilism is so restricted that I am not sure how much useful substance remains. Against Gertler, Horgan, and Kriegel, I offer this chapter. Alston 1971 contains a series of quotes illustrating the widespread acceptable of infallibilism and indubitabilism by leading philosophers from the early modern period through the middle of the twentieth century.

6. Contrast, for example, Dennett's seeming skepticism about the accuracy of introspective reports in chapter 11 of his 1991 book with his apparent claims of infallibility or incorrigibility on pages 81 and 96 of that same book and his 2002 article. On the apparent contradictions in Dennett's view, see Schwitzgebel 2007b. See Dennett 2007 for his reply.

7. Philosophers sometimes say that we introspect our attitudes, such as our beliefs and desires, as well as our conscious experiences. (See Schwitzgebel 2010.) My own view is that we can introspect our attitudes only if those attitudes are consciously experienced, and therefore introspective self-knowledge of attitudes is a type of introspective self-knowledge of conscious experience. (See Schwitzgebel forthcoming a.) However, to what extent attitudes such as belief and desire can be consciously experienced is unclear. Carruthers 2009 argues against the conscious experience of attitudes. The issue is also entangled with the cognitive phenomenology issue discussed below. In Schwitzgebel forthcoming b, I argue for pessimism about our self-knowledge of our morally most important attitudes.

8. Haybron (2008) presents an impressive array of evidence suggesting that we don't know how (un)happy we are. For example, a 2007 Gallup poll of Americans (cited in Haybron 2008) found that 98 percent of respondents with household incomes

over $75,000 reported being happy, while only 2 percent reported being "not too happy" (the closest thing to a negative option); and typically, when polled, more than 90 percent of Americans describe themselves as happy or satisfied with their lives. Given the rates of clinical depression, with about 10 percent of the population suffering from major depression in any given year (Kessler et al. 1999), not to mention other psychological troubles, I, like Haybron, find such avowals very difficult to believe.

Moment-by-moment emotional assessments seem likely to be at least somewhat more realistic. In the best study of this that I'm aware of, Brandstätter (2001) examines the frequency of positive and negative emotions in a variety of situations, based on people's reports about their emotions in "time sampling diaries" when they were beeped unexpectedly at various intervals. He finds negative emotion reports—anger, fear, sadness, stress, exhaustion, etc.—to occur in about one-third of all sampled moments. But even measures like Brandstätter's probably involve positive bias due to self-deception and impression management.

9. It is a matter of some dispute exactly how strongly to read Descartes on this point (e.g., Rozemond 2004), and in the case of emotion, at least, he does (elsewhere) seem to assert the possibility of error: "For experience shows that those who are the most strongly agitated by their passions are not those who know them best, and that the passions are to be numbered among the perceptions which the close alliance between the soul and the body renders confused and obscure." (1649/1985, p. 339)

Although infallibilism isn't my only target in this chapter, let me mention a few other authors, besides Descartes, who make remarks that suggest some sort of general immunity to error, doubt, or correction. Locke: "For a Man cannot conceive himself capable of a greater Certainty, than to know that any *Idea* in his Mind is such, as he perceives it to be." (1690/1975, IV.2, p. 531) Hume: "For since all actions and sensations of the mind are known to us by consciousness, they must necessarily appear in every particular what they are, and be what they appear." (1740/1978, I.4.2, p. 190) Lewis: "[T]here could be no doubt about the presented content of experience as such at the time when it is given." (1946, p. 183) Shoemaker: "Among the incorrigible statements are statements about 'private' experiences and mental events, e.g., pain statements, statements about mental images, reports of thoughts, and so on. These are incorrigible in the sense that if a person sincerely asserts such a statement it does not make sense to suppose, and nothing could be accepted as showing, that he is mistaken, i.e., that what he says is false." (1963, pp. 215–216) Emotion is rarely chosen as the example, but the statements appear to be general.

10. I take this argument to be in the spirit of Armstrong (1963). It needn't require that the phenomenology and the judgment be entirely "distinct existences" in the sense Shoemaker (1996) criticizes, though of course it assumes that the one state is possible without the other. The only reason I see to reject such a possibility is a prior commitment to infallibilism.

11. A published example is Melanie in Hurlburt and Schwitzgebel 2007 (pp. 88–91)—though it isn't the best example, because visual experience wasn't the main topic of inquiry.

12. Oddly, though, people—and I include myself—seem much less willing to concede lack of precision in experienced color outside the foveal area, despite the fact that both shape and color are poorly detected outside the fovea. I don't know whether this reflects a real disparity between our nonfoveal experiences of shape and color (more "filling-in" and implicit inference about the latter, perhaps) or a more stubborn recidivism of introspection.

13. Among recent authors, Dennett (1991), O'Regan (1992), Mack and Rock (1998), Rensink, O'Regan, and Clark (2000), and Blackmore (2002) all deny that visual experience involves a broad expanse of stable clarity, though the various authors and I differ somewhat in our positive views. Some of these authors believe that we don't visually experience what we don't attend to—a question I addressed in chapter 6.

14. The British empiricists—most famously Locke (1690/1975), Berkeley (1710/1965), and Hume (1740/1978)—appear to have believed that conscious thought is always imagistic. So did many later introspective psychologists influenced by them—notably Titchener (1909, 1910), who argued against advocates of "imageless thought," particularly the "Würzburg group" (whose work is reviewed in Humphrey 1951 and in Kusch 1999). Recent discussions include Siewert 1998, Horgan and Tienson 2002, Wilson 2003, Pitt 2004, Robinson 2005, Prinz 2007, Hurlburt and Akhter 2008, and Spener forthcoming. The issue goes back at least to Aristotle, who in *De Anima* 431a (4th c. BCE/1936) appears to espouse the view that thought is always imagistic. See also my brief discussion of this issue in section iii of chapter 3.

15. Related poll results (taken at the end of the seminar) are available at consc.net/neh/pollresults.html. I am inclined to read the disagreement between the "no phenomenology of thought" and the "imagery exhausts it" camps as a disagreement about terms or concepts rather than about phenomenology—a disagreement about whether having an image should count as "thinking." However, I see no similar terminological explanation of the central dispute. As I recall (though this number is not recorded on the website), only two participants, Maja Spener and I, said they didn't know.

16. On classical introspective training, see chapter 5 above. On the possibility of careful interview about randomly sampled experiences, see Hurlburt and Schwitzgebel 2007. Schooler and Schreiber (2004) assess the current scientific situation reasonably, if not quite as pessimistically. (See also Bayne and Spener forthcoming.) Recently there has been some promising work on meditation (e.g., Lutz et al. 2007), but much remains to be done to establish the scientific credibility of meditation as a technique for learning about conscious experience.

17. But see Chalmers 1996 and Dretske 2003 on the possibility that we could be experienceless "zombies" without knowing it. Both Chalmers and Dretske think that we do know that we are conscious, but that it isn't straightforward to see *how* we know that.

18. See Chisholm 1957 and Jackson 1977. Naturally, ordinary and philosophical usage of "appears" is rather more complex than this simply portrayal suggests if one examines the details; but I don't think that affects the basic observation of this section.

19. Epistemologists—for example, Goldman (1986), who calls the second sort of failure a lack of "power"—often define "reliability" so that only the first type of failure counts as a failure of reliability. It's a semantic issue, but I think ordinary language is on my side.

20. Titchener thinks this strategy is common among untutored introspectors and repeatedly warns against it as "stimulus error" or "R-error" (Titchener 1901–1905; Boring 1921; see also chapter 5 above). This strategy bears some relation to the strategy that "transparency theorists" such as Harman (1990), Dretske (1995, 2000), and Tye (2003) think we always use in reaching judgments about our experience. (See note 8 to chapter 5.)

21. I am not certain whether this is the best interpretation of Descartes. My impression is that Descartes is not entirely clear on the point, and sympathetic interpretations of him shift with the mood of the times. The view is also associated with Locke (1690/1975) and Russell (1912).

Chapter 8

1. Goethe's *Theory of Colors* (1810/1840/1967) anticipates Purkinje's work to some extent. Goethe's subjective observations about color range widely but tend to be brief and to lack detail. Contrast, for example, the amount of detail in Goethe's and Purkinje's remarks about the wandering cloudy stripes quoted below.

2. If you are looking at this note, maybe you are just the sort of person who will embarrass me by finding discussions I have missed. They must be out there.

3. Rapport describes "upon the dark background . . . an increasing kaleidoscopic riot" (1949, p. 272). Hurvich and Jameson, apparently summarizing the earlier literature, describe "floating light spots . . . of many forms peculiar to the individual observer," sometimes looking "like curved bands with dark intervals between them," sometimes "cloudlike streamers and ribbons" or "circular waves . . . clouds, specks, ribbons, swirls, and the like" (1966, pp. 20–21). (Hurvich and Jameson 1966 is a partial exception to the statement with which I close section iii. The authors seem to have been very influenced by nineteenth-century physiology and psychology, as—among other things—translators of Hering.) Horowitz quotes the following

verbal report: "When I close my eyes I see darkness but then it lightens to gray. Next I see colored lights and sometimes very complex geometric forms that dance, rotate, or sparkle about." (1970, p. 11) Sorenson describes the experience as initially black, then defaulting to a very dark "brain gray" (the term seems to trace back to G. E. Müller), affected by retinal noise of "shifting clouds of floating light spots" and "retinal light swirls" (2004, p. 476). Discussions also sometimes appear in works intended for non-academic audiences. Bates, in *The Bates Method for Good Sight Without Glasses*, writes: "It is impossible to see a perfect black unless the eyesight is faultless, because only then is the mind at rest; but some people can without difficulty approximate such a black nearly enough to improve their eyesight, and as the eyesight improves the deepness of the black increases. People who fail to see even an approximate black when they [cover their closed eyes with the palms of their hands] state that instead of black they see streaks or floating clouds of gray, flashes of light, patches of red, blue, green, yellow, etc." (1944, p. 54). Note that Bates's view agrees with Fechner's: Seeing colors is symptomatic of pathology (though Fechner may have had more severe pathology in mind). Purkinje and Helmholtz, in contrast, suggest that weak vision makes it impossible to see forms in the Eigenlicht. McCrone, writing for a popular science audience, says: "It is easy to assume that when we shut out [sic] eyes, we should see just blackness. However if we stare into this void, we soon will notice thousands of shimmering points of light. . . . If we remain with our eyes shut, the *eigenlicht* does not fade but in fact becomes more active. Often flashes of colour, like summer lightning, will flare. . . ." (1993, pp. 176–177)

4. In the 1950s, psychologists began to study the effects of days-long "sensory deprivation." Early reports emphasized hallucination (Bexton et al. 1954; Heron 1961). Later investigators often failed to replicate those results (Vernon et al. 1961; Zuckerman 1969; Suedfeld 1980), though Nigel Thomas has convinced me in conversation that at least some of the disagreement may be due to differing ideas about what qualifies as a hallucination. Setting aside the work on (at most occasional) hallucinations, I have found no careful studies of the basic visual phenomenology of subjects spending extended periods in absolute darkness. In any case, the effects of serious, prolonged sensory deprivation are not the topic of this chapter. Another related topic is the experience of the "Ganzfeld" that is induced by presenting an unstructured field of light to the eyes (e.g., by shining light through two ping-pong-ball halves covering the eyes) and which is sometimes deployed in attempts to induce relaxation or discover paranormal phenomena. The Ganzfeld is sometimes casually described as neutral gray. More serious phenomenological descriptions— often characterizing it as a gray cloud or fog with forms or colors—can be found in Metzger 1930, Hochberg et al. 1951, Gibson and Waddell 1952, Avant 1965, and Gur 1989. Also, in what is known as Charles Bonnet Syndrome, people who lose their sight also sometimes report hallucinations (Bonnet 1760/1769, pp. 176–178; Menon 2005).

5. In lightless caves, where not a single photon penetrates the darkness, people often report nonetheless being able to see their hands waving before their faces. They never see their friends' hands. Call this the spelunker illusion. One possible explanation is the brain's motor output is actually creating hints of visual experience in accord with that output. Another possible explanation is that, since you know how you are moving your hand, your visual system interprets the low-level sensory noise in conformity with your knowledge (as you might see a meaningful shape in a random splash of line segments). Or maybe there is no visual experience of motion and the spelunker only mistakenly thinks there is. In the eyes-closed experiment, something similar to the spelunker illusion may partly explain my seemingly better perception of my own hand than of my friend's hand.

References

Ach, N. 1905. *Über die Willenstätigkeit und das Denken.* Vandenhoeck & Ruprecht.

Aglioti, S., J. F. X. DeSouza, and M. A. Goodale. 1995. Size-contrast illusions deceive the eye but not the hand. *Current Biology* 5: 679–685.

Ahsen, A. 1977. Eidetics: An overview. *Journal of Mental Imagery* 1: 5–38.

Ahsen, A. 1985. Unvividness paradox. *Journal of Mental Imagery* 9: 1–18.

Ahsen, A. 1986. Prologue to unvividness paradox. *Journal of Mental Imagery* 10: 1–8.

Ahsen, A. 1987. Epilogue to unvividness paradox. *Journal of Mental Imagery* 11: 13–60.

Ahsen, A. 1990. AA-VVIQ and imagery paradigm: Vividness and unvividness issue in VVIQ research paradigms. *Journal of Mental Imagery* 14: 1–58.

Albutt, J., J. Ling, T. M. Heffernan, and M. Shafiullah. 2008. Self-report imagery questionnaire scores and subtypes of social-desirable responding: Auditory imagery, visual imagery, and thinking style. *Journal of Individual Differences* 29: 181–188.

Allen, F. 1924. On the reflex origin of the self light of the retina. *Journal of the Optical Society of America* 8: 275–286.

Allport, G. W. 1924. Eidetic imagery. *British Journal of Psychology* 15: 99–120.

Allport, G. W. 1928. The eidetic image and the after-image. *American Journal of Psychology* 40: 418–425.

Alston, W. 1971. Varieties of privileged access. *American Philosophical Quarterly* 8: 223–241.

Amedi, A., R. Malach, and A. Pascual-Leone. 2005. Negative BOLD differentiates visual imagery and perception. *Neuron* 48: 859–872.

Ammons, C. H., P. Worchel, and K. M. Dallenbach. 1953. "Facial vision": The perception of obstacles out of doors by blindfolded and blindfolded-deafened subjects. *American Journal of Psychology* 66: 519–554.

Andrews, G. A., and M. W. Calkins. 1900. Minor studies from the psychological laboratory of Wellesley College: Studies of the dream consciousness. *American Journal of Psychology* 12: 131–134.

Angell, J. R. 1910. Methods for the determination of mental imagery. *Psychological Monographs* 13: 61–108.

Angell, J. R. 1911. Imageless thought. *Psychological Review* 18: 295–323.

Antonietti, A. 1999. Can students predict when imagery will allow them to discover the problem solution? *European Journal of Cognitive Psychology* 11: 407–428.

Antonietti, A., D. Bologna, and G. Lupi. 1997. Creative synthesis of visual images is not associated with individual differences. *Perceptual and Motor Skills* 85: 881–882.

Antony, M. V. 2008. Are our concepts CONSCIOUS STATE and CONSCIOUS CREATURE vague? *Erkenntnis* 68: 239–263.

Aristotle. 4th c. BCE/1906. *De Sensu and De Memoria*. Cambridge University Press.

Aristotle. 4th c. BCE/1936. *On the Soul, Parva Naturalia, On Breath*. Harvard University Press.

Aristotle. 4th c. BCE/1996. *Aristotle on Sleep and Dreams*, ed. D. Gallop. Aris and Phillips.

Armstrong, D. M. 1955. Illusions of sense. *Australasian Journal of Philosophy* 33: 88–106.

Armstrong, D. M. 1963. Is introspective knowledge incorrigible? *Philosophical Review* 72: 417–432.

Armstrong, D. M. 1981. *The Nature of Mind*. Cornell University Press.

Ashmead, D. H., and R. S. Wall. 1999. Auditory perception of walls via spectral variations in the ambient sound field. *Journal of Rehabilitation Research and Development* 36: 313–322.

Aubert, H. 1865. *Physiologie der Netzhaut*. Morgenstern.

Austin, J. L. 1962. *Sense and Sensibilia*. Oxford University Press.

Avant, L. L. 1965. Vision in the Ganzfeld. *Psychological Bulletin* 64: 246–258.

Ayer, A. J. 1940. *The Foundations of Empirical Knowledge*. Macmillan.

Baars, B. J. 1988. *A Cognitive Theory of Consciousness*. Cambridge University Press.

Baars, B. J. 1997. *In the Theater of Consciousness*. Oxford University Press.

Bar-On, D. 2004. *Speaking My Mind*. Oxford University Press.

Barry, H., Jr., and W. A. Bousfield. 1934. Implications of the flight of colors. *Psychological Review* 41: 300–305.

Bates, W. H. 1944. *The Bates Method for Good Sight Without Glasses*. Faber and Faber.

Bayle, P. 1702/1734–8. *The Dictionary Historical and Critical of Mr. Peter Bayle*. Knapton.

Bayne, T., and M. Spener. Forthcoming. Introspective humility. *Philosophical Issues*.

Beaunis, H. 1903. Contribution à la Psychologie du Rêve. *American Journal of Psychology* 14 (3/4): 7–23.

Belardinelli, M. O., et al. 2009. An fMRI investigation on image generation in different sensory modalities: The influence of vividness. *Acta Psychologica* 132: 190–200.

Bellamy, R. 1915. The analysis of a nightmare. *Journal of Abnormal Psychology* 10: 11–18.

Belot, G. 2003. Remarks on the geometry of visibles. *Philosophical Quarterly* 53: 581–586.

Bem, D. J. 1972. Self-perception theory. *Advances in Experimental Social Psychology* 6: 1–62.

Bentley, M. 1915. The study of dreams. *American Journal of Psychology* 26: 196–210.

Berger, R. J. 1963. Experimental modification of dream content by meaningful verbal stimuli. *British Journal of Psychiatry* 109: 722–740.

Berkeley, G. 1710/1965. A treatise concerning the principles of human knowledge. In *Principles, Dialogues, and Philosophical Correspondence*, ed. C. Turbayne. Macmillan.

Berry, W. 1922. The flight of colors in the after image of a bright light. *Psychological Bulletin* 19: 307–337.

Berry, W. 1927. Color sequences in the after-image of a white light. *American Journal of Psychology* 38: 584–598.

Betts, G. H. 1909. *The Distribution and Functions of Mental Imagery*. Teachers College, Columbia University.

Bexton, W. H., W. Heron, and T. H. Scott. 1954. Effects of decreased variation in the sensory environment. *Canadian Journal of Psychology* 8: 70–76.

Blackmore, S. 2002. There is no stream of consciousness. *Journal of Consciousness Studies* 9 (5–6): 17–28.

Blajenkova, O., M. Kozhevnikov, and M. A. Motes. 2006. Object-spatial imagery: A new self-report imagery questionnaire. *Applied Cognitive Psychology* 20: 239–263.

Blazhenkova, O., and M. Kozhevnikov. 2009. The new object-spatial-verbal cognitive style model: Theory and measurement. *Applied Cognitive Psychology* 23: 638–663.

Block, N., ed. 1981. *Imagery*. MIT Press.

Block, N. 1995. On a confusion about the function of consciousness. *Behavioral and Brain Sciences* 18: 227–287.

Block, N. 2007. Consciousness, accessibility, and the mesh between psychology and neuroscience. *Behavioral and Brain Sciences* 30: 481–548.

Blum, H. P. 1964. Colour in dreams. *International Journal of Psycho-Analysis* 45: 519–529.

Bolton, R. 1978. Salience of color terms in the dreams of Peruvian mestizos and Qolla Indians. *Journal of Social Psychology* 105: 299–300.

Bonnet, C. 1760/1769. *Essai analytique sur les faculties de l'ame*, second edition, vol. 2. Philibert.

Borges, J. L. 1949/1962. The Zahir. In *Labyrinths*. New Directions.

Boring, E. G. 1921. The stimulus error. *American Journal of Psychology* 32: 449–471.

Boring, E. G. 1927. Edward Bradford Titchener. *American Journal of Psychology* 38: 489–506.

Boring, E. G. 1929/1950. *A History of Experimental Psychology*, second edition. Appleton-Century-Crofts.

Boring, E. G. 1942. *Sensation and Perception in the History of Experimental Psychology*. Appleton-Century-Crofts.

Boring, E. G. 1953. A history of introspection. *Psychological Bulletin* 50: 169–189.

Bornstein, R. F. 1989. Subliminal techniques as propaganda tools: Review and critique. *Journal of Mind and Behavior* 10: 231–262.

Bower, G. H. 1972. Mental imagery and associative learning. In *Cognition in Learning and Memory*, ed. L. Gregg. Wiley.

Brandstätter, H. 2001. Time sampling diary: An ecological approach to the study of emotion in everyday life situations. In *Persons, Situations, and Emotions*, ed. H. Brandstätter and A. Eliasz. Oxford University Press.

Brang, D., and V. S. Ramachandran. 2010. Visual field heterogeneity, laterality, and eidetic imagery in synaesthesia. *Neurocase* 16: 169–174.

Braun, A. R., T. J. Balkin, N. J. Wesensten, F. Gwadry, R. E. Carson, M. Varga, P. Baldwin, G. Belenky, and P. Herscovitch. 1998. Dissociated pattern of activity in visual cortices and their projections during human rapid eye movement sleep. *Science* 279: 91–95.

Brentano, F. C. 1874/1973. *Psychology from an Empirical Standpoint*, ed. O. Kraus and L. McAlister. Routledge.

Brewer, W. F., and M. Schommer-Aikins. 2006. Scientists are not deficient in mental imagery: Galton revisited. *Review of General Psychology* 10: 130–146.

Broad, C. D. 1925. *The Mind and Its Place in Nature*. Humanities Press.

Brown, J. L. 1965. Afterimages. In *Vision and Visual Perception*, ed. C. Graham. Wiley.

Bruner, J. S., and L. Postman. 1949. On perception of incongruity: A paradigm. *Journal of Personality* 18: 206–223.

Bühler, K. 1907. Tatsachen und Probleme zu einer Psychologie der Denvorgänge. *Archiv für die gesamte Psychologie* 9: 297–365.

Burbridge, D. 1994. Galton's 100: An exploration of Francis Galton's imagery studies. *British Journal for the History of Science* 27: 443–463.

Burge, T. 1988. Individualism and self-knowledge. *Journal of Philosophy* 85: 649–663.

Burge, T. 1996. Our entitlement to self-knowledge. *Proceedings of the Aristotelian Society* 96: 91–116.

Burgess, C., and K. Lund. 2000. The dynamics of meaning in memory. In *Cognitive Dynamics: Conceptual and Representational Change in Humans and Machines*, ed. E. Dietrich and A. Markman. Erlbaum.

Burton, L. J., and G. J. Fogarty. 2003. The factor structure of visual imagery and spatial abilities. *Intelligence* 31: 289–318.

Calef, V. 1954. Color in dreams. *Journal of the American Psychoanalytic Association* 2: 453–461.

Calkins, M. W. 1893. Minor studies from the psychological laboratory of Clark University: Statistics of dreams. *American Journal of Psychology* 5: 311–343.

Campos, A., and C. I. Fernández. 1997. Imagen mental e intervalo de retención en el recuerdo de series. *Estudios de Psicología* 58: 105–112.

Campos, A., and C. I. Fernández. 1998. La imagen mental en el sistema de enlace. *Revista de Psicología* 16: 3–17.

Campos, A., and M. J. Pérez. 1997. Mnemonic images and associated pair recall. *Journal of Mental Imagery* 21: 73–82.

Campos, A., M. J. Pérez, and M. A. González. 1997. The interactiveness of paired images is affected by image bizarreness and image vividness. *Imagination, Cognition and Personality* 16: 301–307.

Carretti, B., E. Borella, and R. De Beni. 2007. Does strategic memory training improve the working memory performance of younger and older adults? *Experimental Psychology* 54: 311–320.

Carroll, J. B., P. Davies, and B. Richman. 1967. *The American Heritage Word Frequency Book*. Houghton Mifflin.

Carruthers, P. 2009. How we know our own minds: The relationship between mindreading and metacognition. *Behavioral and Brain Sciences* 32: 121–182.

Chalmers, D. J. 1996. *The Conscious Mind*. Oxford University Press.

Chalmers, D. J. 2003. The content and epistemology of phenomenal belief. In *Consciousness: New Philosophical Essays*, ed. Q. Smith and A. Jokic. Clarendon.

Chara, P. J. 1992. Some concluding thoughts on the debate about the Vividness of Visual Imagery Questionnaire. *Perceptual and Motor Skills* 75: 947–954.

Cherry, E. C. 1953. Some experiments on the recognition of speech, with one and two ears. *Journal of the Acoustical Society of America* 25: 975–979.

Chisholm, R. M. 1957. *Perceiving*. Cornell University Press.

Churchland, P. M. 1985. Reduction, qualia, and the direct introspection of brain states. *Journal of Philosophy* 82: 8–28.

Churchland, P. M. 1984/1988. *Matter and Consciousness*, revised edition. MIT Press.

Clark, A. 2001. Visual experience and motor action: Are the bonds too tight? *Philosophical Review* 110: 495–519.

Cleomedes. Circa 2nd c. CE/2004. *Cleomedes' Lectures on Astronomy*, ed. A. Bowen and R. Todd. University of California Press.

Cohen, P. 2008. The World Science Festival: Oliver Sacks at the MET. http: //artsbeat .blogs.nytimes.com).

Coltheart, M., and M. J. Glick. 1974. Visual imagery: A case study. *Quarterly Journal of Experimental Psychology* 25: 438–453.

Comte, A. 1830. *Cours de philosophie positive*, vol. 1. Bachelier.

Conway, B. R. 2009. Color vision, cones, and color-coding in the cortex. *Neuroscientist* 15: 274–290.

Coren, S., and J. S. Girgus. 1978. *Seeing Is Deceiving*. Erlbaum.

Cornoldi, C. 1995. Imagery and meta-imagery in the VVIQ. *Journal of Mental Imagery* 19: 131--136.

Cotzin, M., and K. M. Dallenbach. 1950. "Facial vision": The role of pitch and loudness in the perception of obstacles by the blind. *American Journal of Psychology* 63: 485–515.

Crawford, H. J., and S. N. Allen. 1996. Paired-associate learning and recall of high and low imagery words: Moderating effects of hypnosis, hypnotic susceptibility level and visualization abilities. *American Journal of Psychology* 109: 353–372.

Crick, F. 1994. *The Astonishing Hypothesis*. Scribner.

Cui, X., C. B. Jeter, D. Yang, P. R. Montague, and D. M. Eagleman. 2007. Vividness of mental imagery: Individual variability can be measured objectively. *Vision Research* 47: 474–478.

Dahl, H. 1979. *Word Frequencies in Spoken American English*. Gale Research.

Danquah, A.N., Farrell, M.J., and O'Boyle, D.J. 2008. Biases in the subjective timing of perceptual events: Libet et al. (1983) revisited. *Consciousness and Cognition*, 17, 616–627.

da Vinci, L. 1519/1989. *Leonardo on Painting*, ed. M. Kemp. Yale University Press.

de Aguilón, F. 1613. *Opticorvm libri sex*. Officina Plantiniana.

Dean, G. M., and P. E. Morris. 2003. The relationship between self-reports of imagery and spatial ability. *British Journal of Psychology* 94: 245–273.

Delboeuf, J. 1865. Note sur certaines illusions d'optique: Essai d'une théorie psychphysique de la manière dont l'oeil apprécie les distances et les angles. *Bulletins de l'Académie Royale des Sciences, Lettres et Beaux-arts de Belgique* 19 (2d serie), 195–216.

de Martino, M. F. 1953. Sex differences in the dreams of Southern college students. *Journal of Clinical Psychology* 9: 199–201.

Dennett, D. C. 1969. *Content and Consciousness*. Humanities Press.

Dennett, D. C. 1991. *Consciousness Explained*. Little, Brown.

Dennett, D. C. 2001. Surprise, Surprise. *Behavioral and Brain Sciences* 24: 982.

Dennett, D. C. 2002. How could I be wrong? How wrong could I be? *Journal of Consciousness Studies* 9 (5–6): 13–16.

Dennett, D. C. 2007. Heterophenomenology reconsidered. *Phenomenology and the Cognitive Sciences* 6: 247–270.

Descartes, R. 1641/1984. Meditations on first philosophy. In *The Philosophical Writings of Descartes*, vol. II. Cambridge University Press.

Descartes, R. 1649/1985. The passions of the soul. In *The Philosophical Writings of Descartes*, vol. I. Cambridge University Press.

Dewey, John. 1886. *Psychology*. Harper.

Dharmakīrti. 7th c./1958. Nyāya-bindu. In T. Stcherbatsky, *Buddhist Logic*. Mouton.

Diderot, D. 1749/1916. Letter on the blind for the use of those who see. In *Diderot's Early Philosophical Works*, ed. M. Jourdain. Open Court.

Dignāga. 6th c./1968. Pramānasamuccaya. In M. Hattori, *Dignāga, on Perception*. Harvard University Press.

Doust, J. W. L. 1951. Studies in the physiology of awareness: The incidence and content of dream patterns and their relationship to anoxia. *Journal of Mental Science* 97: 801–811.

Dretske, F. 1995. *Naturalizing the Mind*. MIT Press.

Dretske, F. 2000. *Perception, Knowledge, and Belief.* Cambridge University Press.

Dretske, F. 2003. How do you know you are not a zombie? In *Privileged Access*, ed. B. Gertler. Ashgate.

Dreyfus, G. B. J. 1997. *Recognizing Reality.* SUNY Press.

Eberman, C., and S. J. McKelvie. 2002. Vividness of visual imagery and source memory for audio and text. *Applied Cognitive Psychology* 16: 87–95.

Einstein, G. O., and M. A. McDaniel. 1987. Distinctiveness and the mnemonic benefits of bizarre imagery. In *Imagery and Related Mnemonic Processes*, ed. M. McDaniel and M. Pressley. Springer-Verlag.

Ellis, H. 1911. *The World of Dreams.* Houghton Mifflin.

Epicurus. 3rd c. BCE/1926. *The Extant Remains.* Oxford University Press.

Epstein, W., J. Park, and A. Casey. 1961. The current status of the size-distance hypotheses. *Psychological Bulletin* 58: 491–514.

Ermentrout, G. B., and J. D. Cowan. 1979. A mathematical theory of visual hallucination patterns. *Biological Cybernetics* 34: 137–150.

Ernest, C. H. 1977. Imagery ability and cognition: A critical review. *Journal of Mental Imagery* 2: 181–216.

Eton, D. T., F. H. Gilner, and D. C. Munz. 1998. The measurement of imagery vividness: A test of the reliability and validity of the Vividness of Visual Imagery Questionnaire and the Vividness of Movement Imagery Questionnaire. *Journal of Mental Imagery* 22: 125–136.

Euclid. Circa 300 BCE/1945. The optics of Euclid. *Journal of the Optical Society of America* 35: 357–372.

Evans, R. B. 1972. Titchener and his lost system. *Journal of the History of the Behavioral Sciences* 8: 168–180.

Evans, W. E. 1973. Echolocation by marine delphenids and one species of freshwater dolphin. *Journal of the Acoustical Society of America* 54: 191–199.

Faw, B. 1997. Outlining a brain model of mental imaging abilities. *Neuroscience and Biobehavioral Reviews* 21: 283–288.

Faw, B. 2009. Conflicting intuitions may be based on differing abilities. *Journal of Consciousness Studies* 16 (4): 45–68.

Fechner, G. T. 1860/1889. *Elemente der Psychophysik*, vol. 2. Breitkopf und Härtel.

Fechner, G. T. 1860/1966. *Elements of Psychophysics*, vol. 1, ed. D. Howes and E. Boring. Holt.

Feldman, M., L. Todman, and M. B. Bender. 1974. "Flight of colours" in lesions of the visual system. *Journal of Neurology, Neurosurgery, and Psychiatry* 37: 1265–1272.

Ferree, C. E. 1908. The intermittence of minimal visual sensations: I. *American Journal of Psychology* 19: 58–129.

Fick, A. 1879. Die Lehre von der Lichtempfindungen. In *Handbuch der Physiologie*, vol. 3. ed. L. Hermann. F. C. W. Vogel.

Flanagan, O. 1992. *Consciousness Reconsidered*. MIT Press.

Ford, J. 2008. Attention and the new skeptics. *Journal of Consciousness Studies* 15 (3): 59–86.

Fortier, R. H. 1951. A Study of the Relationship of Response to Color and Some Personality Functions. Ph.D. dissertation, Case Western Reserve University.

Frayn, D. H. 1991. The incidence and significance of perceptual qualities in the reported dreams of patients with anorexia nervosa. *Canadian Journal of Psychiatry* 36: 517–520.

Freud, S. 1900/1931. *The Interpretation of Dreams*. Carlton House.

Fröhlich, F. W. 1921. Untersuchungen über periodische Nachbilder. *Zeitschrift für Psychologie und Physiologie der Sinnesorgane* 52: 60–88.

Furst, C. J. 1979. The inside and outside of eidetic imagery. *Behavioral and Brain Sciences* 2: 602–603.

Galton, F. 1880. Statistics of mental imagery. *Mind* 5: 301–318.

Galton, F. 1883/1907. *Inquiries into Human Faculty and Its Development*, second edition. J. M. Dent.

Galton, F. 1908. *Memories of My Life*. Methuen.

Ganis, G., W. L. Thompson, and S. M. Kosslyn. 2004. Brain areas underlying visual imagery and visual perception: an fMRI study. *Cognitive Brain Research* 20: 226–241.

Gardner, R. W., and R. I. Long. 1960a. Errors of the standard and illusion effects with L-shaped figures. *Perceptual and Motor Skills* 10: 107–109.

Gardner, R. W., and R. I. Long. 1960b. Errors of the standard and illusion effects with the inverted-T. *Perceptual and Motor Skills* 10: 47–54.

Garma, A. 1961. Colour in dreams. *International Journal of Psycho-Analysis* 42: 556–559.

Gegenfurtner, K. R., and D. C. Kiper. 2003. Color vision. *Annual Review of Neuroscience* 26: 181–206.

Geldard, F. A., and C. E. Sherrick. 1972. The cutaneous "rabbit": A perceptual illusion. *Science* 178 (4057): 178–179.

Gemignani, A., L. Sebastiani, A. Simoni, E. L. Santarcangelo, and B. Ghelarducci. 2006. Hyponotic trait and specific phobia: EEG and autonomic output during phobic stimulation. *Brain Research Bulletin* 69: 197–203.

Gertler, B. 2001. Introspecting phenomenal states. *Philosophy and Phenomenological Research* 63: 305–328.

Gertler, B., ed. 2003. *Privileged Access*. Ashgate.

Gibson, J. J., and D. Waddell. 1952. Homogeneous retinal stimulation and visual perception. *American Journal of Psychology* 65: 263–270.

Gilinsky, A. S. 1951. Perceived size and distance in visual space. *Psychological Review* 58: 460–482.

Girgus, J. J., I. Rock, and R. Egatz. 1977. The effect of knowledge of reversibility on the reversibility of ambiguous figures. *Perception & Psychophysics* 22: 550–556.

Glicksohn, J., I. Steinbach, and S. Elimalach-Malmilyan. 1999. Cognitive dedifferentiation in eidetics and synaesthesia: Hunting for the ghost once more. *Perception* 28: 109–120.

Glover, S. 2002. Visual illusions affect planning but not control. *Trends in Cognitive Sciences* 6: 288–292.

Goethe, J. W. von. 1810/1840/1967. *Goethe's Theory of Colours*. Frank Cass.

Goldman, A. 1986. *Epistemology and Cognition*. Harvard University Press.

Goldman, A. 2004. Epistemology and the evidential status of introspective reports. *Journal of Consciousness Studies* 11 (7–8): 1–16.

Goldman, A. 2006. *Simulating Minds*. Oxford University Press.

González, M., A. Campos, and M. J. Pérez. 1997. Mental imagery and creative thinking. *Journal of Psychology* 131: 357–364.

Goodale, M. A., C. L. R. Gonzales, and G. Króliczak. 2008. Action rules: Why the visual control of reaching and grasping is not always influenced by perceptual illusions. *Perception* 37: 355–366.

Gopnik, A., and P. Graf. 1988. Knowing how you know: Young children's ability to identify and remember the sources of their beliefs. *Child Development* 59: 1366–1371.

Gordon, M. S., and L. D. Rosenblum. 2004. Perception of sound-obstructing surfaces using body-scaled judgments. *Ecological Psychology* 16: 87–113.

Gordon, R. 1949. An investigation into some of the factors that favour the formation of stereotyped images. *British Journal of Psychology* 39: 156–167.

Grandin, T. 1995. *Thinking in Pictures*. Doubleday.

Granrud, C. E. 2009. Development of size constancy in children: A test of the metacognitive theory. *Attention, Perception & Psychophysics* 71: 644–654.

Gray, C. R., and K. Gummerman. 1975. The enigmatic eidetic image: A critical examination of methods, data, and theories. *Psychological Bulletin* 82: 383–407.

Gregory, R. L. 1970. *The Intelligent Eye*. McGraw-Hill.

Griffin, D. 1958. *Listening in the Dark*. Yale University Press.

Guillot, A., S. Champely, C. Batier, P. Thiriet, and C. Collet. 2007. Relationship between spatial abilities, mental rotation, and functional anatomy learning. *Advances in Health Sciences Education : Theory and Practice* 12: 491–507.

Gur, M. 1989. Color and brightness fade-out in the Ganzfeld is wavelength dependent. *Vision Research* 29: 1335–1341.

Gyselinck, V., C. Meneghetti, R. De Beni, and F. Pazzaglia. 2009. The role of working memory in spatial text processing: What benefit of imagery strategy and visuospatial abilities? *Learning and Individual Differences* 19: 12–20.

Haber, R. N. 1979. Twenty years of haunting eidetic imagery: Where's the ghost? *Behavioral and Brain Sciences* 2: 583–629.

Haber, R. N., and L. Haber. 2000. Experiencing, remembering, and reporting events. *Psychology, Public Policy, and Law* 6: 1057–1097.

Haber, R. N., and R. B. Haber. 1964. Eidetic imagery: I. Frequency. *Perceptual and Motor Skills* 19: 131–138.

Haffenden, A. M., and M. A. Goodale. 1998. The effect of pictorial illusion on prehension and perception. *Journal of Cognitive Neuroscience* 10: 122–136.

Hall, C. S. 1951. What people dream about. *Scientific American* 184 (5): 60–63.

Hall, C. S., and R. L. Van de Castle. 1966. *The Content Analysis of Dreams*. Appleton-Century-Crofts.

Hall, D. E. 1980/2002. *Musical Acoustics*, third edition. Brooks/Cole Thomson Learning.

Hall, D. E. 1981. The difference between difference tones and rapid beats. *American Journal of Physics* 49: 632–636.

Hanson, N. R. 1969. *Perception and Discovery*. Freeman, Cooper.

Harman, G. 1990. The intrinsic quality of experience. *Philosophical Perspectives* 4: 31–52.

Hatfield, G. 2009. *Perception and Cognition*. Oxford University Press.

Hausfeld, S., R. P. Power, A. Gorta, and P. Harris. 1982. Echo perception of shape and texture by sighted subjects. *Perceptual and Motor Skills* 55: 623–632.

Haybron, D. 2008. *The Pursuit of Unhappiness*. Oxford University Press.

Hayes, S. P. 1935. *Facial Vision or the Sense of Obstacles*. Perkins Publications.

Heaps, C., and M. Nash. 1999. Individual differences in imagination inflation. *Psychonomic Bulletin & Review* 6: 313–318.

Heavey, C. L., and R. T. Hurlburt. 2008. The phenomena of inner experience. *Consciousness and Cognition* 17: 798–810.

Helmholtz, H. 1856/1909/1962. *Helmholtz's Treatise on Physiological Optics*, ed. J. Southall. Dover.

Hering, E. 1868/1977. *The Theory of Binocular Vision*, ed. B. Bridgeman and L. Stark. Plenum.

Hering, E. 1878. *Zur Lehre vom Lichtsinne*. Carl Gerolds Sohn.

Hering, E. 1905. *Grundzüge der Lehre von Lichtsinn*, vol. 1. Wilhelm Engelmann.

Hering, E. 1920/1964. *Outlines of a Theory of the Light Sense*. Harvard University Press.

Herman, J., H. Roffwarg, and E. S. Tauber. 1968. Color and other perceptual qualities of REM and NREM sleep. *Psychophysiology* 5: 223.

Heron, W. 1961. Cognitive and physiological effects of perceptual isolation. In *Sensory Deprivation*, ed. P. Solomon, P. Kubzansky, P. Leiderman, J. Mendelson, R. Trumbull, and D. Wexler. Harvard University Press.

Higashiyama, A., and K. Shimono. 1994. How accurate is size and distance perception for very far terrestrial objects? Function and causality. *Perception & Psychophysics* 55: 429–442.

Hills, P. J., R. L. Elward, and M. B. Lewis. 2008. Identity adaptation is mediated and moderated by visualisation ability. *Perception* 37: 1241–1257.

Hine, R. (forthcoming). Attention as experience: Through "thick" and "thin." *Journal of Consciousness Studies*.

Hintikka, J. 1962. Cogito ergo sum: Inference or performance? *Philosophical Review* 71: 3–32.

Hochberg, J. E. 1950. Figure-ground reversal as a function of visual satiation. *Journal of Experimental Psychology* 40: 682–686.

Hochberg, J. E., W. Triebel, and G. Seaman. 1951. Color adaptation under conditions of homogeneous visual stimulation (*Ganzfeld*). *Journal of Experimental Psychology* 41: 153–159.

Hochel, M., and E. G. Milán. 2008. Synaesthesia: The existing state of affairs. *Cognitive Neuropsychology* 25: 93–117.

Hochman, J. 2002. *Memory and the Eidetic*. Brandon House.

Holender, D. 1986. Semantic activation without conscious identification in dichotic listening, parafoveal vision, and visual masking: A survey and appraisal. *Behavioral and Brain Sciences* 9: 1–66.

Holender, D., and K. Duscherer. 2004. Unconscious perception: The need for a paradigm shift. *Perception & Psychophysics* 66: 872–881.

Homuth, P. 1913. Beiträge zur Kenntnis der Nachbilderscheinungen. *Archiv für die gesamte Psychologie* 26: 181–268.

Hong, C.-H. H., et al. 2009. fMRI evidence for multisensory recruitment associated with rapid eye movements during sleep. *Human Brain Mapping* 30: 1705–1722.

Horgan, T., and J. Tienson. 2002. The intentionality of phenomenology and the phenomenology of intentionality. In *Philosophy of Mind*, ed. D. Chalmers. Oxford University Press.

Horgan, T., and U. Kriegel. 2007. Phenomenal epistemology: What is consciousness that we may know it so well? *Philosophical Issues* 17: 123–144.

Horgan, T., J. Tienson, and G. Graham. (2005). Internal-world skepticism and the self-presentational nature of phenomenal consciousness. In *Experience and analysis: Proceedings of the 27ʰ International Wittgenstein Symposium*, ed. M. Reicher and J. Marek. ÖBV and HPT.

Horowitz, M. J. 1970. *Image Formation and Cognition*. Appleton-Century-Crofts.

Huet, P.-D. 1694/2003. *Against Cartesian Philosophy*, ed. T. Lennon. Humanity Books.

Hume, D. 1740/1978. *A Treatise of Human Nature*, ed. L. Selby-Bigge and P. Nidditch. Oxford University Press.

Hume, D. 1748/1975. An enquiry concerning human understanding. In *Enquiries Concerning Human Understanding and Concerning the Principles of Morals*, ed. L. Selby-Bigge and P. Nidditch. Clarendon.

Humphrey, G. 1951. *Thinking*. Methuen.

Hurlburt, R. T. 1990. *Sampling Normal and Schizophrenic Inner Experience*. Plenum.

Hurlburt, R. T., and S. A. Akhter. 2008. Unsymbolized thinking. *Consciousness and Cognition* 17: 1364–1374.

Hurlburt, R. T., and C. L. Heavey. 2004. To beep or not to beep: Obtaining accurate reports about awareness. *Journal of Consciousness Studies* 11 (7–8): 113–128.

Hurlburt, R. T., and C. L. Heavey. 2006. *Exploring Inner Experience*. John Benjamins.

Hurlburt, R. T., and E. Schwitzgebel. 2007. *Describing Inner Experience? Proponent Meets Skeptic*. MIT Press.

Hurvich, L. M., and D. Jameson. 1966. *The Perception of Brightness and Darkness.* Allyn and Bacon.

Husband, R. W. 1935. Sex differences in dream contents. *Journal of Abnormal and Social Psychology* 30: 513–521.

Huxley, A. 1956. *Heaven and Hell.* Harper.

Huxley, T. H. 1895. *Hume.* Macmillan.

Ichikawa, J. 2009. Dreaming and imagination. *Mind & Language* 24: 103–121.

Intons-Peterson, M. J. 1983. Imagery paradigms: How vulnerable are they to experimenters' expectations? *Journal of Experimental Psychology. Human Perception and Performance* 9: 394–412.

Isaac, A. R., and D. F. Marks. 1994. Individual differences in mental imagery experience: Developmental changes and specialization. *British Journal of Psychology* 85: 479–500.

Jack, A. I., and T. Shallice. 2001. Introspective physicalism as an approach to the science of consciousness. *Cognition* 79: 161–196.

Jackson, F. 1977. *Perception.* Cambridge University Press.

Jaensch, E. R. 1923. *Über den Aufbau der Wahrnehmungswelt.* Barth.

Jaensch, E. R. 1930. *Eidetic Imagery.* Kegan Paul.

James, W. 1884. On some omissions of introspective psychology. *Mind*, o.s. 9: 1–26.

James, W. 1890/1981. *The Principles of Psychology.* Harvard University Press.

Jankowski, W. L., S. C. Dee, and R. D. Cartwright. 1977. A distribution of colorimetric imagery in REM sleep. *Sleep Research* 6: 123.

Jaynes, J. 1976. *The Origin of Consciousness in the Breakdown of the Bicameral Mind.* Houghton Mifflin.

Johansson, S., and K. Hofland. 1989. *Frequency Analysis of English Vocabulary and Grammar.* Clarendon.

Judd, D. B. 1927. A quantitative investigation of the Purkinje after-image. *American Journal of Psychology* 38: 507–533.

Kahn, E., W. Dement, C. Fisher, and J. E. Barmack. 1962. Incidence of color in immediately recalled dreams. *Science* 137: 1054–1055.

Kaylor, C. W., and R. S. Davidson. 1979. Accuracy of recall as a function of eidetic imagery. *Perceptual and Motor Skills* 48: 1143–1148.

Kellogg, W. N. 1958. Echo ranging in the porpoise. *Science* 128: 982–988.

Kells, K. 2001. Ability of blind people to detect obstacles in unfamiliar environments. *Journal of Nursing Scholarship* 33: 153–157.

Kelly, S. 2008. Content and constancy: Phenomenology, psychology, and the content of perception. *Philosophy and Phenomenological Research* 76: 682–690.

Kenet, T., D. Bibitchkov, M. Tsodyks, A. Grinvald, and A. Arieli. 2003. Spontaneously emerging cortical representations of visual attributes. *Nature* 425 (6961): 954–956.

Keng, C.-J., and H.-Y. Lin. 2006. Impact of telepresence levels on internet advertising effects. *Cyberpsychology & Behavior* 9: 82–94.

Keogh, L., and R. Markham. 1998. Judgements of other people's memory reports: Differences in reports as a function of imagery vividness. *Applied Cognitive Psychology* 12: 159–171.

Kessler, R. C., R. L. DuPont, P. Berglund, and H.-U. Wittchen. 1999. Impairment in pure and comorbid generalized anxiety disorder and major depression at 12 months in two national surveys. *American Journal of Psychiatry* 156: 1915–1923.

Kilgour, A. R., and S. J. Lederman. 2002. Face recognition by hand. *Perception & Psychophysics* 54: 339–352.

Kind, A. 2003. What's so transparent about transparency? *Philosophical Studies* 115: 225–244.

Kish, D. 2009. Human echolocation: How to "see" like a bat. *New Scientist* 201 (2703): 31–33.

Klüver, H. 1933. Eidetic imagery. In *A Handbook of Child Psychology*, second edition, ed. C. Murchison. Russell and Russell.

Knapp, P. H. 1953. The ear, listening, and hearing. *Journal of the American Psychiatric Association* 1: 672–689.

Knapp, P. H. 1956. Sensory impressions in dreams. *Psychoanalytic Quarterly* 25: 325–347.

Koch, C. 2004. *The Quest for Consciousness*. Roberts.

Koch, C., and N. Tsuchiya. 2007. Attention and consciousness: Two distinct brain processes. *Trends in Cognitive Sciences* 11: 16–22.

Kogon, M. M., P. Jasiukaitis, A. Berardi, M. Gupta, S. M. Kosslyn, and D. Spiegel. 1998. Imagery and hypnotizability revisited. *International Journal of Clinical and Experimental Hypnosis* 46: 363–370.

Köhler, P. 1912. Beiträge zur systematischen Traumbeobachtung. *Archiv für die gesamte Psychologie* 23: 415–483.

Köhler, W. 1929/1947. *Gestalt Psychology*. Liveright.

Köhler, W., and H. Wallach. 1944. Figural aftereffects; an investigation of visual processes. *Proceedings of the American Philosophical Society* 88: 269–357.

Koninski, K. 1934. Beitrag zur Kenntnis der entoptischen Erscheinungen. *Kwartalnik Psychologiczny* 5: 337–382.

Kornblith, H. 1998. What is it like to be me? *Australasian Journal of Philosophy* 76: 48–60.

Kosslyn, S. M. 1980. *Image and Mind*. Harvard University Press.

Kosslyn, S. M. 1994. *Image and Brain*. MIT Press.

Kosslyn, S. M., G. Ganis, and W. L. Thompson. 2001. Neural foundations of imagery. *Nature Reviews. Neuroscience* 2: 635–642.

Kosslyn, S. M., L. M. Shin, W. L. Thompson, R. J. McNally, S. L. Rauch, R. K. Pitman, and N. M. Alpert. 1996. Neural effects of visualizing and perceiving aversive stimuli: A PET investigation. *Neuroreport* 7: 1569–1576.

Kouider, S., V. de Gradelle, J. Sackur, and E. Dupoux. 2010. How rich is consciousness? The partial awareness hypothesis. *Trends in Cognitive Sciences* 14: 301–307.

Kozhevnikov, M., S. Kosslyn, and J. Shephard. 2005. Spatial versus object visualizers: A new characterization of visual cognitive style. *Memory & Cognition* 33: 710–726.

Kubie, L. S. 1950. *Practical and Theoretical Aspects of Psychoanalysis*. International Universities Press.

Kučera, H., and W. N. Francis. 1967. *Computational Analysis of Present-Day American English*. Brown University Press.

Külpe, O. 1893/1895. *Outlines of Psychology*. Swan Sonnenschein.

Kundt, A. 1863. Untersuchungen über Augenmaass und optische Täuschungen. *Annalen der Physik und Chemie* 120: 118–158.

Künnapas, T. M. 1955. An analysis of the "horizontal-vertical illusion." *Journal of Experimental Psychology* 49: 134–140.

Kunzendorf, R. G. 1984. Centrifugal effects of eidetic imaging on flash electroretinograms and autonomic responses. *Journal of Mental Imagery* 8: 67–76.

Kunzendorf, R. G., K. Young, T. Beecy, and K. Beals. 2000. Is visual thinking "imageless thought"? *Perceptual and Motor Skills* 91: 981–982.

Kusch, M. 1999. *Psychological Knowledge*. Routledge.

Ladd, G.T. 1892. Contribution to the psychology of visual dreams. *Mind*, n.s 1: 299–304.

Ladd, G. T. 1894. Direct control of the retinal field. *Psychological Review* 1: 351–355.

Ladd, G. T. 1903. Direct control of the "retinal field": Report on three cases. *Psychological Review* 10: 139–149.

Laeng, B., and D.-S. Teodorescu. 2002. Eye scanpaths during visual imagery reenact those of perception of the same visual scene. *Cognitive Science* 26: 207–231.

Lamme, V. A. F. 2003. Why visual attention and awareness are different. *Trends in Cognitive Sciences* 7: 12–18.

Lamme, V. A. F. 2005. The difference between visual attention and awareness: A cognitive neuroscience perspective. In *The Neurobiology of Attention*, ed. L. Itti, G. Rees, and J. Tsotsos. Elsevier.

Lamme, V. A. F., and P. R. Roelfsema. 2000. The distinct modes of vision offered by feedforward and recurrent processing. *Trends in Neurosciences* 23: 571–579.

Lanca, M., and D. J. Bryant. 2001. Metric representations of haptically explored triangles. *American Journal of Psychology* 114: 377–409.

Lavie, N. 2006. The role of perceptual load in visual awareness. *Brain Research* 1080: 91–100.

Leask, J., R. N. Haber, and R. B. Haber. 1969. Eidetic imagery in children. II. Longitudinal and experimental results. *Psychonomic Monograph Supplements* 3: 25–48.

Le Conte, J. 1881/1897. *Sight: An Exposition of the Principles of Monocular and Binocular Vision*, second edition. Appleton.

Lee, D. N. 1990. Getting around with light or sound. In *Perception and Control of Self-Motion*, ed. R. Warren and A. Wertheim. Erlbaum.

Lee, H. S., and A. C. Dobbins. 2006. Perceiving surfaces in depth beyond the fusion limit of their elements. *Perception* 35: 31–39.

Lehar, S. 2003. Gestalt isomorphism and the primacy of subjective conscious experience: A Gestalt Bubble model. *Behavioral and Brain Sciences* 26: 375–444.

Lequerica, L., L. Rapport, B. N. Axelrod, K. Telmet, and R. D. Whitman. 2002. Subjective and objective assessment methods of mental imagery control: Construct validation of self-report measures. *Journal of Clinical and Experimental Neuropsychology* 24: 1103–1116.

Lewis, C. I. 1946. *An Analysis of Knowledge and Valuation*. Open Court.

Lewis, M. B., and H. D. Ellis. 2000. Satiation in name and face recognition. *Memory & Cognition* 28: 783–788.

Libet, B. 1985. Unconscious cerebral initiative and the role of conscious will in voluntary action. *Behavioral and Brain Sciences* 8: 529–566.

Liebowitz, H. W., S. W. Pollard, and D. Dickson. 1967. Monocular and binocular size-matching as a function of distance at various age-levels. *American Journal of Psychology* 80: 263–268.

Lobmaier, J. S., and F. W. Mast. 2008. Face imagery is based on featural representations. *Experimental Psychology* 55: 47–53.

Locke, J. 1690/1975. *An Essay Concerning Human Understanding*, ed. P. Nidditch. Clarendon.

Loftus, E. F. 1979. *Eyewitness Testimony*. Harvard University Press.

Long, G. M., and A. D. Olszweski. 1999. To reverse or not to reverse: When is an ambiguous figure not ambiguous? *American Journal of Psychology* 112: 41–71.

López, A. T., T. J. Sanchéz, A. E. Arriaga, and R. E. Saldivar. 1986. El rol de la memoria visual y el color onirico en la frecuencia del recuerdo de sueños. *Revista Mexicana de Psicología* 3: 143–149.

Lucretius. 1st c. BCE/1910. *Lucretius on the Nature of Things*. Oxford University Press.

Luria, A. R. 1965/1968. *The Mind of a Mnemonist*. Basic Books.

Lutz, A., J. D. Dunne, and R. J. Davidson. 2007. Meditation and the neuroscience of consciousness. In *Cambridge Handbook of Consciousness*, ed. P. Zelazo, M. Moscovitch, and E. Thompson. Cambridge University Press.

Lycan, W. G. 1996. *Consciousness and Experience*. MIT Press.

Mach, E. 1886/1959. *The Analysis of Sensations*. Dover.

MacIntyre, T., A. Moran, and D. J. Jennings. 2002. Is controllability of imagery related to canoe-slalom performance? *Perceptual and Motor Skills* 94: 1245–1250.

Mack, A., and I. Rock. 1998. *Inattentional Blindness*. MIT Press.

Malach, R. 2006. Perception without a perceiver, in conversation with Zoran Josipovic. *Journal of Consciousness Studies* 13 (9): 57–66.

Malcolm, N. 1959. *Dreaming*. Routledge.

Malebranche, N. 1674/1997. *The Search After Truth*. T. M. Lennon.

Manser, A. R. 1956. Dreams, part II. *Aristotelian Society: Supplementary* 30: 208–228.

Marcel, T. 1980. Conscious and preconscious recognition of polysemous words: Locating the selective effects of prior verbal context. In *Attention and Performance, 8*, ed. R. Nickerson.

Marks, D. F. 1973. Visual imagery differences in the recall of pictures. *British Journal of Psychology* 64: 17–24.

Marks, D. F., and P. McKellar. 1982. The nature and function of eidetic imagery. *Journal of Mental Imagery* 6: 1–124.

Massaro, D. W., and G. R. Loftus. 1996. Sensory and perceptual storage: Data and theory. In *Memory: Handbook of Perception and Cognition*, second edition, ed. E. Bjork and R. Bjork. Academic Press.

Mast, F. W., D. M. Merfeld, and S. M. Kosslyn. 2006. Visual mental imagery during caloric vestibular stimulation. *Neuropsychologica* 44: 101–109.

Matilal, B. K. 1986. *Perception*. Clarendon.

Matsuoka, K. 1989. Imagery vividness, verbalizer-visualizer, and fantasy-proneness in young adult eidetikers. *Tohoku Psychologica Folia* 48: 25–32.

Maury, L.-F. A. 1861/1878. *Le sommeil et les rêves*, fourth edition. Dider.

McCarty, B., and P. Worchel. 1954. Rate of motion and object perception in the blind. *New Outlook for the Blind* 48: 316–322.

McCrone, J. 1993. *The Myth of Irrationality*. Carroll & Graf.

McGinn, C. 2004. *Mindsight*. Harvard University Press.

McKelvie, S. J. 1995. The VVIQ as a psychometric test of individual differences in visual imagery vividness: A critical quantitative review and plea for direction. *Journal of Mental Imagery* 19: 1–106.

Meadows, P. J. (forthcoming). Contemporary arguments for a geometry of visual experience. *European Journal of Philosophy*.

Meehl, P. E. 1990. Why summaries of research on psychological theories are often uninterpretable. *Psychological Reports* 66: 195–244.

Mencius. 4th c. BCE/1970. *Mencius*. Penguin.

Menon, G. J. 2005. Complex visual hallucinations in the visually impaired. *Archives of Ophthalmology* 123: 349–355.

Merikle, P. M., D. Smilek, and J. D. Eastwood. 2001. Perception without awareness: Perspectives from cognitive psychology. *Cognition* 79: 115–134.

Metzger, W. 1930. Optische Untersuchung am Ganzfeld: II. Mitteilung: Zur Phän-omenologie des homogenen Ganzfelds. *Psychologische Forschung* 13: 6–29.

Middleton, W. C. 1933. Nocturnal dreams. *Scientific Monthly* 37: 460–464.

Middleton, W. C. 1942. The frequency with which a group of unselected college students experience colored dreaming and colored hearing. *Journal of General Psychology* 27: 221–229.

Miller, S. C. 1964. The manifest dream and the appearance of colour in dreams. *International Journal of Psycho-Analysis* 45: 512–518.

Miller, S., and Peacock, R. 1982. Evidence for the uniqueness of eidetic imagery. *Perceptual and Motor Skills* 55: 1219–1233.

Mohr, H. M., et al. 2009. Orientation-specific adaptation to mentally generated lines in human visual cortex. *NeuroImage* 47: 384–391.

Mole, C. 2008. Attention and consciousness. *Journal of Consciousness Studies* 15 (4): 86–104.

Monroe, W. S. 1898. Einige Experimente über Gesichtsbilder in Traum. *American Journal of Psychology* 9: 413–414.

Monson, C. K., and R. T. Hurlburt. 1993. A comment to suspend the introspection controversy: Introspecting subjects did agree about "imageless thought. In Hurlburt, *Sampling Inner Experience in Disturbed Affect*. Plenum.

Montaigne, M. 1580/1948. *The Complete Essays of Montaigne*. Stanford University Press.

Moore, G. E. 1953. *Some Main Problems of Philosophy*. Allen and Unwin.

Moran, R. 2001. *Authority and Estrangement*. Princeton University Press.

Moray, N. 1959. Attention and dichotic listening: Affective cues and the influence of instructions. *Quarterly Journal of Experimental Psychology* 11: 56–60.

Most, S. B., B. J. Scholl, E. R. Clifford, and D. J. Simons. 2005. What you see is what you set: Sustained inattentional blindness and the capture of awareness. *Psychological Review* 112: 217–242.

Müller, G. E. 1896. Zur Psychophysik der Gesichtsempfindungen: Kapitel 1. *Zeitschrift für Psychologie und Physiologie der Sinnesorgane* 10: 1–82.

Müller, G. E. 1897. Zur Psychophysik der Gesichtsempfindungen: Kapitel 4. *Zeitschrift für Psychologie und Physiologie der Sinnesorgane* 14: 1–76.

Müller, G. E. 1904. *Die Gesichtspunkte und die Tatsachen der Psychophysischen Methodik*. J.F. Bergmann.

Müller, J. 1826/1927. *Über die Phantastischen Gesichtserscheinungen*. Barth.

Müller, J. 1837–1840. *Handbuch der Physiologie des Menschen für Vorlesungen*. Hölscher.

Mundle, C. W. K. 1971. *Perception: Facts and Theories*. Oxford University Press.

Münsterberg, H. 1927. *On the Witness Stand*. Clark Boardman.

Murzyn, E. 2008. Do we only dream in colour? A comparison of reported dream colour in older and younger adults with different experiences of black and white media. *Consciousness and Cognition* 17: 1128–1237.

Nagel, T. 1974. What is it like to be a bat? *Philosophical Review* 83: 435–450.

Nahmias, E. A. 2002. Verbal reports on the contents of consciousness: Reconsidering introspectionist methodology. *Psyche* 8 (21).

Necker, L.A. 1832. Observations on some remarkable optical phænomena seen in Switzerland; and on an optical phænonmenon which occurs in viewing a figure of a crystal or geometrical solid. *(London and Edinburgh) Philosophical Magazine (and Journal of Science)*, third series, 1: 329–337.

Nichols, S., and R. Grantham. 2001. Adaptive complexity and phenomenal consciousness. *Philosophy of Science* 67: 648–670.

Nichols, S., and S. P. Stich. 2003. *Mindreading.* Clarendon.

Nickerson, R. S., and M. J. Adams. 1979. Long-term memory for a common object. *Cognitive Psychology* 11: 287–307.

Nicolas, S. 1995. Joseph Delboeuf on visual illusions: A historical sketch. *American Journal of Psychology* 108: 563–574.

Nijhawan, R. 1994. Motion extrapolation in catching. *Nature* 370: 256–257.

Nir, Y., U. Hasson, I. Levy, Y. Yeshurun, and R. Malach. 2006. Widespread functional connectivity and fMRI fluctuations in human visual cortex in the absence of visual stimulation. *NeuroImage* 30: 1313–1324.

Nir, Y., and G. Tononi. 2010. Dreaming and the brain: From phenomenology to neurophysiology. *Trends in Cognitive Sciences* 14: 88–100.

Nisbett, R. E., and L. Ross. 1980. *Human Inference.* Prentice-Hall.

Nisbett, R. E., and T. D. Wilson. 1977. Telling more than we can know: Verbal reports on mental processes. *Psychological Review* 84: 231–259.

Noë, A. 2004. *Action in Perception.* MIT Press.

O'Brien, G., and J. Opie. 1999. A connectionist theory of phenomenal experience. *Behavioral and Brain Sciences* 22: 127–196.

Ogden, R. M. 1911. Imageless thought: Resume and critique. *Psychological Bulletin* 8: 183–197.

Okada, H., K. Matsuoka, and T. Hatakeyama. 2005. Individual differences in the range of sensory modalities experienced in dreams. *Dreaming* 15: 106–115.

O'Neill, D. K., and A. Gopnik. 1992. Young children's ability to indentify the sources of their beliefs. *Developmental Psychology* 27: 390–397.

Ono, H., A. Fay, and S. E. Tarbell. 1986. A "visual" explanation of facial vision. *Psychological Research* 48: 57–62.

Oppel, J.J. 1854–1855. Über geometrisch-optische Tauschungen. *Jahresbericht des Frankfurter Vereins.*

O'Regan, J. K. 1992. Solving the "real" mysteries of visual perception: The world as an outside memory. *Canadian Journal of Psychology* 46: 461–488.

O'Shaughnessy, B. 2003. *Consciousness and the World*, new edition. Oxford University Press.

Padgham, C. A. 1975. Colours experienced in dreams. *British Journal of Psychology* 66: 25–28.

Paine, P. A. 1980. Eidetic imagery and recall accuracy in preschool children. *Journal of Psychology* 105: 253–258.

Paivio, A. 1971. *Imagery and Verbal Processes*. Holt, Rinehart, and Winston.

Paivio, A. 1986. *Mental Representations: A Dual Coding Approach*. Oxford University Press.

Palmer, S. E. 1999. *Vision Science*. MIT Press.

Panum, P. 1858. *Physiologische Untersuchungen über das Sehen mit zwei Augen*. Schwerssche Buchhandlung.

Papineau, D. 1993. *Philosophical Naturalism*. Blackwell.

Peddie, W. 1922. *Colour Vision*. Edward Arnold.

Pérez-Mata, M. N., J. D. Read, and M. Diges. 2002. Effects of divided attention and word concreteness on correct recall and false memory reports. *Memory (Hove, England)* 10: 161–177.

Perky, C. W. 1910. An experimental study of imagination. *American Journal of Psychology* 21: 422–452.

Peterson, M. A., and J. Hochberg. 1983. Opposed-set measurement procedure: A quantitative analysis of the role of local cues and intention in form perception. *Journal of Experimental Psychology. Human Perception and Performance* 9: 183–193.

Petrova, P. K., and R. B. Cialdini. 2005. Fluency of consumption imagery and the backfire effects of imagery appeals. *Journal of Consumer Research* 32: 442–452.

Philodemus. 1st c. BCE/1978. *On Methods of Inference*, revised edition, ed. P. de Lacy and E. de Lacy. Bibliopolis.

Pillsbury, W. B. 1908. *Attention*. Macmillan.

Pitt, D. 2004. The phenomenology of cognition, or what is it like to think that P? *Philosophy and Phenomenological Research* 69: 1–36.

Plato. 4th c. BCE/1961. *The Collected Dialogues*, ed. E. Hamilton and H. Cairns. Princeton University Press.

Plomp, R. 1976. *Aspects of Tone Sensation*. Academic Press.

Plotinus. 3rd c. CE/1966–1988. *Plotinus*. Heinemann.

Plutarch. c. 100 CE/1918. *Plutarch's Lives*, vol. VI. Heinemann.

Polanyi, M. 1966. *The Tacit Dimension*. Doubleday.

Post, R. B., M. D. O'Malley, T. L. Yeh, and J. Bethel. 2006. On the origin of vertical line bisection errors. *Spatial Vision* 19: 505–527.

Price, H. H. 1932. *Perception*. Methuen.

Price, H. H. 1941. *The Foundations of Empirical Knowledge*, by Alfred J. Ayer. *Mind* 50: 280–293.

Prinz, J. J. 2004. *Gut Reactions*. Oxford University Press.

Prinz, J. J. 2007. All consciousness is perceptual. In *Contemporary Debates in Philosophy of Mind*, ed. B. McLaughlin and J. Cohen. Blackwell.

Prinzmetal, W., and L. Gettleman. 1993. Vertical-horizontal illusion: One eye is better than two. *Perception & Psychophysics* 53: 81–88.

Prior, K. 1999. *Don't Shoot the Dog!* Bantam.

Pritchard, R. M. 1958. Visual illusions viewed as stabilized retinal images. *Quarterly Journal of Experimental Psychology* 10: 77–81.

Ptolemy. 2nd c. CE/1996. *Ptolemy's Theory of Visual Perception*. American Philosophical Society.

Purdy, D. M. 1939. Vision. In *Introduction to Psychology*, ed. E. Boring, H. Langfeld, and H. Weld. Wiley.

Purkinje, J. 1819/2001. *Purkinje's Vision*, ed. N. Wade and J. Brožek. Erlbaum.

Purkinje, J. 1823/1919. *Beobachtungen und Versuche zur Physiologie der Sinne*. Komisi Knihkupectví J. Calve. Reproduced in *Joannes Ev-Purkinje Opera Omnia*, vol. 1. Praze.

Pylyshyn, Z. W. 1973. What the mind's eye tells the mind's brain: A critique of mental imagery. *Psychological Bulletin* 80: 1–24.

Pylyshyn, Z. W. 2002. Mental imagery: In search of a theory. *Behavioral and Brain Sciences* 25: 157–182.

Rao, S. 1998. *Perceptual Error*. University of Hawai'i Press.

Rapport, N. 1949. Overture to dreams. *Psychiatric Quarterly* 23: 266–276.

Rechtschaffen, A., and C. Buchignani. 1992. The visual appearance of dreams. In *The Neuropsychology of Sleep and Dreaming*, ed. J. Antrobus and M. Bertini. Erlbaum.

Reid, T. 1764/1997. *An Inquiry into the Human Mind*, ed. D. Brookes. Pennsylvania State University Press.

Reisberg, D., D. G. Pearson, and S. M. Kosslyn. 2003. Intuitions and introspections about imagery: The role of imagery experience in shaping an investigator's theoretical views. *Applied Cognitive Psychology* 17: 147–160.

Rensink, R. A. 2000. When good observers go bad: Change blindness, inattentional blindness, and visual experience. *Psyche* 6 (9).

Rensink, R. A. 2004. Visual sensing without seeing. *Psychological Science* 15: 27–32.

Rensink, R. A., J. K. O'Regan, and J. J. Clark. 1997. To see or not to see: The need for attention to perceive changes in scenes. *Psychological Science* 8: 368–373.

Rensink, R. A., J. K. O'Regan, and J. J. Clark. 2000. On the failure to detect changes in scenes across brief interruptions. *Visual Cognition* 7: 127–145.

Rice, C. E. 1967. Human echo perception. *Science* 155: 656–664.

Richardson, A., and J. Di Francesco. 1985. Stability, accuracy, and eye movements in eidetic imagery. *Australian Journal of Psychology* 37: 51–64.

Richardson, J. T. E. 1980. *Mental Imagery and Human Memory*. St. Martin's Press.

Riske, M. E., B. Wallace, and P. A. Allen. 2000. Imagining ability and eyewitness accuracy. *Journal of Mental Imagery* 24: 137–148.

Robertson, V. M., and G. A. Fry. 1937. After-images observed in complete darkness. *American Journal of Psychology* 49: 265–276.

Robinson, J. O. 1972. *The Psychology of Visual Illusion*. Hutchinson.

Robinson, W. S. 2005. Thoughts without distinctive non-imagistic phenomenology. *Philosophy and Phenomenological Research* 70: 534–560.

Rock, I., C. M. Linnett, P. Grant, and A. Mack. 1992. Perception without attention: Results of a new method. *Cognitive Psychology* 24: 502–534.

Rosenblum, L. D. *See What I'm Saying*. Norton.

Rosenblum, L. D., and R. L. Robart. 2007. Hearing silent shapes: Identifying the shape of a sound-obstructing surface. *Ecological Psychology* 19: 351–366.

Rosenblum, L. D., M. S. Gordon, and L. Jarquin. 2000. Echolocating distance by moving and stationary listeners. *Ecological Psychology* 12: 181–206.

Rosenthal, R., and K. L. Fode. 1963. The effect of experimenter bias on the performance of the albino rat. *Behavioral Science* 8: 183–189.

Rosnow, R. L., and R. Rosenthal. 1997. *People Studying People*. Freeman.

Rossing, T. D., F. R. Moore, and P. A. Wheeler. 1982/2002. *The Science of Sound*, third edition. Addison Wesley.

Rozemond, M. 2004. Critical notice: Janet Broughton, *Descartes's Method of Doubt*. *Canadian Journal of Philosophy* 34: 591–614.

Russell, B. 1912. *The Problems of Philosophy*. Oxford University Press.

Russell, B. 1914/1926. *Our Knowledge of the External World*, second edition. Allen & Unwin.

Russeil, B. 1914/1986. The relation of sense-data to physics. In *The Collected Papers of Bertrand Russell*, volume 8. Allen & Unwin.

Rüte, C. G. T. 1845/1855. *Lehrbuch der Ophthalmologie*, second edition. Vieweg.

Ryle, G. 1949. *The Concept of Mind*. Barnes and Noble.

Sacks, O. 1995. *An Anthropologist on Mars*. Random House.

Sacks, O. 2006. Stereo Sue. *New Yorker*, June 19: 64–73.

Sanches, F. 1581/1988. *That Nothing Is Known*, ed. E. Limbrick and D. Thomson. Cambridge University Press.

Sanford, E. C. 1892. A laboratory course in physiological psychology (third paper). *American Journal of Psychology* 4: 474–490.

Sanford, E. C. 1901. *A Course in Experimental Psychology*. Heath.

Sanford, E. C. 1917/1982. Professor Sanford's morning prayer. In *Memory Observed*, ed. U. Neisser. Freeman.

Santarcangelo, E. L., E. Cavallaro, S. Mazzoleni, E. Marano, B. Ghelarducci, P. Dario, S. Micera, and L. Sebastiani. 2005. Kinematic strategies for lowering of upper limbs during suggestions of heaviness: A real-simulator design. *Experimental Brain Research* 162: 35–45.

Sartre, J.-P. 1940/1972. *The Psychology of Imagination*, ed. M. Warnock. Methuen.

Savage, G. H. 1908. Dreams: Normal and morbid. *St. Thomas's Hospital Gazette* 18: 24–35.

Schacter, D. C. 1976. The hypnagogic state: A critical review of the literature. *Psychological Bulletin* 83: 452–481.

Schechter, N., G. R. Schmeidler, and M. Staal. 1965. Dream reports and creative tendencies in students of the arts, sciences, and engineering. *Journal of Consulting Psychology* 29: 415–421.

Schienle, A., A. Schäfer, and D. Vaitl. 2008. Individual differences in disgust imagery: A functional magnetic resonance imaging study. *Neuroreport* 19: 527–530.

Schön, W. 1876. Zur Lehre vom binocularen indirecten Sehen. *Albrecht Von Graefe's Archiv für Ophthalmologie* 22 (4): 31–62.

Schön, W. 1878a. Zur Lehre vom binocularen Sehen. II. Aufsatz. *Albrecht Von Graefe's Archiv für Ophthalmologie* 24 (1): 27–130.

Schön, W. 1878b. Zur Lehre vom binocularen Sehen. III. Aufsatz. *Albrecht Von Graefe's Archiv für Ophthalmologie* 24 (4): 47–116.

Schooler, J., and C. A. Schreiber. 2004. Experience, meta-consciousness, and the paradox of introspection. *Journal of Consciousness Studies* 11 (7–8): 17–39.

Schredl, M. 2008. Spontaneously reported colors in dreams: Correlations with atti-tude towards creativity, personality, and memory. *Sleep and Hypnosis* 10: 54–60.

Schredl, M., A. Fuchedzhieva, H. Hëmig, and V. Schindele. 2008. Do we think dreams are black and white due to memory problems? *Dreaming* 18: 175–180.

Schreiber, K. M., J. M. Hillis, H. R. Filippini, C.M. Schor,, and M. S. Banks. 2008. The surface of the empirical horopter. *Journal of Vision* 8 (3): 1–20.

Schwitzgebel, E. 2002a. How well do we know our own conscious experience? The case of visual imagery. *Journal of Consciousness Studies* 9 (5–6): 35–53.

Schwitzgebel, E. 2002b. Why did we think we dreamed in black and white? *Studies in History and Philosophy of Science* 33: 649–660.

Schwitzgebel, E. 2003. Do people still report dreaming in black and white? An attempt to replicate a questionnaire from 1942. *Perceptual and Motor Skills* 96: 25–29.

Schwitzgebel, E. 2004. Introspective training apprehensively defended: Reflections on Titchener's lab manual. *Journal of Consciousness Studies* 11 (7–8): 58–76.

Schwitzgebel, E. 2005. Difference tone training: A demonstration adapted from Titchener's *Experimental Psychology. Psyche* 11 (6).

Schwitzgebel, E. 2006. Do things look flat? *Philosophy and Phenomenological Research* 72: 589–599.

Schwitzgebel, E. 2007a. Do you have constant tactile experience of your feet in your shoes? Or is experience limited to what's in attention? *Journal of Consciousness Studies* 14 (3): 5–35.

Schwitzgebel, E. 2007b. No unchallengeable epistemic authority, of any sort, regard-ing our own conscious experience—contra Dennett? *Phenomenology and the Cognitive Sciences* 6: 107–113.

Schwitzgebel, E. 2008. The unreliability of naive introspection. *Philosophical Review* 117: 245–273.

Schwitzgebel, E. 2010. Introspection. *Stanford Encyclopedia of Philosophy* (http://plato.stanford.edu/).

Schwitzgebel, E. Forthcoming a. Introspection, what? In *Introspection and Conscious-ness,* ed. D. Smithies and D. Stoljar. Oxford University Press.

Schwitzgebel, E. Forthcoming b. Self-unconsciousness. In *Consciousness and the Self: New Essays,* ed. J. Liu and J. Perry. Cambridge University Press.

Schwitzgebel, E., and M. S. Gordon. 2000. How well do we know our own conscious experience? The case of human echolocation. *Philosophical Topics* 28: 235–246.

Schwitzgebel, E., C. Huang, and Y. Zhou. 2006. Do we dream in color? Cultural variations and skepticism. *Dreaming* 16: 36–42.

Scripture, E.W. 1897. Cerebral light. *Science*, n.s. 6 (134): 138–139.

Searle, J. R. 1984. *Minds, Brains, and Science*. Harvard University Press.

Searle, J. R. 1992. *The Rediscovery of the Mind*. MIT Press.

Searle, J. R. 1993. The problem of consciousness. *Consciousness and Cognition* 2: 310–319.

Sebastiani, L., A. Simoni, A. Gemignani, B. Ghelarducci, and E. L. Santarcangelo. 2003. Autonomic and EEG correlates of emotional imagery in subjects with different hypnotic susceptibility. *Brain Research Bulletin* 60: 151–160.

Sextus Empiricus. 2nd c. CE/1933. *Sextus Empiricus*. Harvard University Press.

Sextus Empiricus. 2nd c. CE/1994. *Outlines of Skepticism*. Cambridge University Press.

Sextus Empiricus. 2nd c. CE/1996. *The Skeptic Way*. Oxford University Press.

Sextus Empiricus. 2nd c. CE/2005. *Against the Logicians*. Cambridge University Press.

Shaw, G. A., and S. T. DeMers. 1986. The relationship of imagery to originality, flexibility and fluency in creative thinking. *Journal of Mental Imagery* 10: 65–74.

Sheehan, P. W. 1967. A shortened form of Betts' Questionnaire upon Mental Imagery. *Journal of Clinical Psychology* 23: 386–389.

Shoemaker, S. 1963. *Self-Knowledge and Self-Identity*. Cornell University Press.

Shoemaker, S. 1996. *The First-Person Perspective and Other Essays*. Cambridge University Press.

Shuey, A. M. 1924. The flight of colors. *American Journal of Psychology* 35: 559–582.

Siewert, C. 1998. *The Significance of Consciousness*. Princeton University Press.

Siewert, C. 2004. Is experience transparent? *Philosophical Studies* 117: 15–41.

Siewert, C. 2006. Is the appearance of shape Protean? *Psyche* 12 (3).

Simmons, J. A. 1989. A view of the world through a bat's ear. *Cognition* 33: 155–199.

Simner, J., C. Mulvenna, N. Sagiv, E. Tsakanikos, S. A. Witherby, C. Fraser, K. Scott, and J. Ward. 2006. Synaesthesia: The prevalence of atypical cross-modal experiences. *Perception* 35: 1024–1033.

Simons, D. J. 2000. Attentional capture and inattentional blindness. *Trends in Cognitive Sciences* 4: 147–155.

Simons, D. J., and C. F. Chabris. 1999. Gorillas in our midst: Sustained inattentional blindness for dynamic events. *Perception* 28: 1059–1074.

Simons, D. J., and D. T. Levin. 1998. Failure to detect changes to people during a real-world interaction. *Psychonomic Bulletin & Review* 5: 644–649.

Skinner, B. F. 1945. The operational analysis of psychological terms. *Psychological Review* 52: 270–277.

Skinner, B. F. 1953. *Science and Human Behavior*. Macmillan.

Smeets, J. B. J., and E. Brenner. 2006. 10 years of illusions. *Journal of Experimental Psychology. Human Perception and Performance* 32: 1501–1504.

Smithies, D. Forthcoming. Attention is rational-access consciousness. In *Attention: Philosophical and Psychological Essays*, ed. C. Mole, D. Smithies, and W. Wu. Oxford University Press.

Smythies, J. R. 1957. A preliminary analysis of the stroboscopic patterns. *Nature* 179 (4558): 523–524.

Snodgrass, M., E. Bernat, and H. Shevrin. 2004. Unconscious perception: A model-based approach to method and evidence. *Perception & Psychophysics* 66: 846–867.

Snyder, F. 1970. The phenomenology of dreaming. In *The Psychodynamic Implications of the Physiological Studies on Dreams*, ed. L. Madow and L. Snow. Thomas.

Solomon, S. G., and P. Lennie. 2007. The machinery of colour vision. *Nature Reviews. Neuroscience* 8: 276–286.

Sommer, R. 1978. *The Mind's Eye*. Delacorte.

Sommer, R. 1980. Strategies for imagery research. *Journal of Mental Imagery* 4: 115–121.

Sorenson, R. 2004. We see in the dark. *Noûs* 38: 456–480.

Spence, C., D. I. Shore, and R. M. Klein. 2001. Multisensory prior entry. *Journal of Experimental Psychology. General* 130: 799–832.

Spener, M. Forthcoming. Disagreement about cognitive phenomenology. In *Cognitive Phenomenology*, ed. T. Bayne and M. Montague. Oxford University Press.

Sperling, G. 1960. The information available in brief visual presentation. *Psychological Monographs* 74 (11): 1–29.

Srinivasan, N. 2008. Interdependence of attention and consciousness. *Progress in Brain Research* 168: 65–75.

Stamper, D. A., D. J. Lund, J. W. Mochany, and B. E. Stuck. 2000. Laser-induced afterimages in humans. *Perceptual and Motor Skills* 91: 15–33.

Stepansky, R., B. Holzinger, A. Schmeiser-Rieder, B. Saletu, M. Kunze, and J. Zeitlhofer. 1998. Austrian dream behavior: Results of a representative population survey. *Dreaming* 8: 23–30.

Stickney, S. E., and T. J. Englert. 1975. The ghost flute. *Physics Teacher* 13: 518–522.

Stoffregen, T. A., and J. B. Pittenger. 1995. Human echolocation as a basic form of perception and action. *Ecological Psychology* 7: 181–216.

Stout, G. F. 1899/1977. *A Manual of Psychology*, ed. D. Robinson. University Publications of America.

Stwertka, S. 1993. The stroboscopic patterns as dissipative structures. *Neuroscience and Biobehavioral Reviews* 17: 69–78.

Suedfeld, P. 1980. *Restricted Environmental Stimulation*. Wiley.

Suinn, R. M. 1966. Jungian personality typology and color dreaming. *New York Mental Hygiene Department Psychiatric Quarterly* 40: 659–666.

Supa, M., M. Cotzin, and K. M. Dallenbach. 1944. "Facial Vision": The Perception of Obstacles by the Blind. *American Journal of Psychology* 62: 133–183.

Tapia, F., J. Werboff, and G. Winokur. 1958. Recall of some phenomena of sleep. *Journal of Nervous and Mental Disease* 127: 119–123.

Tatibana, Y. 1938. Grundtypen der Traumfarben. *Tohoku Psychologica Folia* 6: 127–144.

Tauber, E. S., and M. R. Green. 1962. Color in dreams. *American Journal of Psychotherapy* 16: 221–229.

Taya, R., and S. Ohinata. 2002. Afterimage oscillation after a brief light flash. *Japanese Psychological Research* 44: 99–106.

Thomas, I. E. 1956. Dreams, Part I. *Aristotelian Society: Supplementary* 30: 197–207.

Thomas, N. J. T. 1989. Experience and theory as determinants of attitudes toward mental representation: The case of Knight Dunlap and the vanishing images of J. B. Watson. *American Journal of Psychology* 102: 395–412.

Thomas, N. J. T. 1999. Are theories of imagery theories of imagination? An active perception approach to conscious mental content. *Cognitive Science* 23: 207–245.

Thomas, N. J. T. 2010. The multidimensional spectrum of imagination: Images, dreams, hallucinations, and active, imaginative, perception. Unpublished manuscript.

Thouless, R. H. 1930–1931. Phenomenal regression to the real object. I. *British Journal of Psychology* 21: 339–359.

Titchener, E. B. 1896/1906. *An Outline of Psychology*, revised edition. Macmillan.

Titchener, E. B. 1898/1900. *A Primer of Psychology*, revised edition. Macmillan.

Titchener, E. B. 1901–1905. *Experimental Psychology: A Manual of Laboratory Practice*. Macmillan.

Titchener, E. B. 1901. Idio-retinal light. In *Dictionary of Philosophy and Psychology*, ed. J. Baldwin. Macmillan.

Titchener, E. B. 1908. *Lectures on the Elementary Psychology of Feeling and Attention*. Macmillan.

Titchener, E. B. 1909. *Lectures on the Experimental Psychology of the Thought-Processes.* Macmillan.

Titchener, E. B. 1910. *A Text-Book of Psychology.* Macmillan.

Titchener, E. B. 1912a. Prolegomena to a study of introspection. *American Journal of Psychology* 23: 427–448.

Titchener, E. B. 1912b. The schema of introspection. *American Journal of Psychology* 23: 485–508.

Titchener, E. B. 1915. *A Beginner's Psychology.* Macmillan.

Titchener, E. B. 1929. *Systematic Psychology: Prolegomena.* Cornell University Press.

Tomes, J. L., and A. N. Katz. 1997. Habitual susceptibility to misinformation and individual differences in eyewitness memory. *Applied Cognitive Psychology* 11: 233–251.

Tomes, J. L., and A. N. Katz. 2000. Confidence-accuracy relations for real and suggested events. *Memory* 8: 273–283.

Trappey, C. 1996. A meta-analysis of consumer choice and subliminal advertising. *Psychology and Marketing* 13: 517–530.

Troland, L. T. 1922/2008. *The Present Status of Visual Science.* BiblioBazaar.

Tye, M. 1991. *The Imagery Debate.* MIT Press.

Tye, M. 1995. *Ten Problems of Consciousness.* MIT Press.

Tye, M. 2000. *Color, Consciousness, and Content.* MIT Press.

Tye, M. 2003. Representationalism and the transparency of experience. In *Privileged Access*, ed. B. Gertler. Ashgate.

Tye, M. 2009. *Consciousness Revisited.* MIT Press.

Unger, P. 1975. *Ignorance.* Clarendon.

Van Cleve, J. 2002. Thomas Reid's geometry of visible. *Philosophical Review* 111: 373–416.

Vernon, J., T. Marton, and E. Peterson. 1961. Sensory deprivation and hallucinations. *Science* 133 (3467): 1808–1812.

Volkmann, A. W. 1846. Sehen. In *Handwörterbuch der Physiologie*, vol. 3. ed. R. Wagner. Vieweg.

Wade, A., M. Augath, N. Logothetis, and B. Wandell. 2008. fMRI measurement of color in macaque and human. *Journal of Vision* 8 (10): 1–19.

Walczyk, J. J. 1995. Between- versus within-subjects assessments of image vividness. *Journal of Mental Imagery* 19: 161–176.

Walczyk, J. J., and R. W. Taylor. 2000. Reverse-spelling, the VVIQ, and mental imagery. *Journal of Mental Imagery* 24: 177–188.

Wallace, B. 1979. Hypnotic susceptibility and the perception of afterimages and dot stimuli. *American Journal of Psychology* 92: 681–691.

Wallace, B. 1990. Imagery vividness, hypnotic susceptibility, and the perception of fragmented stimuli. *Journal of Personality and Social Psychology* 58: 354–359.

Wallace, B., P. A. Allen, and R. E. Propper. 1996. Hypnotic susceptibility, imaging ability, and anagram-solving activity. *International Journal of Clinical and Experimental Hypnosis* 44: 324–337.

Wang, K., T. Jiang, C. Yu, L. Tian, J. Li, Y. Liu, Y. Zhou, L. Xu, M. Song, and K. Li. 2008. Spontaneous activity associated with primary visual cortex: A resting-state fMRI study. *Cerebral Cortex* 18: 697–704.

Wang, Yangming. Early 16th c./1963. *Instructions for Practical Living and Other Neo-Confucian Writings*. Columbia University Press.

Ward, J. 1918. *Psychological Principles*. Cambridge University Press.

Washburn, M. F. 1899. Subjective colors and the afterimage: Their significance for the theory of attention. *Mind*, N.S., 8: 25–34.

Wasinger, K., P. F. Zelhart, and R. P. Markley. 1982. Memory for random shapes and eidetic ability. *Perceptual and Motor Skills* 55: 1076–1078.

Watson, J. B. 1913. Psychology as the behaviorist views it. *Psychological Review* 20: 158–177.

Wehrle, R., M. Czisch, C. Kaufmann, T. C. Wetter, F. Holsboer, D. P. Auer, and T. Pollmächer. 2005. Rapid eye movement-related brain activation in human sleep: A functional magnetic resonance imaging study. *Neuroreport* 16: 853–857.

Weve, H. 1925. The colours of after-images. *British Journal of Ophthalmology* 9: 627–638.

Wheatstone, C. 1838/1983. Contributions to the physiology of vision—Part the first. On some remarkable, and hitherto unobserved, phenomena of binocular vision. In *Brewer and Wheatstone on Vision*, ed. N. Wade. Academic Press.

Wilson, R. A. 2003. Intentionality and phenomenology. *Pacific Philosophical Quarterly* 84: 413–431.

Wilson, T. D. 2002. *Strangers to Ourselves*. Harvard University Press.

Winograd, E., J. P. Peluso, and T. A. Glover. 1998. Individual differences in susceptibility to memory illusions. *Applied Cognitive Psychology* 12: S5–S27.

Wittgenstein, L. 1967. *Zettel*, ed. G. Anscombe and G. von Wright. University of California Press.

Wolgast, E. H. 1958. Perceiving and impressions. *Philosophical Review* 67: 226–236.

Worchel, P., and K. M. Dallenbach. 1947. "Facial vision": Perception of obstacles by the deaf-blind. *American Journal of Psychology* 60: 502–553.

Wright, W. 2005. Distracted drivers and unattended experience. *Synthese* 144: 41–68.

Wundt, W. 1888. Selbstbeobachtung und innere Wahrnehmung. *Philosophische Studien* 4: 292–309.

Wundt, W. 1896/1897. *Outlines of Psychology*. Stechert.

Wundt, W. 1907. Über Ausfrageexperimente und über die Methoden zur Psychologie des Denkens. *Psychologische Studien* 3: 301–360.

Wundt, W. 1908a. *Grundzüge der physiologischen Psychologie*, vol. 1. Wilhelm Engelmann.

Wundt, W. 1908b. Kritische Nachlese zur Ausfragemethode. *Archiv für die gesamte Psychologie* 9: 445–459.

Wyra, M., M. J. Lawson, and N. Hungi. 2007. The mnemonic keyword method: The effects of bidirectional keyword training and of ability to image on foreign language vocabulary recall. *Learning and Instruction* 17: 360–371.

Xitco, M. J., and H. L. Roitblat. 1996. Object recognition through eavesdropping: Passive echolocation in bottlenose dolphins. *Animal Learning & Behavior* 24: 355–365.

Xunzi. 3rd c. BCE/1999. *Xunzi*. Hunan People's Publishing House.

Yaffe, G. 2002. Reconsidering Reid's geometry of visible. *Philosophical Quarterly* 52: 602–620.

Yamanaka, T., Y. Morita, and J. Matsumoto. 1982. Analysis of the dream contents in college students by REM-awakening technique. *Folia Psychiatrica et Neurologica Japonica* 36: 33–52.

Yazmajian, R. V. 1964. Color in dreams. *Psychoanalytic Quarterly* 33: 176–193.

Yazmajian, R. V. 1968. Dreams completely in color. *Journal of the American Psychoanalytic Association* 16: 32–47.

Yost, R. M., Jr., and D. Kalish. 1955. Miss MacDonald on sleeping and waking. *Philosophical Quarterly* 5: 109–124.

Young, F. A. 1948. The projection of after-images and Emmert's Law. *Journal of General Psychology* 39: 161–166.

Zhuangzi (Chuang Tzu). 3rd c. BCE/1968. *The Complete Works of Chuang Tzu*. Columbia University Press.

Zuckerman, M. 1969. Hallucinations, reported sensations, and images. In *Sensory Deprivation*, ed. J. Zubek. Appleton-Century-Crofts.

Index